Generation Denied

Generation Denied

The Broken Promise of Education in Iran

REZA KHANZADEH

University of Texas Press *Austin*

First edition, 2026

♾ The paper used in this book meets the minimum requirements of ANSI/NISO Z39.48-1992 (R1997) (Permanence of Paper).

Cataloging-in-Publication Data is available from the Library of Congress

ISBN 978-1-4773-3485-0 (hardcover)
ISBN 978-1-4773-3574-1 (paperback)
ISBN 978-1-4773-3486-7 (PDF)
ISBN 978-1-4773-3487-4 (ePub)

doi:10.7560/334850

بسم الله

به نام خدا

In the name of God

Thank you to all my participants. Thank you to my family, friends, and colleagues who helped make this book possible. Rest in peace my beloved grandmother Madar Tooba, Amoo Hassan, Amoo Ali, Ameh Behjat, and my brother Ricardo.

Figure 0.1. From The World Factbook, by Central Intelligence Agency, 2021. https://www.cia.gov/the-world-factbook/countries/iran/map.

Contents

Tables and Illustrations

Tables

Illustrations

Abbreviations

BERA	British Educational Research Association
BLS	Bootstrapped Lean Start-ups
CEO	chief executive officer
CIA	Central Intelligence Agency
COVID	coronavirus disease
CUREC	Central University Research Ethics Committee
DISC	dominance, inducement, submission, compliance assessment
DREC	Departmental Research Ethics Committees
Engr.	engineering
GPA	grade-point average
GRE	Graduate Record Examinations
GPS	global positioning system
HR	human resources
IBM	International Business Machines Corporation
ID	identity document
ILO	International Labor Organization
IQ	intelligence quotient
IRGC	Islamic Revolutionary Guard Corps
IRPHE	Institute for Research and Planning in Higher Education
IT	information technology
JCPOA	Joint Comprehensive Plan of Action
MBA	master of business administration
MBTI	Myers-Briggs Type Indicator
MI6	Military Intelligence Section 6
MIT	Massachusetts Institute of Technology
NDA	nondisclosure agreement
OECD	The Organization for Economic Cooperation and Development

STEM	science, technology, engineering, math
STEMM	science, technology, engineering, math, medicine
TOEFL	Test of English as a Foreign Language
TV	television
URL	uniform resource locator
US	United States
USD	United States Dollars

Preface

The Islamic Republic forces you down a one-dimensional path of obedience to the State or they push you to leave. Why? Because you are not a member of the establishment. Because you don't think like us. Your ideology is different. It is you who go to the streets and protest, so it's better that you leave. So, we'll lie to you during your youth and say yes, human capital is good, invest in yourself, but we won't tell you that is a lie. Then when you find out and it's too late, what do you do? You acquiesce to a submissive life, or you leave.
MAJID

The research and fieldwork that went into this book was inspired by quotes like this that I have repeatedly heard throughout my time in and outside of Iran. Thus, my interest in this project stems from a paradoxical life of two worlds. The first, in the United States, where I have been fortunate to seize the opportunities afforded to me in attending some of the finest universities and succeeding in a career I passionately care about. The second, in the Islamic Republic of Iran, where I have visited, lived, or worked—off and on—for nineteen years. During this time, I have witnessed the struggles of many Iranians trying to build a standard of living above the poverty line. This has constantly left me comparing my life to theirs and theorizing why and how they have been comparatively less fortunate.

My generation (I was born in Shiraz in 1982) has been called "the children of war" due to the eight-year war versus Iraq from 1980 to 1988. However, I do not consider myself a "child of war" since my parents, older sister, and I left for America when I was two, maybe three. Unlike those who stayed in Iran, I did not endure eight years of war, decades of sanctions, a clerical oligarchical government, an uncertain future, and limited freedoms (speech, press, religion, etc.). What followed for the next eighteen years of my life, however, was a series of life-altering events that crystallized my purpose and led me to this book. Not only have I witnessed far too many of my cousins and friends continuously struggle to find a job, gain independence, and start a family of their own, but I have also heard countless stories of the same struggles from both my generation and in the generations since. All the while, politicians, economists, and academics have assessed the problem and prescribed solutions that have not helped the youth.

Every year I discovered an increase in unemployment coupled with a decrease in the standard of living. Throughout this time, I continuously heard stories of how dreams were found outside the geographical borders of Iran and aspirations were seldom attained within. This outlook inspired me to conduct a series of exploratory interviews between 2006 and 2013. Speaking with anyone willing to talk, I engaged with relatives, friends, neighbors, and strangers at coffee shops, hookah bars, sporting facilities, and private family/social gatherings. What I deduced from these conversations was that the root problem could be traced back to the last two years of high school, the *konkur* exam (or university entrance exam), and the four years of undergraduate study. In brief, society espoused a shortsighted mindset toward education that was viewed primarily through a human capital lens. There was no simultaneous focus on the integration of educational attainment with one's future labor market positioning.

After discovering this problem, I devoted my professional career (from 2013 to 2017) to Iran-related matters. I worked for and with major Iranian organizations on human rights, public policy, foreign relations, international business, and international law to determine what possibilities existed in improving Iran's employment opportunities. But despite my best efforts, all my professional endeavors failed to really help the people of Iran. And to make matters worse, not only did the standard of living continue to decline, but the job market also worsened due to a multitude of foreign and domestic issues. Thus, I rigorously reengaged with all forms of literature (in English and Persian) pertaining to Iran in the hopes of uncovering any pertinent material I was unable to obtain up to that point. What I discovered was that the voice of the youth within Iran was missing within the political and economic discussions that monopolized so many debates.

While there are many superb books on Iran, with some authors conducting their research inside the country, I have very seldom come across a contribution like this book. And I believe the only true reason I could complete it was that I was able to safely conduct an almost nine-month longitudinal and ethnographic study within Iran, during which I followed and engaged with my participants. Many authors and researchers are unable to do this out of fear of being detained by the Iranian government. In chapter 3 I explain in depth how and why I was able to do this, but, in short, I maintained a low profile throughout my adult life so as to not draw any attention to myself.

Thus, after twenty-five years in this field, I am cognizant of how I am positioned in this research and juxtaposed with the participants. Nevertheless, to curb my biases, strengthen my ethical compass, and further ensure the rigor of the research, I remained self-critical, reflexive, and reflective. I also self-monitored throughout my fieldwork, data analysis, and writing of this book. The translation of my interviews from Farsi to English was literal, with no supplemental interpretation. I purposely include in my work many direct quotes from my interviewees in order to fully and accurately present their story. My approach is a constant process of self-reflection and attempting to gauge the nuances between careful analysis and reflected biases. I made a conscious effort to remain reflexive throughout and be forthright about my own positionality. Such an endeavor is not an outcome but a process upon which I continue to reflect. There is also a continuous balancing act between outsider and insider, and objectivity and subjectivity, particularly as someone who was born (and briefly lived) in Iran but was raised and educated in America (and a little in England).

Thus, as a halfie—as Abu-Lughod (1991) describes it: people whose national or cultural identity is mixed by virtue of migration, overseas education, or parentage—I am further sensitive to my positionality as a Shia Muslim with Western tendencies and a Persian-Iranian with American thought-processes. However, I do subscribe to Abu-Lughod's argument that to assume that someone from the same nationality cannot be impartial in their research is to accept that the other is impartial in their research. Both types of researchers deliver their own value systems that must be acknowledged. It is not possible to dissociate identities and biases completely; researchers should instead be mindful of minimizing them. I have spent significantly more time in America, even though I have strong professional and personal ties with(in) Iran. As a result, I was able to draw from the advantages of being both an outsider and insider.

While I do not support the Islamic Republic in any way, nor am I an apologist of the regime, I do acknowledge there are many people from many different countries who do support what the Islamic Republic stands for. The regime's anti-West, anti-American, anti-Israeli, anti-colonialism policies and rhetoric does resonate with many who feel they have suffered greatly at the hands of America, the West, Israel, and the like. At the same time, many Iranians have suffered greatly at the hands of their own government because of its policies that seem to neglect or dismiss the needs and wants of its own people. The dichotomous sentiment that surrounds this regime is not lost on me, and the polarizing effect it has that forces one to pick one side (support the regime) or the other (against) is where my academic discipline keeps me prudent in navigating between them. Unfortunately, I did not feel safe soliciting supporters of the regime on my own for this research, as prior attempts led to an increased risk to my well-being. Alternatively, I trusted my sources to connect me with regime supporters or sympathizers.

As a result of my wariness, my access in and around the major cities of Iran (Tehran, Isfahan, Shiraz, and Mashhad) was mostly unencumbered. There were some limitations for myself and my participants based on safety protocols, as well as constraints based on religious, cultural, and societal edicts. At times we had to observe safety protocols during times of protests and riots. For example, during my second trip to Iran (June 2019 to January 2020), there were multiple protests that led to the government shutting down the internet for a week, which sparked further protests. Also, international crises escalated tensions, with the United States assassinating Iran's top general—Qasem Soleimani in Iraq—and Iran shooting down a Ukrainian commercial airplane (Flight 752) mistaken for a US cruise missile. Therefore, I restricted my mobility throughout Tehran during that time and shortened my stay in Iran.

My decision to focus on Sharif graduates resulted from decades of personal, professional, and academic research. First, according to the literature (Appadurai, 2013), individuals who graduate from an elite university, like Sharif, are believed to have an easier path to success. While there are counterarguments to this claim (Deresiewicz, 2008), my focus was on the lived experiences inside Iran to possibly help uncover new reasons, other than what has already been discussed in the literature, why Iran's youth struggled—for example, economic concerns (Hamdhaidari et al., 2008; Livanos, 2010), job-skills mismatch (Alibaygi et al., 2013; Liagouras et al., 2003), disconnect between higher education and the job market (Al-Dosary, 2006; Bazargan, 2000), career indecision (Lent & Brown, 1996; Mojgan et al., 2011), or positional conflict within a globalized job market (Amuzegar, 2004; Brown et al., 2010).

Second, I too discovered an apparent anomaly within the narrative of youth struggles in Iran's job market. The life trajectories of Sharif graduates were viewed by Iranian society as success stories, regardless of whether the graduate stayed in or left Iran. Sharif University was and still is considered the most prestigious university in Iran, even with its academic focus being on STEM programs. Despite engineering graduates in general struggling with double-digit unemployment rates (Alibaygi et al., 2013; Habibi, 2015), Sharif engineering graduates were not categorized in the same statistics. Sharif is considered the "MIT of Iran" and arguably the best university in Iran (Habibi, 1989; Matthews & Lord, 2017, p. 27). However, unlike MIT, Sharif is a public university and therefore free to anyone who can score high enough on the *konkur* (a formidable exam I will discuss at length later in the book). Moreover, the legacy admissions policy that is found at most elite American universities does not exist at Sharif. Thus, while Sharif's admissions criteria present a more meritocratic policy, it is a State-owned institution and still beholden to the regime and in particular the *khodi*.

Nevertheless, on the international stage, *U.S. News & World Report* (2026) ranks Sharif University 50th in the world in mechanical engineering, and 141st in engineering overall. As a result of its global recognition, Sharif has historically been partially excluded from certain sanctions that have left most Iranian universities isolated from the global academic community. For example, Sharif had a collaborative agreement with the University of California, Davis (Matthews & Lord, 2017). And because of its domestic appeal, most STEM (science, technology, engineering, math) students aim to attend Sharif, despite its highly competitive and limited admissions process.

However, my experience and research inside Iran from 2017 to 2020 showed that the success of Sharif graduates primarily coincided with them leaving Iran. These conflicting views—Iran's graduates struggling in the job market versus Sharif graduates finding success abroad—inspired me to explore how the lived experiences of Sharif graduates inside Iran would be described by these individuals. Moreover, if society believes that Sharif's graduates have an increased likelihood of gaining employment inside Iran, then their moments of struggle, underemployment, mismatched expectations, unemployment, and disillusion are compelling in potentially uncovering issues with the country's education system and job market that have yet to be identified. Also, if Sharif graduates' success stories do coincide with them leaving Iran, then the specific aspect of their lived experiences inside Iran could further highlight the limitations of the human capital argument inside Iran and how Sharif graduates' job market expectations are possibly realistic when viewed beyond the borders of Iran.

Thus, one contribution of this book is that, in addition to human capital, an observation of ideological capital also needs to be considered when examining an individual's experience through and with their country's education system, job market, society, and government. It is important to use the term *ideological capital* because my fieldwork uncovered a number of colloquial terms—like *khodi*, *ghayre-khodi*, and *khusulati*—that were ubiquitous to the youth experience, which resulted in the concept of ideological capital. I will discuss this new concept in more depth throughout the book, but, in short, it is the measure of one's ability to increase their standard of living through active participation in the ideology of the ruling elite—which in the case of Iran is the *khodi*. This is a concept that (a) represents the lived experiences of my participants, (b) contributes to the debate on Iran's youth struggles, and (c) contributes to the conversations on youth struggles within the global south and/or a nondemocratic government—like in Iran, Russia, China, Nicaragua, and North Korea. Governments like the Islamic Republic have developed a complex yet simple system of how they govern their country in order to ensure that threats to the regime's existence are minimized while complete control is maximized. Within this complex yet simple system lies a specific combination of one's religious, political, social, cultural, artistic, grooming, and fashion beliefs, to name a few, that dictates, influences, and alters that individual's successes and failures inside Iran when faced with the *khodi* and the Islamic Republic. And these pieces are some of the parts of what makes up the ideological capital I will discuss throughout this book.

One quick example is how the Islamic Republic has a branch within the government, called the Guardian Council, that decides who is allowed to run for political office. Their decision is primarily based on how closely aligned the individual's ideological beliefs are with that of the *khodi* and the regime. In other words, if a potential political candidate is fully qualified and has great ideas to help his/her city, town, or province, but whose ideological beliefs conflict with the *khodi*'s, then the Guardian Council will prohibit them from running. This means, as long as you are ideologically aligned with the Islamic Republic, you could be the least qualified individual but still be allowed to run for public office. This then means that your human capital investment is not comparatively significant to your ideological capital investment. Thus, similar to how we investigate an individual's efforts in strengthening all forms of capital—whether it is human, social, cultural, or religious—we must also investigate their efforts in strengthening their ideological capital. Hence, this book makes the argument that a government, like the Islamic Republic of Iran, reframes promises of human capital theory and employability to reduce its youth to a one-dimensional aspiration irrespective of how much the individual invests in human capital, improves their employability, and exercises their agency.

Generation Denied

Introduction

The khodi *does not allow you to grow in this society. They beat the hell out of you . . . if you want to raise your head just a little, they hit you back down. Either shut up and live in this society . . . or else.*
CYRUS

From the hundreds of hours of interviews, spanning over three years, this comment from Cyrus still remains one of the most visceral depictions of my participants' lived experiences inside Iran. Even though the Islamic Republic's (mis)treatment of many of its citizens is no secret, and the country's brain drain is well documented, along with the government's high corruption, there are still unanswered questions about how and why many of the country's young men are unable to actualize their aspirations inside Iran. This book answers some of these questions directly from the perspectives of young men navigating Iran's education system and job market. Questions include:

1. How does the Islamic Republic shape, obstruct, or redirect the aspirations of its youth from education to employment? This question interrogates the role of the State not as a passive background actor but as an active agent in shaping life trajectories through ideological, institutional, and economic mechanisms.
2. Why do traditional frameworks like human capital theory fail to explain the lived experiences of some individuals in their pursuit of aspirational attainment? This question challenges the global applicability of human capital theory by asking, what happens when investments in education do not yield expected returns? How do nondemocratic regimes reframe or distort the promise of employability through human capital investments?

3. How do young men in Iran navigate the tension between personal agency and structural constraints imposed by the State, society, and family? This question explores the internal conflict between individual aspirations and externally imposed expectations, as well as the strategies of resistance, adaptation, or resignation employed by these young men in the face of systemic barriers.
4. What is the role of ideological capital in determining success or failure in Iran's job market and society? This question introduces a new conceptual lens that asks if success in Iran can be understood not just through human, social, or cultural capital but also through ideological alignment with the regime. And how does one's position on the *khodi* (insider) vs. *ghayre-khodi* (outsider) spectrum affect access to opportunity and realizing one's aspirational goals? The *khodi* and *ghayre-khodi* terms are key themes within this book.
5. And finally, what does the Iranian case reveal about youth struggles in other nondemocratic or Global South contexts? This question situates Iran within a broader comparative framework where we can better examine how youth in countries like Russia and China experience similar tensions, particularly since access to these countries, from an investigative standpoint, is limited and oftentimes restricted or forbidden.

Answering these questions is critical to better understanding Iran and more specifically the relationship between the Islamic Republic and its youth. This understanding is more important now than ever before due to the continued unrest—e.g., the 2009 Green Movement, the 2019 Bloody November (during which I was in Iran), and the 2022 Women, Life, Freedom movement—that has consistently plagued the regime. Also, considering the conflict between Iran and Israel and the US in 2025 and 2026, there has been a constant threat to the Islamic Republic's existence from within and abroad. And yet, the regime still stands (as I write this sentence in June of 2026) and controls a nation of ninety million citizens. Experts have debated as to how and why the people are repeatedly unsuccessful in either changing the regime—at the very least—or toppling the Islamic Republic, and one aspect that is overlooked is the psychological long game the regime seemingly plays on its youth that this book will uncover.

Thus, I begin this book by setting the scene from the broader framework of aspirational attainment as well as the employability and unemployment of youth. I then zoom in on Iran and the recent and long-standing issues that impede youth aspirations. Much of these issues are caused by the regime's efforts to control its citizens, of which the control of its education system is a key element, framed by in-depth discussions on their underlying history and ideology. I then gradually focus on the lived experiences of a group of young men as they detail their pre-university, within-university, and postgraduation journeys in trying to realize their aspirations inside Iran while navigating their country's school system, higher education system, and job market. The stories from my forty-six participants are juxtaposed against sixty-two stakeholders (educators, administrators, counselors, government officials, and employers) across many of Iran's public and private sectors. The stories from these interviews suggest that the Islamic Republic's establishment—or the *khodi*—reframes promises of human capital investment to eventually either corral my participants into submissive citizens or push them as emigrants. The argument is that since the regime's existence is increasingly under threat, its focus has increasingly intensified on (a) holding on to power; (b) procuring and controlling major revenue streams to help them stay in power and circumvent economic sanctions; and (c) superimposing a status quo rooted in the regime's ideological, social, political, and religious beliefs in order to influence its citizens' thought processes and behaviors to counteract threats to (a) and (b). Chapter 2 goes into great depth on the background of Iran and how the country has reached its current state of capriciousness.

The findings from my fieldwork inside Iran are significant because the existing literature on youth struggles in trying to actualize their aspirations and future within their country does not appear to give sufficient consideration to the covert and psychological tactics of the State as it obstructs one's journey. Therefore, this book problematizes the human capital argument and how we understand employability, unemployment, and aspirational attainment inside a nondemocratic country like Iran. Additionally, this book highlights the promises and failures of education posed as a pathway to success through the human capital model. And while these issues are not unique to Iran, what my research has uncovered adds to conversations on the global south as well as other nondemocratic countries—e.g., Russia, China, North Korea, Nicaragua, and the like—in order to help us better understand youth struggles in these parts of the world that are seemingly underresearched due to safety concerns brought on by government restrictions and crackdowns.

Therefore, the term *ideological capital* is proposed as a necessary addition to the existing arguments of human, social, cultural, political, and religious capital. Ideological capital conceptualizes my participants' experiences through the Islamic Republic's education system and job market. Since the participants were considered the other (or *ghayre-khodi*), and most were unable or unwilling to invest in their ideological capital, they were seemingly unable to realize their aspirations inside Iran. I detail throughout the book what it means to invest in one's ideological capital. In short, this investment spans a spectrum—from a superficial facade to a genuine adoption of the regime's belief system—undertaken to either pose as or ingratiate oneself with the *khodi* in order to secure monetary, professional, political, and/or social benefits.

I also discuss ideological capital in more detail throughout the book, but considering the significance of my fieldwork uncovering this new concept, I will briefly explain it here. One way to understand ideological capital is in the moments where human capital fails to explain youths' continued job market struggles. In other words, it is when an individual continuously invests in their human capital and makes the appropriate (re)adjustments and (re) calibrations in order to best position themselves to succeed, yet they continuously fail, particularly when those failures seem to only occur within a specific environment—and in this case within Iran. Then perhaps an examination into one's ideological capital is necessary. And what this entails is the assessment of whether the successes and failures of an individual can be better understood/ explained through their (in)ability to outwardly project an allegiance to and/ or investment in the ideology of the State. And in the case of Iran, the State specifically signifies the "establishment"—or the *khodi* as they say in Iran—who hold the most power and influence over the country.

The type of fieldwork I conducted that led to this concept consisted of a biographical study focusing on the individual lived experiences of forty-six young men. I intimately engaged with five in particular but conducted in-depth interviews with each one of my participants. I also interviewed sixty-two stakeholders. A combination of purposeful and snowball sampling was used to select participants who varied in terms of their economic status, geographical upbringing, religious beliefs, ethnicity, pre-university education, and career specialization. All interviews were conducted face-to-face in Iran—primarily in the city of Tehran but also in the cities of Isfahan, Mashhad, and Shiraz. I made two separate trips in December 2017 to January 2018, and then from June 2019 to January 2020. I decided to focus on a specific demographic of the country that has continued to struggle in actualizing their personal and professional aspirations inside Iran. Unfortunately, this specificity required omitting women from my research and does leave this book partially incomplete.

There were two main reasons why I chose to limit my empirical study by not interviewing young women. The first was due to religious, social, cultural, legal, safety, security, and reputational reasons. I would have been unable to properly conduct biographical narrative interviews with women where I would need to spend hours and days, one-on-one, observing, participating with, and conversing with the opposite sex. Such encounters could have put myself and my female participant at risk, and to avoid such risks would have meant altering my research in a way that would have undermined the full story of the female participants. The second reason was due to my own naivety. While women are affected more by un(der)employment,[1] the attention warranted by gender issues within Iran goes beyond the scope of my expertise, and my attempt to cover it in this book would be a disservice. Moreover, there are many scholars conducting exceptional work on women in Iran: Moghadam (2009), Bahramitash and Esfahani (2011), Behdad and Nomani (2012), and Salehi-Isfahani and Taghvatalab (2019), to name a few.

With that said, however, the issue of unemployment and employability has been discussed across many disciplines, generations, and countries. In recent history, the global debate had to evolve twice due to the 2008 recession and the 2019 coronavirus pandemic. Most existing conversations, however, have continued to pivot around arguments of structure and agency, and how the two should collectively, and/or individually, adapt and persevere to lead to improved job market successes. Contrarily, these debates are not entirely sufficient when examining Iran's youth—and more broadly, youth within the global south and/or within a nondemocratic country. What if current understandings of unemployment, vis-à-vis agency within a human capital argument, do not accurately explain or depict youth experiences in Iran? Should this argument be revised if it fails to explain Iran's unemployment problem and youth struggles? Or have leading thinkers avoided fieldwork inside Iran out of fear of being detained, thus resulting in few in-depth analyses regarding educational opportunities, aspirations, and agentic maneuverings of Iran's youth?

Thus, the way we look at the effectiveness of one's employability and the causes of unemployment in some major cities (e.g., Tehran, Shiraz, Isfahan, Mashhad) within Iran may suggest an added (f)actor when examining these terms: the role of the State in an adversarial capacity, for example. In other words, youth experience in Iran's job market may require an assessment of the Islamic Republic and the *khodi* that limit the parameters in which an individual can navigate in order to succeed in the job market and attain their aspirations. Similar to Brown et al.'s (2010) argument of broken promises of human capital theory through globalization, there may also be broken promises in the way the Islamic Republic guarantees a successful life for the youth but eventually limits job market returns in accordance with the *khodi*'s expectations and job market stipulations. Therefore, if an individual becomes unemployed, the problems may go beyond economic and political factors. There may also be an ideological component, i.e., an us-versus-others tension, or the *khodi* versus *ghayre-khodi*. With that said, my research aimed to uncover how bachelor graduates' professional aspirations were shaped by their pre-university, within-university, and postgraduation experiences.

By focusing my fieldwork inside Iran, and conducting in-depth biographical interviews, I revealed findings that problematize human capital theory. If I had included the portions of my findings and data where the lived experiences of my participants went beyond the borders of Iran, then human capital theory—specifically, the theory's emphasis on personal responsibility for employment outcomes through investment in human capital (in the form of education), which presupposes individual agency within both the education system and the job market—would more accurately explain their journey. Moreover, I believe the human capital perspective also proves problematic within a nondemocratic context due to the tense relationship between the youth and their government, an institution that initially offers promises of returns on their human capital investments but eventually limits those returns within a set of parameters built by the *khodi*.

Thus, in the case of the Islamic Republic, my participants did not believe they could achieve their aspirations inside Iran because of their reported experiences, and often struggles, with certain obstacles they felt were overtly or covertly imposed upon them by the institutions they were told to pursue and trust, hoping they would lead to a guaranteed successful life. There were three facets in their experiences that led to this skepticism. The first took place within the educational institutions they attended—particularly from the gifted schools to high school and pre-university courses, as well as the Science Olympiad, *konkur* prep schools, and university. The second facet occurred within society and the ideological, cultural, religious, and societal norms that were propagated by State-run media outlets, television, cinema, radio, print, online, and social media. And the third was from governmental and quasi-governmental entities of the Islamic Republic—such as mosques, ministry departments, the Islamic Revolutionary Guard Corps (IRGC), *khusulati* companies, as well as the financial sector—that furthered the *khodi* parameters the participants felt confined within.

Two pivotal actors of the Islamic Republic that benefited from the imposition of the parameters were the *khodi* and *khusulati*. The literal translation of *khodi* is "of us" or "us." *Khodi* members are individuals with a connection to the regime. This connection can be through—but not limited to—employment, family, marriage, association, or allegiances. With this connection, certain benefits—including but not limited to social, economic, religious, political, financial, business, investment, and cultural concessions, privileges, advantages, and other benefits—are available to these individuals. As a member of the *khodi*, one upholds, advocates, and at times enforces the ideology of the Islamic Republic, which ensures the *khodi*'s longevity, financial security, and power and influence over how the government operates and what direction the country is headed as it relates to most aspects of life inside Iran. *Khusulati* is a type of company that is partially owned by a private party and partially owned by the *khodi*—i.e., elements of the Islamic Republic, the IRGC, and/or the clerical establishment, to name a few. *Khusulati* companies have become another tool that the *khodi* has used to monopolize the business sector—in addition to the religious, financial, and media sectors—and therefore the job market.

All of this is compounded by the people in the participants' life—e.g., immediate family, relatives, friends, neighbors, cab drivers, store clerks, strangers, teachers, counselors, professors, coworkers, bosses—who the participants felt were either (a) passively indifferent to alleviating these obstacles, tensions, and struggles or (b) actively perpetuating them to where the participants felt, and often times believed, there was only one specific path they were to take, which they later called the one-dimensional path.[2] The participants described how the tension with these institutions and the adults within them resulted in underdeveloped decisions for their short-term future and no decisions for their long-term future, thus leading to unrealized aspirations inside Iran. When we further explored how the participants detailed their experiences with these tensions, obstacles, and parameters, they explained the feeling of being pushed down a one-dimensional path that shaped their aspirations for them. The participants used phrases such as "hitting a ceiling," "being stuck on a rail," "going down a track," or "forced down this road." Chapters 4, 5, and 6 each represent a stage—pre-university, within-university, and postgraduation—of their lives that focus, in-depth, on their encounters and experiences, as well as on perceived tensions, obstacles, and limitations with Iran's educational institutions, governmental entities, and job market, and the *khodi*, society, and family.

The findings revealed that the participants were active in strengthening their weaknesses to improve their employability in order to increase their chances of realizing their aspirations inside Iran. They were also self-aware and able to articulate their own shortcomings while making pragmatic adjustments with their job market expectations. Thus, the participants' maturation led to an increased sense of agency despite being affected by the education system, the job market, and the regime's tentacles of influence. Nevertheless, the participants reported how they eventually realized the difficulties and often impossibilities of achieving their own aspirations inside Iran. One fascinating aspect of this paradox is that the participants developed these skills and knowledge within the same system that they later criticize and blame for their inabilities to succeed within Iran.

Such an irony has an unintended consequence of creating critical thinkers capable of resisting the regime or being active *ghayre-khodi*. This dichotomy is discussed throughout the book, but I will provide a brief synopsis here. It appears that this risk by the *khodi* is a calculated one that is counteracted by two equally consequential possibilities that play to the *khodi*'s favor. First, if such critical thinkers are created, they may decide to leave Iran—which is one less threat to the regime—and many are doing just that with the country suffering from a brain drain. And second, if these critical thinkers decide to stay and use their talents inside the country to create a successful/lucrative business like Snapp (Iran's version of Uber), the *khodi* can acquire such a company, turn it into a *khusulati* company, and reap the benefits.

Chapter Breakdown

In chapter 1, "Setting the Scene Within the Global Debate on Youth Aspiration, Employability, and Unemployment," I provide a review of the relevant scholarly work on professional aspirations, employability, and graduate unemployment. In particular, I examine unemployed individuals' professional aspirations, how those professional aspirations developed or were formed, and how pre-university, within-university, and postgraduation influenced that development or formation. The global conversations I examine are also juxtaposed with the Iranian literature to further highlight where this study contributes to the current discourse. I also examine the literature on structure and agency as well as employability while drawing comparisons with local documents in order to highlight the significance of how these understandings relate to the participants' professional aspirations inside Iran. I do this by first reviewing the literature on aspirations in four parts—inspired by the works of Spenner and Featherman (1978)—in order to understand this concept, see how it is measured and theorized, and uncover what kind of relationship it has with an individual. I then examine the literature on employability through the works of Bourdieu (1977), Brown et al. (2010), and Tomlinson (2008). I also examine the literature on graduate unemployment in juxtaposition with the Iranian literature to highlight where a deeper investigation into the role of the State may be necessary when discussing professional aspirations and graduate employability.

In chapter 2, "Setting the Scene Within Iran's Modern History," I provide a historical overview of Iran in order to situate my work within the context of Iran. This chapter provides the reader a foundational understanding of how Iranian society has been transformed throughout generations of global, social, political, and economic change, which has led to this book's argument of the *khodi*-versus-*ghayre-khodi* dynamic and the ideological capital that challenges the human capital argument. Therefore, I begin by briefly presenting a short background of a nation that had consistently been in domestic and international turmoil since the 1941 Anglo–Soviet invasion during World War II (Alizadeh, 2000). I then focus on the 1979 revolution and subsequent changes with the nation's social, cultural, political, and economic landscape that effected Iran's primary, secondary, and higher education systems. I close out the chapter with a critique of the current scholarly, policy, and media debates on Iran's youth struggles, while highlighting the literature's shortcomings and how this book has moved the conversation forward.

In chapter 3, "Conducting Fieldwork Inside Iran," I detail my fieldwork experience that led to this book. I recount the good experiences and bad, safe practices and dangerous missteps, and dos and donts for any aspiring researcher thinking of conducing fieldwork inside a precarious country like Iran, Russia, China, or the like. I then highlight what I was able to accomplish during my fieldwork and list all the individuals I interviewed, along with each of their most notable comments and thoughts. I close out the chapter by also detailing the local literature I was able to access. The breadth of literature I was able to find contributed significantly to supplementing—and at times confirming—my participants' stories and shaping a fuller picture of their experiences.

In chapter 4, "A One-Dimensionality to Human Capital During Pre-university: School, Family, and Society Postponing Living," I detail the process of aspiration formation as described by the participants through their lived experiences of growing up in Iran's school system, prior to entering university. The time frame of this pre-university stage is from the first year of middle school (or sixth grade, when students are twelve years old) up to entering Sharif. The school curriculum is formulated by the Islamic Republic; thus, the participants had to follow a set of teachings disproportionately focused on upholding the regime's ideology instead of attending a variety of classes or participating in an academic environment to expand their minds, discover their interests, and explore their options. Thus, a tension appeared to exist in this relationship between the participants and the educational institutions. There was also a tension between the participants and their families, who either induced or forced a short-sighted mentality. My interviews with high school guidance counselors and government officials are included in this chapter.

The participants detailed how they felt that their aspirations were being shaped for them, that their individual agency was not developing, and that they were being pushed down a one-dimensional path while simultaneously being promised a guaranteed successful life if they blindly obeyed. This pathway consisted of a human-capital-like focus on short-term goals revolving around exams and studying—specifically, the national entrance exam for the gifted, the National Science Olympiad entrance exam, and the national higher education entrance exam or *konkur*. The participants described the *konkur* as a "monster," an "obstacle," or a "mythical being" that "needed to be conquered" in order to succeed.

Thus, the participants also reported a disposition of ignoring their future and aspirations; they did "not [know they] could think about it," so they felt they could "only see what was in front of" them. They also explained how "everyone wants you to be a certain way, follow a certain path." One influential (f)actor within this tension was the *khodi*, which the participants felt impeded calls for change. Moreover, the participants reported how the Islamic Republic enabled such a culture to persist and strengthen by overlooking those impediments by the *khodi*. I also share my personal experiences with such tensions during my time in Iran. The participants later realized the effects of this tension when they discovered how unprepared they felt for the future and how the promises they were given did not coincide with their lived experiences. As the participants' descriptions became increasingly definitive—using absolute words such as "only" and "everyone"—I challenged them on their own faults. The participants acknowledged their shortcomings, but they counterargued that they felt the environment in which they grew up shaped their aspirations for them. These stories from my participants are the first examples of how theories born out of the global north come up short on explaining the practicalities of my participants' maturation through Iran's education system.

The participants' narrative depicted a culture that would label them either as stupid, lazy, and sloppy or intelligent and gifted. And irrespective of their successes or failures, the participants felt pushed toward the one-dimensional human capital path. They also described sacrificing their personal interests, areas of their social life, and other aspects of their youth due to the feeling of having to take this path in order to reach that guaranteed and successful future they were promised. The participants described this journey as an unhealthy competition with a "wrong culture" in place. Their sense of agency while recounting their pre-university stage was recognizable in retrospect due to their adaptability and perseverance. However, the participants felt their agency was inconsequential during this stage because they felt limited within specific parameters. Thus, while transitioning from their pre- to within-university stage, the participants recalled feeling unable to aspire to their own future. They also described a level of confusion as to why this path was the direction they must take and what professional purpose it may serve.

Chapter 5, "A Tense Realization Within University: A Feeling of Isolation and Ejection," I detail the inflation of the one-dimensional human capital path as described by the participants. They illustrated a highly centralized context that they felt was working against them in trying to identify their own aspirations, even while they tried to improve their employability in the process. My interviews with students, professors, administrators, and government officials are included in this chapter. The time frame of this within-university stage is the participants' four years of undergraduate study at Sharif—which also included an additional year during which they prolonged their graduation in order to assess what course of action to take toward their future. They used this period to consider their own uncertainty, the volatility of the country's economy and job market, and the *sarbazi*, or mandatory military service, they were obligated—but did not want—to enlist in.

As the participants' perceived tensions with the education system and Sharif University continued, I queried their views and tendencies of blaming societal norms, State expectations, educational institutions, and governmental entities. They went on to conceptualize a tense relationship with these institutions that demonstrated how the linear path continued to persist within university, and with the government enabling that persistence. This concept was *khodi* versus *ghayre-khodi*. In short, the *khodi* constitutes any individual/entity who has any kind of affiliation, directly or indirectly, with the Islamic Republic—i.e., Sharif University, which is owned by the regime. And the *ghayre-khodi* is everyone else—particularly my participants. The participants described five experiences as a result of their tension with the *khodi*: (1) a sense of hopelessness toward Sharif's willingness or capability in helping *ghayre-khodi Sharifis*; (2) the pressure to leave Iran at a time when they did not want to; (3) an inaction from the top down and bottom up for change; (4) misguidance from family as the participants tried to navigate the parameters they felt were limiting their academic and professional maturation; and (5) a disconnect between Sharif and the job market. I too encountered this tension during my time in Iran and share my experiences with these five points. At this juncture, more is revealed about ideological capital through the *khodi*-versus-*ghayre-khodi* dynamic, and therefore, I engage further with these concepts.

As a result of the five experiences, the participants actively pursued their own aspirations. However, this pursuit created another tension as the participants realized their uncertainty in what their own aspirations were. This was further compounded by their struggles to distance themselves from the one-dimensional human capital path. Simultaneously, the participants still tried to find ways to manifest their agency and employability to an extent where they had an increased likelihood in realizing their aspirations inside the limited parameters of Iran. In doing so, the participants changed their environment, pursued extracurricular activities, became multidimensional, worked on their employability, and became more self-critical. I close the chapter by briefly highlighting two issues—the *sarbazi* (or conscription) and the economy—that added to the participants' struggles in forming their own aspirations and to the increased tension with the *khodi* as they transitioned into the job market. It is at this point where human capital theory comes under question and the concept of ideological capital takes form as we further examine the participants' experiences.

In chapter 6, "A Clash of Ideologies in Postgraduation: A *Khodi*-Versus-*Ghayre-Khodi* Tension," I detail the participants' accounts of the depreciation of the one-dimensionality to human capital as a result of the increasing obstacles they perceived within the job market, as well as the empty promises made by the Islamic Republic that investing in themselves through education would yield returns in the job market. My interviews with professionals in the human resources, career services, and civil society sectors are included in this chapter. I also integrate my interviews with government officials and professionals. The prime (f)actors at play in this third stage of the participants' lives include the regime's tentacles of influence.

Three discoveries occurred in this stage for the participants that led them feeling defeated, hopeless, or uncertain about their future inside Iran. The first is the monopolizing of the job market by the *khodi*. According to the participants, this tension illustrates a highly structured context that they believed denied them the realization of their aspirations inside Iran despite their continued efforts in improving their employability. What resulted for the participants was an unhealthy environment within the job market that left them with unethical, immoral, and/or illegal decisions they were unwilling to make. The participants also reported a tension between trying to realize their aspirations inside Iran and navigating the parameters of the job market that had limitations resulting from the *khodi*'s monopolization and the subsequent unhealthy environment. The participants and I also discussed their agency in the face of these experiences and how they adapted and responded.

The second discovery for the participants was how the *khodi* and *ghayre-khodi* tension became more of a tactile experience. They reported direct involvement by the tentacles of the State in attempting to prevent their pursuits of trying to realize their aspirations inside Iran. It is here where we first discover the wall at the end of the linear path that limited the participants' standard of living inside Iran and thus the depreciating of the one-dimensionality to human capital. A deeper engagement with ideological capital is conducted at this realization. Moreover, the *khodi* were depicted as more active in their efforts to maintain the status quo that benefited the *khodi* while opposing efforts for change. The participants also experienced the *khodi*'s pursuit of *khusulati* companies that further monopolized the job market. *Khusulati* is a combination of private (***khususi***) and State (***dolati***) entities that primarily consists of current, former, and/or retired officials of the Islamic Republic, members of their families, friends, and/or associates, and some individuals with no ties to the Islamic Republic. Thus, the participants described an uncertain and highly structured job market, and social context, that they felt continued to restrict them while they continued to exert their agency within those parameters.

The third was the participants' experiences of hitting the *ghayre-khodi* wall. For the participants, this experience took on many forms. One was the daily volatility that I briefly experienced with them, such as internet blackouts, overnight price increases, and confrontations with authorities. We expanded on these by further discussing what they believed the volatility was connected to: the economy and national security, both being tied to the Islamic Republic and, more specifically, the *khodi*. The participants explained how the denial for them in trying to realize their aspirations inside Iran led them to either lower their aspirations and accept their state of affairs—which they understood as becoming an "obedient citizen"—or leave the country and increase their likelihood in realizing their aspirations—which reassured them that their job market expectations were realistic in an American environment, for example, where a human capital approach was comparatively and appropriately more applicable.

In chapter 7, "The Role of the State and Ideological Capital," I assemble a comprehensive analysis of the lived experiences of my participants. I recap my concept of ideological capital, the ideological-employability scale, and the *khodi*-versus-*ghayre-khodi* dynamic within the broader literature and conversation. First, I discuss the role of the Islamic Republic and the wall it has established at the end of the participants' distorted version of a human capital path. Then I detail the effects of this path and subsequent tensions that my participants experienced and perceived. I then discuss the limitations of employability and human capital theory within a *ghayre-khodi* context and how my book moves these conversations forward, particularly how the various tensions situate this book among existing literature discussing the same issues—e.g., India (Jeffrey, 2010), Ethiopia (Mains, 2012), Egypt (Pettit, 2017), and Kenya (Thieme, 2017). I also juxtapose this book with the theoretical literature of human capital arguments by reexamining the works of Bourdieu (1972/1977), Schultz (1961), Becker (1993), Brown et al. (2010), and Tomlinson (2008).

CHAPTER 1

Setting the Scene Within the Global Debate on Youth Aspiration, Employability, and Unemployment

I had overcompensated in favor of an idealized vision of agency, thus reproducing the resistance/domination dynamic already found in much of the existing literature. I had done so because I was looking for dramatic or expressed bursts of opposition or bouts of justice seeking under authoritarian rule, rather than seeking out how people negotiate with what can be a suffocatingly tedious and impenetrable bureaucratic setting in order to improve their own lives.

MALEKZADEH

This realization by one of my peers—Shervin Malekzadeh (2016, p. 866)—highlights the complexities and biases of many of the issues we Iran experts wrestle with in our attempts to uncover the realities within Iran. What makes this process more difficult are the global debates within which Iran is situated. In other words, much of the conversations surrounding youth struggles with employability, unemployment, and realizing one's aspirations of a higher standard of living falls short in fully and accurately capturing the situation within Iran. This is partly due to the biases of the researcher as well as the difficulties in being able to properly and safely conduct research inside Iran. But more importantly, it is also partly due to the differences that a country like Iran (and Russia, China, North Korea, and Nicaragua, for example) has with the typical countries (Europe and North America) the global debate has primarily analyzed.

Thus, to fully understand how this book fits within this global debate, it is important to briefly examine how Iran is situated within the conversations on aspiration, employability, and unemployment, of which, an extensive array of issues is discussed: frustration and anger in the United States (Hochschild, 2016), waithood in India (Jeffrey, 2010), boredom in Senegal (Ralph, 2008) and Romania (O'Neill, 2014), inequality and precarity in France (Murphy,

2017), hustling in Kenya (Thieme, 2017), or a broader examination of purposelessness and detachment (Berlant, 2011; Bourdieu, 2000).

There are also the works of Mains (2012) on Ethiopia and Pettit (2017) on Egypt, both of which share many similarities to my own. For Mains (2012), shame and honor were uncovered and explored in the absence of unrealized professional aspirations for his participants in Ethiopia. For Pettit's (2017) participants in Egypt, it was waithood and mismatch. And for the participants of both scholars, hope, masculinity, and unrealistic expectations persisted. The similarities that my research has with Mains and Pettit exist in our findings' paradoxical juxtaposition with the theories—human capital in particular—that attempt to explain an individual's ability, probability, and valence in achieving their professional aspirations. Mains and Pettit, for example, depict their participants' repeated attempts, and subsequent failures, in trying to achieve their aspirations.

Mains (2012, pp. 3–4) looks at young, unemployed Ethiopian men whose aspirations for the future do not fit with economic realities, and what happens when they are "unable to attain their desires for the future." Mains describes a highly social dynamic among his participants where particular social engagements, rituals, and customs are more valuable and honorable than just working any job that is available. Moreover, his participants remain unemployed, living with their parents, unable to marry and start a family, possessing these "unprecedented aspirations" and "elevated ambitions" (p. 3). They also continue to hold on to this hope that one day they will attain the job they want within government. However, his participants are cautious about the positions they pursue in order to ensure that key aspects of their life—e.g., a government job—lead to a rise in their social standing. Mains further argues that one's aspiration can persist despite these conditions as long as the individual retains the "ability to continually imagine a desirable future" which will "enable hope to persist" (p. 43).

Pettit (2017) goes one step further and presents a group of unemployed Egyptian men on the brink of losing hope. Pettit writes about his participants going through the motions of job hunting and seeing themselves as strugglers or *mukafeh*. Pettit also explains how his participants continue to manage their employability while clutching to this hope that eventually they will reach their professional aspirations. Similar to Mains (2012), Pettit's participants are content in remaining unemployed until a suitable job is found; in the meantime, they attend job fairs, training centers, entrepreneurship events, and the like. Pettit portrays his participants as attempting "to make the transition from education to 'aspired to' employment" while "continuing to hold on to this cruel form of hope" (p. 283).

While the lived experiences of our (Mains's, Pettit's, and my) participants bore many similarities, the differences lay in how our participants perceived their experiences and how that manifested through their decision-making. Mains's and Pettit's findings revealed issues of shame, honor, masculinity, mismatch, waithood, and hope, whereas my findings identify a tense relationship between my participants (or the *ghayre-khodi*) and key elements of the Islamic Republic, like the *khodi*. For example, where Mains's participants aspire toward government jobs or Pettit's participants utilize government(-backed) programs, my participants experience a government that seemingly plays an active role in obstructing, diverting, or opposing their professional aspirations inside Iran—despite their best efforts of investing in their human capital. Therefore, how does aspirational attainment within an Islamic Republic context fit in with the global debate?

Aspiration

The literature on aspiration has been discussed across many disciplinary approaches, each employing different terminologies, measures, theories, and concepts. Inspired by Spenner and Featherman's (1978) four variations of aspiration, this section is divided into four parts.

1. Aspirations in objects, such as education, occupation, and material well-being, to identify terminologies and definitions of aspiration.
2. Aspirations in time, such as age-specific and short/mid/long-term, to identify measures of aspiration.
3. "The way in which subjective probability and valence are conceptualized" (p. 376)—vis-à-vis how important, realistic, feasible, and attainable the aspiration is.
4. The procedural relationship between the individual and their aspirations—i.e., their level of desire, inclination, hope, and willingness to work for/toward their aspiration.

The first variation lends itself to the multitude of terms and definitions of aspiration. Reissman (1953) and Kahl (1953) define *aspiration* as one's level of willingness to change to a higher-prestige job, or one's desire and expectation for college attendance. There are also terms such as *educational aspiration* (Sewell et al., 1957), *career* or *occupational aspiration* (Haller & Miller, 1971), and *mobility aspiration* (Van Zeyl, 1974). The literature has shown that students with high aspirations set loftier goals (Hodis et al., 2015; Trice & McClellan,

1993), have increased motivation toward those goals (Mahoney et al., 2003; McGaha & Fitzpatrick, 2010), and are future oriented with clear plans and a directed focus (Nurmi, 2004). However, what happens if aspirations are not achieved? Do students recalibrate their goals or continue with their plan and remain focused on trying to achieve what they have set out to do? Are they able to overcome these setbacks?

If they are able to overcome setbacks and failures, this process may occur incrementally over time depending on their ability to make adjustments and adapt. Thus, the second variation lends itself to the measures of aspiration. One example is personal initiative, defined as "an individual taking an active and self-starting approach to work, goals, and tasks, and persisting in overcoming barriers and setbacks" (Fay & Frese, 2001, p. 97). Another example focuses on the extracurricular activities—such as sports, music, social and academic clubs, volunteering—an individual engages in to promote and set personal goals, evaluate what is needed to attain them, and actively acquire the abilities and resources to achieve them (Larson et al., 2006; Seow & Pan, 2014). These measures of aspiration discuss how an individual's aspirations develop and fluctuate over time with the aim (and hope) of achieving one's goals. However, what happens with the individual if he is still unable to reach his goals even when incremental aspirations are achieved? This book resides in these moments of unrealized aspirations by exploring the participants' lived experiences and seeing how and why they feel unable to attain their desired future inside Iran.

What explanation can be discovered if my participants made adjustments after failing—by acknowledging their unrealistic goals or mismatched expectations and lowering their aspirations—but continued to experience or feel that their aspirations inside Iran were unrealizable? The third variation lends itself to theories trying to answer this question. For example, goal-setting theory argues that setting goals and being goal oriented leads to an increased likelihood of attaining aspirations (Forster & Souvignier, 2014; Locke & Latham, 2006; Schunk, 2001). There is also social cognitive career theory, which looks at self-efficacy, outcome expectation, and goals. Lewin et al. (1944, p. 335) discusses one's level of aspiration, which he defines as "the level of future performance in a familiar task which an individual, knowing their level of past performance in that task, explicitly undertakes to reach."

These explanations have been argued as (a) "essential agency variables that enable individuals to develop personal control over their career development" (Sawitri et al., 2014, p. 562) and (b) ways to express the influence that aspiration has in driving motivation and future goals (Ingram, 2017; Lent et al., 1994; Locke & Latham, 1990). However, I find these explanations limited in describing aspirations within a *ghayre-khodi* context for two reasons. First, such agency-focused theories underestimate the influential importance that structure has on an individual—particularly when that structural influence is anchored in a nondemocratic system. And two, the influence from structure appears to manifest and be perceived differently within a nondemocratic government like the Islamic Republic. Therefore, how can we explain an individual's experience after multiple adjustments, recalibrations, and compromises continue to result in failure? What do aspirations look like to an individual after multiple setbacks?

The fourth variation lends itself to the procedural relationship between the individual and their aspiration—i.e., their willingness to work and their level of desire despite failures. One example is achievement motivation and the extent to which one has the drive to work toward the goals they want to reach (Gregor & O'Brien, 2016; Lens et al., 2002; Ryan & Deci, 2000). There is also Appadurai's (2013) capacity to aspire, which offers an interesting viewpoint from a global south position. For Appadurai (2013, p. 189), the capacity to aspire is a navigational one consisting "of a dense combination of nodes and pathways." Individuals who are less fortunate or have inadequate resources have fewer "aspirational nodes and thinner/weaker pathways" to help them achieve their goals (p. 189). He gives the example of a community in Mumbai, India, that struggled to maintain adequate sanitary facilities due to their low socioeconomic status but also to a political and slumlord situation that stymied progress. Appadurai (2013, p. 190) argues that to remedy such setbacks and strengthen one's ability to reach one's goals "requires strengthening among communities." And for the community in Mumbai, they united their efforts and were able to hire a contractor to "build a large number of community toilets on a scale previously reserved for private [companies or the] government" (pp. 190–191).

This argument by Appadurai is significant because it posits two claims. First, if institutions and governments operate in an adverse capacity—as they appear to my participants in Iran to be doing—a possible remedy is a collective effort from within the marginalized community to increase/expand their capacity to aspire. And two, if an individual is not considered among the less fortunate (or a marginalized community), then their capacity to aspire should be stronger with adequate resources and achievable aspirations. Keeping this in mind, my participants would be considered more fortunate because they attended a top-tier university (like Sharif or Tehran) and earned a prestigious (and lucrative) degree in the field of engineering. However, what if this argument only seems to hold water when examining my participants' lived experiences within a global context whereby they leave Iran? What explanation can be discovered if we examine their journey inside Iran? What if the criterion of being more or less fortunate, within a *ghayre-khodi* context, is not a socioeconomic or human capital understanding but rather an ideological one? What if the dense combination of nodes and pathways inside Iran are more strategically valuable to a different demographic, like Iran's *khodi* (the establishment), instead of the *ghayre-khodi* (my participants)? How would a *ghayre-khodi* individual maneuver these parameters?

Employability

To better understand how a *ghayre-khodi* individual maneuvers this landscape, we must now briefly examine employability. If a global north, human capital, agentic understanding of aspirations does not appear to be applicable within a *ghayre-khodi* context, perhaps the same could be true regarding our understanding of employability. Bourdieu's (1972/1977, 1990) work on habitus and capital has been influential on the discourse of employability and one's ability to realize their aspirations. Bourdieu (1972/1977) argues that an individual's aspirations are in line with their chances of realizing those aspirations, and if that realization is unlikely to occur, they will not aspire for certain things he believes is unattainable. Bourdieu (1972/1977) goes on to explain that the individual knows which aspirations are realizable—and therefore, worth acting on—due to a historical-structuralist understanding where the individual continuously experiences, unconsciously acquires, and internalizes a set of dispositions from their surrounding structures. Thus, the individual's relationship with their surrounding structures is recursive and arguably subordinate to those structures. Ahearn (2001, p. 118) explains how this interaction is "a generative process that produces practices and representations that are conditioned by the structuring structures from which they emerge."

Giddens (1984) goes further than Bourdieu (1972/1977)—with structuration theory—in his understanding of this recursive relationship between structure and agency by moving away from, what he calls, a dualism of structure-agency into a mutually interacting duality where structure and agency have a collaborative relationship. He explains how structure plays the dual role of the "medium and the outcome of the social practices they recursively organize" (1984, p. 25). In other words, the individual's actions are shaped in a constraining and enabling way by the very social structures that his/her actions create and serve to reinforce (Ahearn, 2001). Thus, Giddens claims that this duality provides more space for the agent to affect change through reflexivity (Giddens, 1984).

However, Bourdieu and Giddens have been criticized for being deterministic and seeing agency as "so tightly bound to structure that one loses sight of the different ways in which agency actually shapes social action" (Emirbayer & Mische, 1998, p. 963). Thus, a Bourdieu-inspired or Giddens-inspired view illustrates that although the individual is able to navigate the job market by using different types of capital and employability to aid them in realizing their aspirations, the aspirations they are pursuing have been influentially constructed by their surrounding structures. This view may be a less problematic argument when trying to explain youth's experience inside a developed and/or democratic country, or perhaps a country where the government is amenable to change, with fewer limitations on youth's ability to manifest their employability and types of capital to an extent where their aspirations have an increased likelihood of being realized inside their own country. Bourdieu's work, in fact, if applied within an authoritarian context, can help explain how citizens can be conditioned to have a fatalistic view where they self-censor and self-regulate. And over time, those who show loyalty are rewarded—like the *khodi*—and those who resist—like some of the *ghayre-khodi*—are kept away from some (or all) of those rewards.

One of Giddens's main critics, for example, argues that the conflation of structure and agency elides the possibility of identifying "the properties and powers pertaining respectively to structure and to agents" (Archer, 2007, p. 34). Therefore, some scholars have argued more in favor of agency and globalization in employability enhancements and aspirational attainment that is not necessarily bound within the borders of one's country or within the parameters of one's government. For example—and with criticism on Bourdieu's work—Sewell (1992) argues how the individual is the master of their own future and capable of shaping their own history, and Beck (1992) argues how the individual has complete control of their life due partly to international mobility.

Moreover, the current discourse on employability argues that it is incumbent on the individual (Baruch, 2001; Garavan, 1999) to be able to "move self-sufficiently" within the job market (Hillage & Pollard, 1998, p. 2), find ways to enhance their attractiveness within that job market (Iles et al., 1996), "anticipate changes in tasks and work environment and react to these changes in a proactive way" (Sanders & de Grip, 2004, p. 76), and/or exercise an "active adaptability that enables them to identify and realize job opportunities" (Fugate et al., 2004, p. 16). These debates have a continued focus on the individual, maintaining that one's employability derives from the different types of capital—such as human, cultural, personal, reputational, and/or social—one can invest in (Tholen, 2017). This agentic understanding of employability offers viable explanations on why and how an individual can improve their employability. By investing in oneself—through education, training, and other pertinent activities—youth can realize their aspirations. Even if their environment and conditions are not conducive, they will find a way to realize their aspirations. If they do not, then there is something wrong with their approach and they must restrategize (Becker, 1993).

Such arguments from the human capital perspective have continued to dominate the global debate (Ashwin, 2020; Marginson, 2019). However, similar to my criticism of a structuralist approach, this agentic framework is also less problematic if the individual is from a country where the government is amenable to change. And therefore, fewer limitations are placed on the youth's capacity to manifest their employability and types of capital to an extent where their aspirations have an increased likelihood of being realized. Thus, how do we explain the effectiveness of one's employability if these broader debates—either from a structuralist viewpoint or an agentic one—appear to not be applicable within a *ghayre-khodi* context? Perhaps an alternative explanation is required.

My criticism is shared by some scholars (Brown et al., 2001; Piketty, 2014; Tholen, 2015) who argue that human capital theory is flawed within certain contexts that are not comparable with a twentieth-century Western lens, especially those with a neoliberal premise of a capitalistic market of privatization, deregulation, and competition. For example, the human capital argument does not appear to be entirely sufficient when examining Iranian youths' lived experiences from higher education to Iran's job market specifically because the Islamic Republic is not viewed as an amenable government that creates or leaves opportunities for professional growth, societal progress, and institutional change, like in most contexts where human capital theory is discussed. However, the literature that does criticize this theory does not sufficiently problematize the power of the government in the broken promise of human capital. This book, therefore, deepens and extends that critique on human capital theory by mapping the power of the government in relation to the individual.

I build on the wider discourse by problematizing the existing literature rooted in human capital theory (Becker, 1993; Schultz, 1961), as well as policy rooted in neoliberal approaches, that frame employability and aspirational attainment in terms of individual agency (Fugate et al., 2004; Nilsson, 2010; Tholen, 2015). Thus, I draw inspiration from the work of Brown et al. (2010) in their critique of the broken promises of human capital theory. Where Brown et al. (2010) discuss broken promises of education, jobs, and income, this book adds a broken promise in the complex dynamic between the *khodi* (or a nondemocratic government) and the *ghayre-khodi* (or the individual citizen). Within the *ghayre-khodi* context specifically, my participants seem to have a tense relationship with certain elements of the Islamic Republic that initially promise returns on their human capital investments but eventually limit those returns within specific parameters established by the *khodi*, *khusulati* companies, and certain mafias (in sectors like education and economy).

Given the likelihood that there is an overt and covert resistance to change by the Islamic Republic (that will be discussed in more detail in the next chapter), along with the broken promise of human capital investment, I will examine employability through a subjective understanding. Many scholars have recognized the importance in the subjective nature of the individual experience of employability and the historical, economic, and social context surrounding one's journey (Estienne, 1997; Holmes, 2001; McQuaid & Lindsay, 2005; Tholen, 2017). Tomlinson (2007, p. 286), for example, criticizes the current discourse from "continually overlooking the subjective dimension of employability, . . . how it relates to the way individuals come to perceive and understand the job market [and] the types of dispositions, attitudes, and identities they develop around their future work and employability." This book, therefore, will examine how my participants understand, construct, and manage their employability throughout their journey of trying to explore, identify, and realize their aspirations inside Iran while facing the uncertainties, struggles, and barriers in achieving them in an education system and job market controlled and/or influenced by the *khodi*.

Unemployment

The literature on Iran's unemployment can be categorized into two perspectives. The first comes from Western and diasporic analysts who, in most instances, have examined and debated this issue through the lens of a corrupt government that has caused the country's international isolation, crippling sanctions, political nepotism, financial corruption, economic instability, and inflationary pressures. These conversations (Khosravi, 2008; Mahdavi, 2009; Varzi, 2006; Yaghmaian, 2002) bear compelling arguments; however, they have been criticized for a homogeneous interpretation of complex issues (Olszewska, 2013). Olszewska (2013, p. 844) further criticizes this perspective as "the existence of a unitary society positioned in irreconcilable opposition to a monolithic State [where] there is little accounting for diversity and hierarchies [and] the assumption is that there is a single fault line of struggle in society." Khosravi (2017), for example, acknowledges in his later work that a strong tendency toward a politically oriented narrative exists in the literature. Similarly, Shervin Malekzadeh describes his moment of clarity regarding the aforementioned during his fieldwork in the epigraph at the beginning of this chapter. The "suffocatingly tedious and impenetrable bureaucratic setting" is one area this book examines, as I believe it has to do with the *khodi*-versus-*ghayre-khodi* tension that is manifested through broken promises of human capital and covert resistance to change (2016, p. 866).

The second perspective comes from local scholars (from within Iran) who have mostly examined Iran's unemployment problem though a quantitative lens (Amini et al., 2013; Hashemi et al., 2012; Naji et al. 2016; Sakurai, 2004). Abbas Bazargan is arguably the leading thinker in Iran on the country's education system, and his publications span over five decades and two regimes. Bazargan's work on higher education mainly focuses on institutional performance, evaluation schemes, quality satisfaction ratings, internal evaluations, and access to education. His 2000 article points to a number of shortcomings in the higher education system that he argues has led to unemployment—for example, the inflexibility of higher education institutions to quickly react to the job market. Bazargan (2000, p. 176) goes on to admit that further research on this issue is needed: "Follow-up studies on university graduates are needed to show the current trends of unemployment."

Alashloo et al. (2005, p. 132) conducted a structured questionnaire "to identify the impeders of strategy implementation in the higher education sector of Iran." They identify thirty-two impeders, some of which are mentioned in Bazargan's (2000) article from five years earlier, such as lack of adequate internal communication, unsuitable training systems, and competition rather than cooperation between people and departments (Alashloo et al., 2005, p. 141). Alashloo et al. also echoes a similar sentiment to that of Bazargan regarding the dearth of qualitative work on Iran's higher education system. In 2011, Mojgan et al. published an article discussing the anxiety undergraduate students have over career indecision. This is another quantitative approach employing the career decision scale and the state and trait anxiety inventory on 150 students. Mojgan et al. concludes that "it would be beneficial to explore the possible sources of anxiety in either individual or group counseling sessions" with "further research . . . to investigate the influence of other factors on career indecision" (2011, p. 33). Alibaygi et al. (2013, p. 680) also conducted a quantitative study looking at the skill-mismatch phenomenon, where they concluded not only that there was a worrying and significant mismatch but also that "the employability of students [must] be further investigated utilizing qualitative methodologies."

These aforementioned debates around the causes and factors of unemployment for Iran's youth are similar to the global conversation. Discussions on the different types of job market mismatches, for example, have been debated within political and economic arenas. Issues like a mismatch between supply and demand (Liagouras et al., 2003), a disconnect between knowledge and skills (Dabalen et al., 2001), geographic mismatch (Barker, 2007), mismatched expectations (Mains, 2012), and vertical and horizontal mismatch (International Labor Organization, 2013) have been examined. Iran also joins the wider conversation on socioeconomic concerns (Denny & Harmon, 2000; Granovetter, 1995; Livanos, 2010), (rapid) growth of higher education (Bai, 2006), a surplus of graduates into the job market (Bowers-Brown & Harvey, 2004), and societal influences on career choice (e.g., Hoffman, 1974; Jackson et al., 1993; Lent & Brown, 1996).

As scholars argue which cause or factor is more impactful on unemployment, their lack of consensus highlights Bee and Dolton's (1990, p. 32) argument that "unemployment trends are derived from a complex interaction of forces, and it is difficult to identify the individual impact." This argument by Bee and Dolton was true when the global conversation on unemployment reached more complex debates from the 2008 recession (Livanos, 2010; Oreopoulos et al., 2012; Tomic, 2014), as well as the COVID-19 pandemic. Bee and Dolton's argument is also true within the Iranian context. Not only has Iran endured the complexities of the Great Recession and COVID-19, but the country has continuously struggled with the complexities of unemployment since the 1979 Islamic Revolution. Since 1980 Iran has been under international sanctions by the United States, the European Union, and the United Nations (Amuzegar, 2004; Hamdhaidari et al., 2008; Kousha & Abdoli, 2004).

Moreover, it can be argued that unemployment in Iran has been—and continues to be—structural, as it is explained by Barker (2007, p. 177):

> Job opportunities do not increase fast enough to absorb those already unemployed and those newly entering the job market. Some examples of this inability can be the rapid growth of the labor force, the use of capital- or skills-intensive technology, an inflexible job market, skills mismatch, and geographic mismatch.

The "inflexible job market" Barker mentions is significant in the Iranian context when considering the inflexible nature of those who have monopolized it—i.e., the *khodi* and *khusulati* companies. For example, where Iranian academics and analysts have offered policy proposals to help reduce unemployment, these have been met with much resistance from many within the regime (Ansari et al., 2008; Farasatkhah et al., 2008; Mirzaei, 2019; Seif, 2020). Thus, the next chapter will set the scene as to possible explanations of how and why such a "suffocatingly tedious and impenetrable bureaucratic setting" developed within the Islamic Republic (Malekzadeh, 2016, p. 866), which seemingly led to an "inflexible job market" (Barker, 2007, p. 177) and a covert resistance to change along with the broken promise of human capital investment.

CHAPTER 2

Setting the Scene Within Iran's Modern History

In most cases "they" do not allow change to happen. . . . These conversations have been going on for a very long time and very little has changed.
DR. MAHDI

Anyone who has spent enough time inside Iran, or has studied the intricacies of Iranian society, knows that "they" means the *khodi*. Dr. Mahdi's choice of words was deliberate, especially since he is an employee of the regime. While his comment may not be a surprise given what we know about the Islamic Republic through public knowledge, it still warrants attention for the reasons I explained at the end of the previous chapter. Understanding why someone like Dr. Mahdi would need to be careful with his words goes deeper than just the apparent risks to himself, his loved ones, and/or their livelihood. There is also a hidden or covert element in this resistance to change by the regime, and to understand this aspect we must first unpack what brought the Islamic Republic to this reality.

For at least the past eighty-five years (from 1941 to 2026) a number of foreign and domestic events have stymied Iran's economic growth. In spite of this, Iran has become a self-sufficient regional power and a serious political actor throughout the Middle East. However, the government continues to struggle in strengthening various sectors of its economy—particularly (un) employment, a lingering impediment that many believed would be mitigated with the presidential election of Hassan Rouhani in 2013 and the signing of the nuclear deal in 2015. Thus, Iran analysts and Middle East experts reverted to familiar debates on economic and political circumstances—but couched within current events—in their analysis on Iran's economic struggles. These struggles, most notably, include: (1) the Iranian government's ineffective domestic policies in attempts to revitalize the country's economy; (2) its prioritization of international affairs—vis-à-vis US President Donald Trump and Israeli Prime Minister Benjamin Netanyahu—over domestic issues; (3) further economic uncertainties as a result of the war with the US/Israel, as well as continued sanctions; and (4) the international community's continued reluctance to enter—and at times, prohibition on entering—the Iran market, which has hindered foreign investment.

Even though the aforementioned analyses are important, the assessment of these four issues is incomplete because these conditions are confined within current economic and political circumstances and it is difficult to maneuver within them. As a result, the subsequent recommendations by Iran analysts are dependent on a plethora of variables—such as elections (presidential, congressional, and parliamentary) and conflicts (military, cyber, terrorism, revolution, or sanctions)—that are unpredictable at best and volatile at worst, and which can change the political and economic landscape at any given moment. A prime example is the war between Iran, Israel, and the United States. Moreover, such debates that criticize the Islamic Republic have seemingly overlooked one aspect of the regime's shortcomings in improving the standard of living inside Iran. The issue is not just the inability but more so a purposeful and strategic unwillingness of certain demographics of the regime's citizenry to make improvements.

To best understand this, we must first consider that Iran has consistently been in domestic and international turmoil since the 1941 Anglo-Soviet invasion of Iran during World War II (Alizadeh, 2000). This was quickly followed by the British forced abdication of King Reza Shah that led to his son—Mohammad Reza Pahlavi—being placed on the throne (Kinzer, 2003). Then, in 1951, Iran's oil was nationalized away from the British, a move led by Iran's democratically elected Prime Minister Mohammad Mosaddegh (A. Milani, 2011). This was soon followed by the 1953 coup orchestrated by America's CIA and Britain's MI6, who ousted Mosaddegh, resulting in a foreign nation once again putting Pahlavi back on the throne (Abrahamian, 2013). This event, along with the image of Pahlavi having to crown himself, was seen by many Iranians as the end of his legitimacy (Abrahamian, 2013). In 1963, Pahlavi started the White Revolution aimed at modernizing Iran and Westernizing its people (Abrahamian, 2008). The next fifteen years saw policies, such as land reform and privatization of companies, that did help segments of the population, but Pahlavi's government also alienated, disenfranchised, and marginalized many groups who did not support such a "Westoxification"—a term with negative connotations meaning to infect one's own culture with the unhealthy dependence on and fascination with Western culture, values, and systems—of their country (Al Ahmad et al., 1984).

The residual effects from these events culminated with the 1979 Revolution. From the multitude of groups opposing the monarchy—such as the intellectuals, Marxists, communists, proletariat, and theologians—it was the religious mullahs who gained control (M. Milani, 2018), leading to the ascent to power of Ayatollah Sayyid Ruhollah Khomeini, who had opposed the shah since the White Revolution. Shortly after, the Islamic Republic was formed, and Khomeini became the supreme leader or *Velayat-e Faqih*. In 1980, Iraq invaded Iran hoping to weaken this new government, but for the next eight years the war further helped the mullahs solidify their control over the country through their use of nationalistic and religious zeal and propaganda. The structural makeup of the Islamic Republic and the country's new constitution developed out of Khomeini's religious and theocratic teachings—specifically his book *Islamic Government: Governance of the Jurist* (1970/2005). His claim that a country must be governed by Islamic law with a supreme leader to provide guardianship over its citizens laid the foundation for an ideologically driven government, society, and culture.

However, Khomeini's time as Iran's supreme leader was short and distracted. Eight of the ten years of his rule were occupied by the war with Iraq. So when he passed in June of 1989, the country was still recovering and rebuilding from the war. Ali Khamenei took over as supreme leader two months later, and ten days after that Iran's fourth president—Akbar Hashemi Rafsanjani (1989–1997)—assumed office and launched the reconstruction era to try to strengthen the economy through "expansive privatization, deregulation, and reduction of subsidies, which weakened collective contracts, increased the class gap, and caused the loss of job security" (Khosravi, 2017, p. 62). Such policies transformed the country from a welfare state to a quasi-socialist and free-market state, leading to a rise in cost of living and unprotected workers (Bahramitash, 2003). Additionally, the average growth rate of public (free) universities from 1989 to 1997 was 9.8 percent, compared to a 20.8 percent growth rate of private (paid) universities (Daneshgah Azad Islami; Bayat, 2009, p. 174). The establishment and rapid growth of private universities was seen as a lucrative business by the Islamic Republic, but also a way to widen access to higher education since public universities only accepted 10 percent of their applicants each year (Department of Statistics & Information Technology, 2017; Hamdhaidari et al., 2008; Kalb, 2017; Kamyab, 2008; Sakurai, 2004). The reason for this upsurge in enrollment was threefold: (1) Societal significance was placed on the prestige of higher education; (2) student enrollment rates increased at a faster pace than the country's population; and (3) private and semi-public universities expanded at a rapid rate (Hamdhaidari et al., 2008). This rapid growth of higher education institutions and enrollment rates coincided with President Rafsanjani's mission in widening access irrespective of one's age, gender, class, and hometown (Hamdhaidari et al., 2008).

The expansion of higher education institutions went on to include semi-public universities of the following types: (1) *Payame Noor* (distance learning universities), (2) *Ghayre Entifayi* (specialized universities), (3) *Fani-herfayi* (two-year technical colleges), (4) *Pardis Benulmilal* (international universities), (5) *Daneshgah Shabaneh* (night school, which despite the name is considered a type of university and is typically for adults and professionals), (6) vocational colleges, and (7) junior colleges (Al-Agha et al., 2009; Clark, 2017; Habibi, 2015; Hassani & Mir Ghasemi, 2016). With these many options, students are able to strategically decide which type of university will increase their chances in enrolling in the major they want based on their *konkur* ranking. Ever since Rafsanjani's presidency, some of these universities have struggled to remain half full, and some others have shut down. No official study has been conducted as of yet, but I have been told by my participants that a combination of (a) cost, (b) lack of prestige and credibility, (c) overexpansion of higher education institutions, and (d) newer generations seeking alternatives to higher education are the reasons. The latter half of Rafsanjani's presidency continued to show little economic improvement. With his government oscillating between socialism and free-market policies, as well as experiencing intrapolitical turmoil, not only was economic growth slow, but there was much resistance from the workforce. This led to a series of worker strikes as the insecurities of job protection and inflation rates continued (Bayat, 2009). The government's mission to improve the economy grew more challenging when by 1996 the youth population (under the age of thirty) had drastically increased to account for two-thirds of the total population (Bayat, 2009).

With a reformist-moderate entering office the following year, Iran's new president, Mohammad Khatami (in office from 1997 to 2005), shouldered a great responsibility in trying to improve the economy and increase job growth, especially for the youth. Whereas Rafsanjani had the reconstruction era, Khatami promoted dialogue among civilizations in attempts to thaw relations with America through means other than politics (e.g., literature, arts, culture, history, and music). By 2000, private universities had over 130 campuses nationwide (Hamdhaidari et al., 2008). The total number of enrolled students by that same year reached 1.3 million (Bayat, 2009). By 2001, 61 percent of all admitted students into universities were women (Bahramitash & Esfahani 2011). The pressure on Khatami's government to create job growth for these soon-to-be graduates led his administration toward unconventional and difficult initiatives. Between 2001 and 2003, over one thousand nongovernmental startup organizations were able to register throughout the country, an endeavor difficult to accomplish since the Islamic Republic viewed most NGOs as a threat to the regime (Bayat, 2009). Furthermore, a joint vocational project with Germany, Italy, and Belgium was also established to better prepare half a million Iranians entering the job market (Hamdhaidari et al., 2008). By the end of his second term—specifically from 2001 to 2006—Khatami oversaw an increase by seven hundred thousand in job growth (Habibi, 2015, p. 2). However, the youth unemployment rate remained in double digits (Bayat, 2009).

Khatami's successor, Mahmoud Ahmadinejad (2005 to 2013), had a more conservative agenda, thus reversing many of his predecessor's work (Amuzegar, 2007; Bahramitash, 2013). Many media outlets and NGOs were banned or shut down. Women were prohibited from majoring in seventy-seven academic fields across thirty-six universities at the graduate level (Khosravi, 2017). The country's nuclear program resumed operations, which led to further sanctions. Job growth increased by only twenty thousand from 2006 to 2011 (Habibi, 2015). Unemployment remained in double digits at 19 percent overall and 40 percent in Tehran alone (Arani et al., 2018). Ahmadinejad's government responded by adopting the International Labor Organization definition of employment to an "individual who works at least one hour per week" (International Labor Organization, n.d.; Khosravi, 2017, p. 75). He also increased access to State distance-learning universities (*Payām-e Nur*) without requiring the *konkur* (Arani et al., 2018). The *Payām-e Nur* was promoted as a "direct competitor to the rapidly growing private universities" (Kalb, 2017, p. 12). However, this was seen more as a business opportunity than a policy shift in helping unemployment.

Over time, distance-learning universities had played an important role in extending State education, making up almost 30 percent of Iran's total State university enrollment in 2014 (Kalb, 2017). However, this added to the 270,000 graduates already entering the job market every year, which further complicated the nation's unemployment problem (Azizi & Hosseini, 2006, as cited in Alibaygi et al., 2013). In the span of these eight years during Ahmadinejad's presidency, Iran's economy continued to worsen due to increased inflation, corruption, and sanctions coupled with decreased foreign investment and job growth. Simultaneously, unemployment remained in double digits as it had since 2000: 12 percent overall and almost 27 percent for young people (Khosravi, 2017). In some major cities, such as Tehran, youth unemployment was upward of 40 percent (Khosravi, 2017). Ahmadinejad's legacy, however, has been cemented with the 2009 Green Movement and his alleged rigged reelection.

Iran's next president, Hassan Rouhani (2013–2021), brought much hope to the youth with a plan to reverse some of his predecessor's policies and primarily focus on sanctions relief through a nuclear agreement to help the country's economy. In 2014, the minister of Labor and Social Security warned that approximately four million graduates would enter the job market in the next few years, further complicating the country's unemployment problem (Habibi, 2015). Moreover, due to the continued sanctions, the country's supreme leader, Ali Khamenei, implored his citizens to endure this hardship through what he called "resistance economy" (Khosravi, 2017, p. 11). Parallel to this, President Rouhani's foreign affairs ministry worked with its counterparts from the United States, China, Russia, France, Germany, the United Kingdom, and the European Union to reach an agreement on curbing Iran's nuclear program in exchange for sanctions relief and foreign investments. By 2015, they came to an agreement called the JCPOA, or Joint Comprehensive Plan of Action. However, for the next three years Iran's youth saw minimal improvements in their living standards and employment opportunities. By 2018, US President Trump backed out of the JCPOA and reimposed the sanctions that were lifted in 2015, also imposing additional sanctions for the next four years in what the White House called a maximum pressure campaign. After eight years and closing out his presidency with COVID-19, Rouhani had very little to show in regard to an improved job market not only for its youth but for all its citizens.

Rouhani's successor, Ebrahim Raisi (2021–2024), inherited the COVID issue, maximum sanctions, high unemployment rates, and a crippling economy; his presidency was defined by the death of Jina Mahsa Amini on September 16, 2022, and the subsequent Women, Life, Freedom protests. The metamorphosis of these protests enveloped a myriad of grievances that the citizenry held against the Islamic Republic. One of those grievances is the regime's continued corruption and botchery of domestic issues (Fahim, 2021). For over four decades Iran's youth have struggled with countless international and domestic issues that have directly or indirectly affected their ability to create a standard of living conducive to the acquisition of gainful employment, home ownership, marriage, children, and an overall life inside Iran that is not held hostage by the daily whims of the *khodi*. These struggles and frustrations have seemingly come to a head since the death of Jina Mahsa Amini, and the regime's legitimacy and existence has been under threat ever since from multiple fronts, especially with the passing of Raisi, who was seen by many to be Khamenei's successor. Raisi died in a helicopter crash on May 19, 2024.

With a rushed and truncated election, the only reformist candidate on the ballot, Masoud Pezeshkian (2024–2028 and an additional four years if reelected), was elected on the platform of focusing on domestic issues. However, with the multitude of regional conflicts[1]—most notably, Israel and America's 2025–2026 war against Iran—further threatening the regime's existence and the country's safety, Pezeshkian's administration was unable to implement its policies. And since multiple failed nuclear negotiations with the United States and later with Europe led to further sanctions, Pezeshkian had to fall in rank and file to support Khamenei's decision to continue the anti-West/America policy. This decision was made easy with a second Trump presidency, the bombing of Iran's nuclear sites, and the continuing sanctions, despite Trump's rhetoric of wanting peace but bombing Iran and killing top officials like Khamenei.

Thus, the Islamic Republic needed to shift into survival mode in order to secure the regime's safety and longevity, and Khamenei's son Mojtaba was chosen as his successor for continuity reasons. Another measure has been the possibility of moving the capital from Tehran to a remote and distant region in southern Iran called Makran, which is far away from the threats of citizen protests and revolts. And even with the country's currency falling to an all-time low and inflation climbing to an all-time high, the Islamic Republic did very little to improve its citizens' standard of living. Moreover, there has been a shift in how Iran's younger generations are protesting. More and more women are entering the public sphere without wearing the State-compulsory hijab (or headscarf), and protest chants are increasingly aimed at regime change and revolution. But the Islamic Republic is doubling down on their compulsory hijab law with increased surveillance cameras in public areas, increased fines, vehicle impoundment, and jail time to name a few. Iran's youth, however, refuse to be silenced by the regime, and this book attempts to highlight this tension of constraints and opportunities that balance on a tightrope, with ideological conformity on one side and the ability to develop highly critical perspectives on the other.

These past forty-seven years (1979–2026) have seen a plethora of conflicts and crises arise that have strengthened the Islamic Republic's control over the country while its citizens' standard of living has slowly and consistently deteriorated. On the one hand, the nation has suffered from domestic problems: poor policy decisions, financial corruption, political nepotism, widening ideological gaps, social injustices, economic instability, very limited freedoms (of press, speech, and religion), human rights violations, energy shortages, and civil unrest (protests, demonstrations, and riots) met with government crackdown (Barsamian, 2020). On the other hand, the Islamic Republic has prioritized its foreign influence throughout the Middle East much to the detriment of its citizens. As a result, the regime has been preoccupied with international conflicts: crippling sanctions due to its human rights violations and nuclear program; cyber warfare; proxy wars versus the United States in Syria, Iraq, and Afghanistan; a (maritime) shadow war with Israel, and proxy wars versus Israel through Palestine, Lebanon, and Jordan; proxy wars versus Saudi Arabia in Yemen (until their rapprochement in 2023); and then the 2025–2026 war versus Israel/America.

In trying to explain the perspective of the Iranian youth within this context, the existing literature can be largely categorized in two ways: the local debates inside Iran, and the nonlocal debates between external observers or within the diasporic community. Regarding the former, local Iranian scholars primarily stay away from criticizing the regime in order to avoid risking any threats to their career and/or livelihood. Therefore, they have discussed issues such as unemployment through a quantitative, operational, and economic lens (Alashloo et al., 2005; Amini et al., 2013; Bazargan, 2000; Hashemi et al., 2012; Naji et al., 2016). The tense relationship between Iranian youth and the institutions they navigate has also been debated in local conversations outside academia. One commonality within these local discussions is the years—and often decades—in which public debates have become repetitious and persist to identify shortcomings and recommended reforms. Many of the issues that were brought to light in the local literature shared similarities with the wider literature. One key difference, however, appears to be the very limited change recorded in Iran's local discourse. For example, Iran's school system shares similar problems with the rest of world, from insufficient funding (Leachman et al., 2017; Payne & Biddle, 1999), limited facilities and capabilities (Asiyai, 2012; Schneider, 2003), substandard teaching quality (Darling-Hammond, 2000; Singh & Sarkar, 2012), and lack of guidance and support (House & Hayes, 2002; Johnson & Rochkind, 2010).

Unlike many countries aiming to improve these problems, the calls for change within Iran have reportedly been ignored (Ghanuni & Ghaltash, 2019; Tasmin News, 2016). Similarly, private schools have comparable shortcomings with the broader discourse (Caddell, 2006; Dronkers & Robert, 2003), but again the Iranian government has reportedly overlooked calls for change (H. Hashemi, 2020; Rabiei & Salehi, 2007). Moreover, local conversations on misguidance or directed guidance that relates to the push toward or pull away from certain majors are similar to global debates (Corwin et al., 2004; Ireh, 1999; Lee & Ekstrom, 1987; Orndorff & Herr, 1996; Staff et al., 2010; Tien et al., 2005; Wambu & Fisher, 2015). However, the very limited change reported within the Iranian context is again visible (Afrooz, 2002; "Chera daneshamuzane nokhbeh," 2014; "Ejraie siasate tosiye," 2019; "Ertebate madares," 2018; "Tahre ertebate madares," 2018; Talebi, 2012; "Ulume ensani dar Iran," 2019).

These scholarly and local debates suggest that the Islamic Republic is not as amenable as its global north counterparts to working with its youth to enable positive change. This may further suggest that the complex tension between youth and their educational institutions, job market, and governmental entities within the Iranian context goes beyond political and economic struggles. This then further problematizes the argument that a youth's journey from higher education, investing in human capital, and improving their employability bears a return within the job market. Moreover, experts argue that most of the published work on Iran by nonlocal authors in the twenty-first century is homogenously focused on political and social struggles between the citizens and the Islamic Republic (Malekzadeh, 2016). Although such literature (Khosravi, 2008; Mahdavi, 2009; Varzi, 2006; Yaghmaian, 2002) has received critical acclaim, my book extrapolates from Olszewska's (2013, p. 842) criticism that the work from the diasporic academic community focuses on the narrative of "acts of resistance to and rebellion against the political establishment," particularly when that tension is much more complex and not as rebellious or confrontational as many authors discuss.

The well-documented stories of youth struggles in Iran are mostly confrontational and rebellious because such stories are relatively easier to find throughout varying media sources. It typically does not require one to travel inside Iran and conduct interviews or research—which is a risky endeavor that has led to many individuals being detained on charges of espionage. Furthermore, these stories capture the experiences of the "active *ghayre-khodi* youth"—a term I have developed and will explain in more detail in chapter 7 with table 7.1. But what about the stories of the youth who do not make it on social media or at the top of your newsfeed? This is where my book aims to unearth the complexities of the tensions between the Islamic Republic and its youth and look at the lived experiences of the "passive *ghayre-khodi* youth"—another term that will be discussed in chapter 7 with table 7.1. I believe the vast majority of Iran's youth can be categorized as passive *ghayre-khodi*. Very briefly, an active *ghayre-khodi* is someone who outwardly opposes the Islamic Republic and actively participates in public displays of defiance and resistance—which often leads to imprisonment, abuse, and/or death. While a passive *ghayre-khodi* is someone who also opposes the regime, their acts of defiance and resistance are more subtle or covert in order to minimize the chance and degree to which their livelihood will be at risk. One way to understand how an individual becomes a passive *ghayre-khodi* is to examine their maturation through the Islamic Republic's education system.

Iran's tertiary education institutions date back to the nineteenth century, with the establishment of its first university in Tehran in 1934 (Khan & Wenk, 1974). Due to a series of foreign and domestic conflicts explained above, the nation struggled to develop its economy, job market, and education system for the majority of the twentieth century. By 1957, Iran had only three universities, each with fewer than 9,000 students (Kalb, 2017). After Pahlavi launched the "White Revolution" in 1963, the next fifteen years showed a modest growth in the number of higher education institutions, from three to eight universities, and an increase to 136,000 students (Khan & Wenk, 1974). However, as university applicants increased from 16,000 in 1961 to 235,000 by 1978, the acceptance rate decreased from 36 percent to 12 percent (Boroujerdi, 1996, p. 38; Menashri, 1992, p. 207).

By 1979, the tertiary student population reached 176,000, accounting for 5 percent of the age group 18 to 29 (Bazargan, 2000, p. 173). Following the 1979 revolution, the Islamic Republic closed all universities for four years in order to change textbooks, subject matter, curriculum, and faculty to be in alignment with the regime's new ideology (Arani et al., 2018; Mahdi, 1999). This also included a substantial shift away from and an alteration in the social sciences, humanities, literature, and history, which Hamdhaidari et al. (2008) called the "Islamicisation" of the academic system. The eight-year war versus Iraq also occurred during this time, and as a result the 1980s became known as the lost decade, where $40 billion US was spent on a war instead of directly invested in domestic policies and social projects (Hunter, 1992).

What developed as a result, and over the decades, was an educational curriculum from first grade through higher education that was decided by the supreme leader of the country and a forty-one-member council that he selected called the Supreme Council of the Cultural Revolution (شورای عالی انقلاب فرهنگی; Hamdhaidari et al., 2008). In other words, neither Iran's Ministry of Education nor the provincial or local governments had significant authority over the direction of their education system. The primary duties of the Supreme Council of the Cultural Revolution were to ensure that the education and culture of Iran remain in accordance with Islamic teachings—or more specifically, the teachings of Twelver Shia Islam—as it was understood by the Islamic Republic. In Islam, there are two main denominations: Sunni and Shia. Then within Shia Islam, there are two main branches: Twelver and Ismaili. The difference is Twelver Shias follow the teachings of the Twelve Imams—who are believed to be the descendants of the Prophet Muhammad. Ismailis, on the other hand, follow the teachings of the first Six Imams. In Iran, Twelver Shias account for almost 90 percent of the Muslim population. Islam is the official religion of the country; Twelver Shia Islam is the religion of the Islamic

Republic and a fundamental component of the regime's ideology and, thus, the education system.

As a result, there are between three to seven classes every student must take throughout their twelve or sixteen years of education (twelve years of school and four years of undergrad study) regardless of their religious beliefs or academic interest: Quranic studies, Islamic ethics, Islamic theory, Islamic history, and the Islamic Revolution of Iran, to name a few. Table 2.1 is a translated list of these mandatory courses that I obtained from one of the professors at Sharif (the original document, Table 2.2, in Farsi, is included). This curriculum ensured that every student grew up learning key aspects of the regime's ideology. Furthermore, many classes within the humanities and social sciences (history, art, music, philosophy, politics, and religion) were either tailored to the regime's ideology or omitted from the curriculum. As Darius—one of my participants—explained, "It was very natural not to know what was taking place in [those subjects], and they kept us far away from everything at school, since those people control these places."

Thus, Iran's high school structure and admissions to university process are set up as follows. The first two years of high school (freshman and sophomore years) consist of a standard curriculum that includes some of the courses listed in table 2.1. Upon entering their junior year of high school, students must declare their intended area of study from four choices: math, science, humanities, or arts. Their final two years of high school consist of a specialized concentration, with their senior curriculum tailored toward their collegiate major (as a result, many seniors attend vocational schools). Toward the end of high school, students prepare for the *konkur*, which is the national entrance exam and the sole deciding factor in admittance to higher education (Kamyab, 2008). The literature written about the *konkur* is limited, and at times dated. Sakurai explained in 2004 that "only one study[2] in English exists which addresses" the *konkur* (p. 387). She goes on to explain that the "effects and impact [of the *konkur*] have not been studied thoroughly because its method is complicated and is subject to change" (Sakurai, 2004, p. 387). For example, many of the quota and allocation methods she discusses regarding an egalitarian approach to admissions have since changed. Another example is from Kamyab's 2008 article in which he briefly mentions a separate *konkur* exam for private universities—a policy that has since been altered. He concludes by saying that "authorities are contemplating a replacement mechanism for student selection" into university, which may be their high school grade-point average (Kamyab, 2008, p. 22). I have read and heard similar debates in local media outlets in Iran, but after seventeen years, such reforms have not reached

Table 2.1. List of Mandatory Islamic (and Other) Courses Required for the Bachelor's Program at Sharif University (in English)

Category	*Required credits*	*Course no.*	*Course title*	*Credits*
Islamic Theoretical Foundations	2	37445	Islamic Thought 1, Origin and Resurrection	2
	2	37446	Islamic Thought 2, Prophethood and Imamate	2
		37447	Human in Islam	2
		37448	Social and Political Rights in Islam	2
Islamic Ethics	2	37126	Philosophy of Ethics, Educational Topics	2
		37123	Islamic Ethics, Principles, and Concepts	2
		37127	Way of Life, Applied Ethics	2
		37128	Practical Mysticism of Islam	2
Islamic Revolution	2	37626	Islamic Revolution of Iran	2
		37627	Introduction to the Constitution of the Islamic Republic of Iran	2
		37628	Political Thought of Imam Khomeini	2
History and Civilization of Islam	2	37618	History of Islamic Culture and Civilization	2
		37620	Analytical History of Early Islam	2
		37622	History of the Imamate	2
Islamic Sources	2	37489	Thematic Interpretation of the Qur'an	2
		37490	Thematic Interpretation of Nahj al-Balagha	2
Literature	3	37991	Persian Literature	3
Languages	3	31101	General English	3
Physical Education	2	30001	Physical Education 1	1
		30002	Physical Education 2	1
Family Planning	0	37510	Family Planning and Population	0
Total				**20**

Table 2.2. List of Mandatory Islamic (and Other) Courses Required for the Bachelor's Program at Sharif University (in Farsi)

واحد	نام درس	شماره درس	واحد مورد نیاز	گرایش
2	اندیشه اسلامی ۱ (مبدا و معاد)	37445	2	مبانی نظری اسلام
2	اندیشه اسلامی ۲ (نبوت و امامت)	37446	2	
2	انسان در اسلام	37447		
2	حقوق اجتماعی و سیاسی در اسلام	37448		
2	فلسفه اخلاق (مباحث تربیتی)	37126	2	اخلاق اسلامی
2	اخلاق اسلامی (مبانی و مفاهیم)	37123		
2	آیین زندگی (اخلاق کاربردی)	37127		
2	عرفان عملی اسلام	37128		
2	انقلاب اسلامی ایران	37626	2	انقلاب اسلامی
2	آشنایی با قانون اساسی ج.ا. ایران	37627		
2	اندیشه سیاسی امام خمینی (ره)	37628		
2	تاریخ فرهنگ و تمدن اسلامی	37618	2	تاریخ و تمدن اسلامی
2	تاریخ تحلیلی صدر اسلام	37620		
2	تاریخ امامت	37622		
2	تفسیر موضوعی قرآن	37489	2	منابع اسلامی
2	تفسیر موضوعی نهج البلاغه	37490		
3	ادبیات فارسی	37991	3	ادبیات
3	انگلیسی همگانی	31101	3	زبان
1	تربیت بدنی ۱	30001	2	تربیت بدنی
1	تربیت بدنی ۲	30002		
0	تنظیم خانواده و جمعیت	37510	0	تنظیم خانواده
20		**جمع**		

fruition. Thus, with the limited research and literature, I relied on my participants and stakeholders to explain the *konkur* process.

A high school student's yearlong preparation for the *konkur* (typically during their last year of high school) leads up to a four-subject general exam (Persian, Arabic, religion, and English) and a three- to five-subject specific exam (depending on their area of study). Once the *konkur* rankings are publicly released, each student has two weeks to submit a list of up to 150 majors and

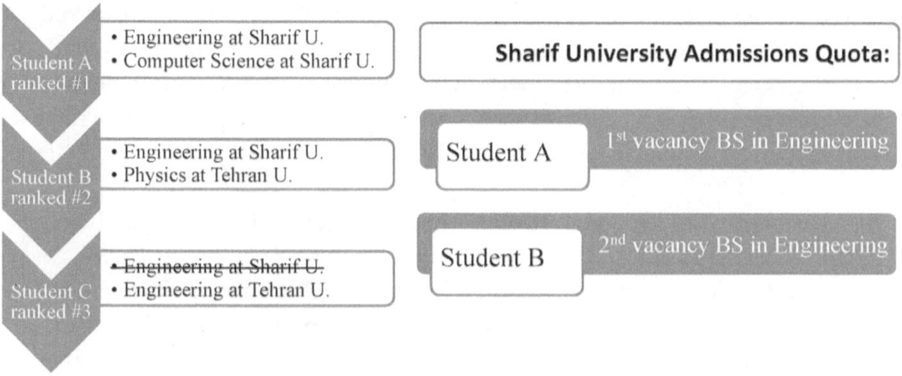

Figure 2.1. University admissions quota cross-referenced with students' 150-major list of major/university.

the corresponding university they would like to attend. To ensure that each program has a proportionate number of students, a national quota is imposed on all public universities. Therefore, every academic year, public universities must submit their list of vacancies for each major. The Sazman Sanjesh, or the National Organization for Educational Testing, cross-references these two lists and offers admissions to each student in the first major/university on the 150-major list the student is eligible for. For example, in figure 2.1, Sharif University has a quota of two vacancies in engineering. Students A and B will be offered admissions, but Student C will now be considered for their second selection on their 150-major list. However, instead of ranking third, what if Student C was ranked three hundredth? Once it is Student C's turn, most university quotas will be filled, and the student's admissions offer could be a major ranked much lower on their list, and perhaps a major they have little interest in. This means that even those who are admitted are not typically offered the major or university in the top half of their 150-major list, unless their *konkur* ranking is one of the highest in their area of study and/or region of the country. Thus, while the prestigious universities of Iran—like Sharif and Tehran University—are public (or State run) and therefore free to anyone who can score high enough on the *konkur*, the parameters in which one can be admitted are highly competitive and often changing.

Moreover, prior to the start of their collegiate career, students may already be majoring in a field they have little interest in pursuing professionally. Once enrolled—and regardless of their major or university—undergraduates who wish to change majors cannot simply request or declare it. In most cases, they must retake the *konkur*, and hope their ranking is high enough to be accepted in the major they want. Doing so will cause them to fall behind at least one year as they prepare, but it may be two or three years depending on when they change majors and how much of their previous credits transfer. Because changing majors is so difficult, most undergraduates decide to continue their education in a field that was not one of their top choices just to graduate (Kamyab, 2008).

Contrarily, students and graduates told me that students can pay higher tuition costs and enroll in the major they want at a private university (Shahrzad, 2008). Moreover, private universities have slightly changed their "rules." The word "rules" is in quotation marks because the professors, guidance counselors, and administrators I spoke with stated that the regulation books—either from the Ministry of Education or from each individual university/college—do not have a clause that explicitly explains the conditions of how an undergraduate can change their major. One guidance counselor from a private university in Isfahan showed me a list of majors (see translated table 2.3 and the original Farsi figure 2.2) his students can freely change to as long as their current major is within this list. Furthermore, they can change majors as many times as they want, whenever they want, without having to retake the *konkur* or greatly fall behind in their studies. There is also a list of majors his students can change to, but they would have to retake the *konkur* to do so (also see translated table 2.3 and the original Farsi figure 2.2). Fortunately, they can take the exam while still enrolled, and if their ranking is not high enough, they can continue with their current major without falling behind or incurring any penalty.

Table 2.3. Islamic Azad University of Isfahan (Khorasgan) List of Majors Students Can Change to (in English)

Department	*Programs not requiring the* konkur *exam*	*Degree*	*Capacity*	*Gender*
Physical Education and Sport Sciences	Physical Education	Bachelor's	60	Men and women
Foreign Languages	English Translation	Bachelor's	60	Men and women
Foreign Languages	French Language and Literature	Bachelor's	60	Men and women
Humanities	Accounting	Bachelor's	60	Men and women

Department	Programs not requiring the konkur exam	Degree	Capacity	Gender
Humanities	Accounting	Bachelor's, noncontinuous	60	Men and women
Basic Sciences	Applied Mathematics	Bachelor's	60	Men and women
Basic Sciences	Geology	Bachelor's	60	Men and women
Basic Sciences	Environmental Chemistry	Bachelor's	60	Men and women
Basic Sciences	Chemistry of Pesticides	Bachelor's	60	Men and women
Educational Sciences and Psychology	Psychology	Bachelor's	60	Men and women
Educational Sciences and Psychology	Educational Sciences, Educational Planning	Bachelor's	60	Men and women
Educational Sciences and Psychology	Educational Sciences, Management and Educational Planning	Bachelor's	60	Men and women
Educational Sciences and Psychology	Educational Sciences, Education of Children with Intellectual Disabilities	Bachelor's	60	Men and women
Engineering	Urban Engineering	Bachelor's	60	Men and women
Engineering	Computer Engineering, Software	Bachelor's	60	Men and women
Engineering	Computer Software Technology Engineering	Bachelor's, noncontinuous	60	Men and women
Engineering	Architecture	Bachelor's, noncontinuous	60	Men and women
Nursing and Midwifery	Nursing	Bachelor's	60	Men and women
Nursing and Midwifery	Midwifery	Bachelor's	60	Women only

(*continues*)

Table 2.3. (*Continued*)

Department	*Programs requiring the* konkur *exam*	*Degree*	*Capacity*	*Gender*
Dentistry	Dentistry	Professional Doctorate	40	Men and women
Humanities	Law, Judicial	Bachelor's	60	Men and women
Engineering	Electrical Engineering, Electronics	Bachelor's	60	Men and women
Engineering	Civil Engineering	Bachelor's	100	Men and women
Engineering	Architecture	Bachelor's	60	Men and women
Agriculture and Natural Resources	Landscape Engineering	Bachelor's	60	Men and women
Agriculture and Natural Resources	Water Science and Engineering	Bachelor's	60	Men and women
Agriculture and Natural Resources	Soil Science Engineering	Bachelor's	60	Men and women
Agriculture and Natural Resources	Agronomy and Plant Breeding Engineering	Bachelor's	60	Men and women
Agriculture and Natural Resources	Horticultural Engineering	Bachelor's	60	Men and women
Agriculture and Natural Resources	Animal Science Engineering	Bachelor's	60	Men and women
Agriculture and Natural Resources	Plant Protection Engineering	Bachelor's	60	Men and women
Agriculture and Natural Resources	Plant Production Engineering	Bachelor's	60	Men and women
Agriculture and Natural Resources	Food Science and Technology Engineering	Bachelor's	60	Men and women
Agriculture and Natural Resources	Pesticide Chemistry	Bachelor's	60	Men and women
Agriculture and Natural Resources	Natural Resources Engineering	Bachelor's	60	Men and women

Of Isfahan (Khorasgan)

پذیرش ظرفیت	مقطع	دانشکده پرستاری و مامایی
60 نفر مرد – زن	مقطع کارشناسی	رشته پرستاری
60 نفر زن	مقطع کارشناسی	رشته مامایی
		دانشکده دندانپزشکی
40 نفر مرد – زن	مقطع دکتری حرفه ای	رشته دندانپزشکی
		دانشکده علوم انسانی
60 نفر مرد – زن	مقطع کارشناسی	رشته حقوق قضایی
		دانشکده فنی و مهندسی
60 نفر مرد – زن	مقطع کارشناسی	مهندسی برق – الکترونیک
100 نفر مرد – زن	مقطع کارشناسی	مهندسی عمران
60 نفر مرد – زن	مقطع کارشناسی	مهندسی معماری
		دانشکده کشاورزی و منابع طبیعی
60 نفر مرد – زن	مقطع کارشناسی	مهندسی فضای سبز
60 نفر مرد – زن	مقطع کارشناسی	علوم و مهندسی آب
60 نفرد مرد – زن	مقطع کارشناسی	مهندسی خاکشناسی
60 نفرد مرد – زن	مقطع کارشناسی	مهندسی زراعت و اصلاح نباتات
	مقطع کارشناسی	مهندسی باغبانی
60 نفرد مرد – زن	مقطع کارشناسی	مهندسی علوم دامی
60 نفرد مرد – زن	مقطع کارشناسی	مهندسی گیاه پزشکی
60 نفرد مرد – زن	مقطع کارشناسی	مهندسی تولیدات گلخانه ای
60 نفرد مرد – زن	مقطع کارشناسی	مهندسی صنایع غذایی
60 نفرد مرد – زن	مقطع کارشناسی	شیمی افت کش ها
60 نفرد مرد – زن	مقطع کارشناسی	مهندسی منابع طبیعی

رشته های با آزمون

شرایط ثبت نام:

۱. داشتن دیپلم کامل نظام قدیم متوسطه یا گواهی پایان دوره پیش دانشگاهی نظام جدید متوسطه و مدرک فوق دیپلم برای کارشناسی پیوسته جهت ثبت نام الزامی است.

۲. ثبت نام داوطلبان در رشته های بدون آزمون بر اساس ضوابط دفتر آزمون دانشگاه آزاد اسلامی و از طریق آدرس www.azmoon.org انجام می شود.

۳. علاقمندان جهت کسب اطلاع بیشتر و اطلاع از رشته های بدون آزمون می توانند به وب سایت دانشگاه آزاد اسلامی واحد اصفهان (خوراسگان) به نشانی www.khuisf.ac.ir مراجعه نمایید و یا با شماره تلفن های ۰۳۱-۳۵۳۵۴۲۱۵-۱۸ و ۰۳۱-۳۵۳۵۴۰۴۹ تماس حاصل فرمایید.

Figure 2.2. Islamic Azad University of Isfahan (Khorasgan) list of majors that students can change to (in Farsi).

He went on to explain that these two lists are different for every private university, and the lists change slightly (by one or two majors) each year.

While there are options for horizontal and upward changes at private universities, the issue of paying (higher) tuition for such latitude is not justifiable for most families when confronted with high inflation, a weak economy,

Figure 2.2. (*continued*).

energy (electricity and water) shortages, and a poor job market that leaves them struggling to put food on the table. And it is here where the passive *ghayre-khodi* individual takes shape. When it comes down to having to survive in Iran or fight the regime, most people choose the former, but the struggles and uncertainties still persist. But as I mentioned above, the literature and media coverage regarding those who passively resist the Islamic Republic are underresearched and underdocumented—primarily because gathering such information requires one to be inside the country to conduct fieldwork, collect data, and interview people, which, again, runs the risk of jeopardizing one's safety and livelihood. That is why I feel it is necessary to detail how I was able to successfully do all of this and safely leave Iran to write this book. Because while there are limitations to my work—which I will discuss in the next chapter—these limitations were a result of safety precautions, not of biases or neglect.

CHAPTER 3

Conducting Fieldwork Inside Iran

There are freedoms here . . . but depending on what you do or say, there's no freedom after that.

GOVERNMENT OFFICIAL

Historically, the academic community inside Iran has looked unfavorably toward qualitative research as unnecessary, unproductive, and lacking scientific rigor (Nadjmabadi, 2009; Naficy, 2018). I recall that, during my first trip in the winter of 2017/2018, professors would try to convince me to conduct a quantitative study and argued that a qualitative approach would not be taken seriously. I even tried a quantitative approach when I conducted a questionnaire with fourteen graduates in Shiraz, but I quickly discovered they each had a lot more to say about their lived experiences, and we ended up having more in-depth conversations. Thus, decades-old arguments by scholars like Bromberger were still timely when he explained that "whole sectors of the social and cultural experience [in Iran] have been neglected and research on present-day . . . Iran has barely begun" (2009, p. 196). This continued neglect from academics within Iran can also be explained by another complication that is shared with most Iran scholars/analysts living outside the country—and that is the personal risk of jeopardizing one's own safety. Considering the Islamic Republic's suppression of certain freedoms, the risk one takes when interviewing individuals within Iran increases the likelihood of that individual being detained, or worse. Many human rights organizations, like Amnesty International, have documented the number of cases where this has occurred; for example, Jason Rezaian in 2014, Matthew Trevithick in 2015, Ahmadreza Djalali in 2016, Kylie Moore-Gilbert in 2018, and Fariba Adelkhah in 2019, to name a few. Therefore, while the lived experiences inside Iran reveal amazing stories and uncover underresearched issues, conducting fieldwork in Iran comes with great personal risk.

However, despite the risk, I continued with my qualitative approach, relying heavily on extensive fieldwork inside Iran with in-depth biographical interviews. During unsafe times where dual nationals and foreigners have been detained inside Iran on charges of espionage, and access to the country has been difficult, I successfully conducted eight-and-a-half months of fieldwork inside Iran, spanning two trips. My first trip was for six weeks over December 2017 and January 2018. During this month and a half, I visited four cities (Mashhad, Shiraz, Isfahan, and Tehran) and ten universities, and interviewed thirty-five individuals. In Mashhad, I visited Ferdowsi University and interviewed three professors. In Shiraz, I visited Shiraz University and Salman Farsi University; I interviewed two professors and fourteen graduates. In Isfahan, I visited Isfahan University, Farhangian University, Shayenshar University, and Isfahan Azad University; I interviewed three professors and one statistician. In Tehran, I visited Tehran University, Amirkabir University, and Sharif University; I interviewed four professors, one admissions counselor, two librarians, one administrator, and four graduates. I was even granted temporary access to Tehran University's library; see figure 3.1.

During my second trip, from June 2019 to January 2020, I primarily focused on Sharif University and Tehran University, but I also made a trip to Shiraz and Isfahan. Within these seven months I interviewed seventeen professors, one journalist, two university administrators, two university admissions

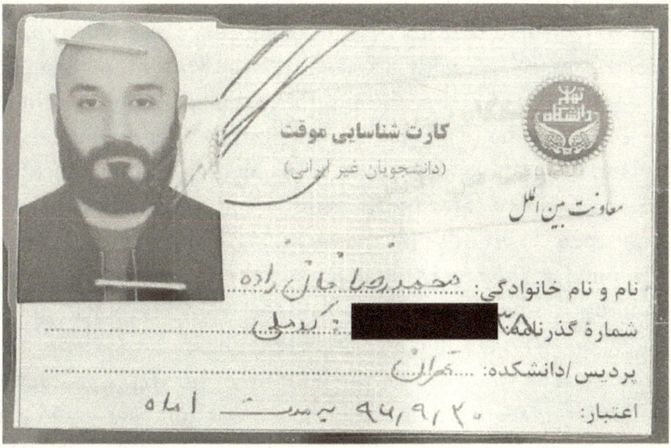

Figure 3.1. Temporary library card at Tehran University.

counselors, two university guidance counselors, five university career counselors, twenty-nine graduates, four employment companies, two think tanks, one high school guidance counselor, and eight government employees within six offices of the Islamic Republic: the Ministry of Education, the Ministry of Health, the Institute of Humanities and Cultural Studies, the Institute for Research and Planning in Higher Education (IRPHE), the Statistical Center of Iran, and the Iranian Research Institute for Information Science and Technology (or IranDoc, which houses all Iranian academic publications).

The ability to successfully conduct my research and safely leave Iran stems from my deep understanding of the complex yet simple system of how the Islamic Republic governs the country in order to ensure threats to the regime's existence are minimized while complete control over its citizenry is maximized. This deep understanding developed over twenty years of traveling to Iran, which informed every minute detail of my eight-and-a-half-month itinerary. In other words, I projected the perception that I was one of the *khodi*, or at the very least sympathetic to the regime. Which, in a way, was me investing in my ideological capital. For starters, I had the legal documents that would identify me as a native Iranian if I were ever stopped for questioning: my *kart-e-meli* (national ID card), *shenasnameh* (birth certificate), and *gozarnameh* (passport); I did not have a driver's license since I used public transportation. Second, and at that time my only internet presence was a dormant LinkedIn profile, so if anyone were to Google me, they would not find, for example, antiregime social media posts. Third, my religious beliefs as a Twelver Shia were in accordance with the regime. I would often go to local mosques to pray so while this aspect was not a charade it still played to my favor. Fourth, I ensured that my outward appearance resembled that of what Iranian society associates with a *khodi*, a pious Muslim, or a supporter of the regime (see figure 3.2). Specifically, this entailed staying within a monochromatic color scheme (e.g., gray, brown, black, and dark blues and greens), wearing plain, nongraphic long-sleeve shirts, never wearing a necktie, always wearing pants, having a short beard, maintaining a basic short hairstyle, and keeping my gaze down in public. On two separate occasions I was called a *Hezbollahi* and a *Talibani* by strangers on the street because of the way I looked (adding the letter *i* to the end of the word Hezbollah and Taliban signifies someone who is a member of these groups).

While these four strategies on my part are in no way a guarantee of my safety, I knew any gradational divergence from this approach could incrementally increase the risks of jeopardizing not only my safety but also that of my participants. Moreover, I had to at least control these four aspects of my fieldwork because although I was born in Iran, I was raised in the United

Figure 3.2. Example of how men in Iran should dress and groom themselves according to the Islamic Republic.

States, so I have an American accent when speaking Farsi and my nonverbal cues (walking, hand gestures, and facial expressions) are not those of a native Iranian—which are added risks depending on who I interacted with. Also, while some aspects of who I am—a Persian-Iranian and a practicing Shia Muslim—fit the regime's acceptable norms, I am not a supporter, sympathizer, or apologist of the Islamic Republic. Therefore, I needed to maintain a sophisticated level of discretion to successfully and safely conduct my research, which limited the scope to which I could conduct interviews, explore institutions, and further research sensitive issues like the *khodi*-versus-*ghayre-khodi* tension. For example, there are schools and universities that children of the *khodi* attend. There are also places frequented by the *khodi*, particularly members of the Basij, a plainclothes paramilitary volunteer militia of the IRGC who are considered staunch supporters of the regime.

These locations would have revealed compelling stories that would have complemented and contradicted my findings, but for my own safety I stayed clear of such places. For example, there are members of the *khodi* who are considered passive *khodi* who also feel stuck on a one-dimensional path. However, their path is restricted to the purposes of defending the regime and upholding its tenets. There are many passive *khodi* members who would prefer to leave the Islamic Republic but do not since there is no better alternative for them to financially support themselves and their families. Finding such individuals is extremely risky due to an absence of trust. Also, as explained in the introduction, I did not conduct extensive interviews with women for safety reasons, among other things. But interviewing such individuals would have uncovered a fascinating tension that I hope future research can examine.

Nevertheless, there were also domestic and international crises during my second trip that created limitations to my fieldwork. First, for one week in November 2019, there were protests, riots, and a partial internet blackout due to an overnight increase in gas prices. I was not able to conduct my research during this time, but I also knew it would be risky if I tried. Then, in January 2020, the United States assassinated Iran's Major General Qasem Soleimani, which subsequently led to threats of war—at that point I decided to leave Iran. Given how Iranian society has become a ticking time bomb where every wrong move by the regime is an opportunity for the people to protest, I spent the majority of my time at my apartment or at my office. I also limited my time in public spaces in order to decrease the chances of encountering a questionable situation that could potentially put me at risk. For instance, one mistake some visiting individuals have made that I believe contributed to their arrest was their formal or official announcement to the Islamic Republic on the nature of their trip to Iran and their plans within the country. I did not officially inform any entity of the Islamic Republic of my presence. In fact, precautions were taken regarding who I spoke to and how much information I divulged to each individual about myself and my research. This level of discretion was vital in keeping me below the regime's radar so as to not draw more attention to myself than needed—which, in turn, decreased the likelihood of jeopardizing not only my safety but that of my participants.

Participants

Thus, when it came to finding my participants, I began with the people I trusted with the details of my research (approximately seventy-seven people) and incorporated a snowball sampling approach that led to 180 potential participants. The criteria in finding participants were that they attended and/or graduated from Sharif University and then experienced Iran's job market before moving on to: (a) returning to university for their master's, (b) completing their two-year mandatory military service (*sarbazi* in Farsi), (c) leaving Iran, (d) founding their own startup company, or (e) failing to find employment. Other sources of evidence were also utilized—my personal lived experiences inside Iran, local and nonlocal documents, literature, and media reports—for contextual, evidentiary, empirical, and accuracy purposes. I also investigated other universities, public and private institutions, and the tense relationship between my participants and Iran's education system, job market, society, and the regime. Of the 180 graduates I initially contacted, 77 did not reply, 57 were not interested in participating, and 46 were interested. I therefore met with each of the 46 individuals in person and conducted face-to-face interviews with each of them individually. Appendix A provides the list of the 46 graduates along with some of their most notable comments. I have used pseudonyms and generalized some of their education in order to protect their identities. After hundreds of hours of interviews, there were five graduates in particular with compelling stories and extremely different upbringings that I chose to speak with in more depth: Cyrus, Darius, Ismail, Karim, and Nader. The following is a synopsis of each of these five men.

Cyrus

In the upscale parts of Tehran, Cyrus grew up with a wealthy family—their fortunes dated back to his grandfather. He attended one of the elite private schools in Tehran from first to twelfth grade. The pressures from his private school were so stressful that some of his classmates became ill, had mental breakdowns, or developed spasms—and during the *konkur*, some became so sick they vomited and/or fainted. Although Cyrus also experienced a breakdown during the exam, it was not as severe, and though he failed the *konkur*, he was accepted into Sharif (in computer engineering) as a result of political nepotism. This was possible because the father of a fellow test taker who also failed the *konkur*—a very powerful political figure within the *khodi*—enacted a law that allowed students, like his son, with specific circumstances to attend Sharif, and Cyrus also qualified under this law.

Nevertheless, Cyrus was one of the top students in his computer engineering department during his four years at Sharif. Throughout his bachelor's, Cyrus worked part-time as a coach, teacher, counselor, and *konkur* tutor. He graduated in 2017 and quickly went into entrepreneurship. In one year he founded two startups. The first was lucrative and in demand. However, he shut down operations after a year because he could no longer afford paying what he phrased "under-the-table bribes" to the government in order to stay in business. His altercations with municipal, provincial, and federal officials left him "frustrated and hopeless." I was surprised at how openly and freely he spoke of the government, but he said, "I don't care. I want them to know what they did." Somehow, he moved on and founded the second startup for a mobile app. He again had confrontations with the government and was not allowed to take his company public. Having experienced the failure of two startups, then being unemployed for one year, and having shouldered the stress of the *sarbazi*, Cyrus unenthusiastically went for his master's—and that was when we met.

Cyrus attended three job fairs during his time at Sharif and entertained an adequate number of job offers, a reflection of his degree in computer engineering, which was considered the top field at that time. What was difficult for him was, on the one side, aspiring to build a successful company that could improve society without being stymied by the government, and, on the other side, constantly feeling pushed toward jobs that did not contribute to the betterment of society or paid low wages that could not support an independent life or a family. In the time that I got to know Cyrus, he battled with feelings of depression, failure, and hopelessness against his personal drive and determination to achieve his goals. By the time I was preparing to leave Iran, Cyrus found a job. He told me he was enjoying his new job and the pay was good, but he considered his professional life a failure up to that point because of the obstacles that denied him the realization of his aspirations. Cyrus felt he had reached a ceiling he could not go beyond because of what the *khodi* did to him, and he accepted that this was his life, for now.

Darius

Darius grew up in a town twelve hours (by car) from Tehran in a family considered middle class. He had little trouble with schoolwork, exams, and tests, even though he considered himself (as did others) a "disorderly student." One of his rationales for this was his indifference toward certain subjects he considered uninteresting or useless. Nonetheless, he attended the school for the gifted and participated in the national science Olympiad (receiving the silver medal in astronomy). Throughout this time, Darius struggled with low self-confidence. When teachers and peers would tell him he was not intelligent or skilled, or that he did not belong where he was because of where he came from, Darius would not try as hard, but still received high marks.

Darius also grew up with a computer. He was fascinated with the hardware and software. He taught himself some programming languages and software applications. On occasions when he would retreat from the competition of school and the Science Olympiad, he would play video games on his computer. He was also interested in graphic art and even took the art *konkur* in addition to the math *konkur*. He scored very well on both but chose the latter because of the pathway he was on. He was accepted into Sharif, where he majored in mechanical engineering. Darius described his educational journey as a specific path that required him to be one-dimensional and not deviate from the path set in front of him.

Therefore, he followed this track and enrolled for a master's in mechanical engineering but dropped out after two weeks when he realized there was no future in it—regardless if he had a bachelor's or master's—within Iran.

He then changed track and pursued an MBA at Amirkabir University. My time with Darius began during his second year at Amirkabir, and by then he had experienced many failed attempts in the job market and faced problems similar to those of the other participants. However, unlike my other participants, Darius had a medical exemption (weak eyesight) from the *sarbazi*, and therefore one less problem to worry about, but he was still unsure about his future. He planned on going abroad to further his education but favored the possibility of returning to Iran because he wanted to help his country. However, his experiences up to this point demonstrated that far too many obstacles existed within Iran for him to realize this aspiration.

Ismail

Ismail, on the other hand, was convinced that there was no future in Iran. An equally intelligent man, Ismail relied on himself to overcome the obstacles he experienced. Ismail grew up in a town one hour outside of Tehran. His family was considered middle class, and his parents each had a modest education and career. He attended public school because he was unaware of the schools for the gifted, but his attendance at public school was brief. Two weeks into his final, pre-university year of high school, Ismail dropped out. He realized that his school, and particularly his teachers, were not going to prepare him for the *konkur*. He studied on his own and was the only student from his high school to be accepted into Sharif. He majored in chemical engineering because he enjoyed it and thought since Iran was an oil-rich country, he would have no trouble finding a job—but he was mistaken.

Similar to most of my participants, Ismail prolonged his bachelor's to evade the *sarbazi* (he graduated in 2015). During his senior year, he took the engineering master's *konkur* and ranked eleventh. He researched the job market for chemical engineer graduates and discovered it was weak. There were very few opportunities, and those that existed were in the hands of the *khodi*—which meant low pay, remote job sites, and boring repetitive work with minimal job growth. Thus, with much condemnation from the people in his life, Ismail decided against a master's in chemical engineering. Similar to his choice of dropping out of high school, Ismail made decisions that he felt were in his best interest. Very seldom did he listen to those around him.

During his extra semester at Sharif, Ismail took the MBA *konkur* but failed due to bizarre circumstances that he asked me not to divulge. Afterward, he worked on a startup with two of his friends while also searching for a job. The mobile app his startup was developing would have been the first of its kind inside Iran. In circumstances similar to Cyrus's, Ismail's team was confronted by the government and prevented from obtaining the required paperwork and equipment. Soon after, a *khusulati* company launched a similar app that provided the same service, and it has become very lucrative.

It was at this point that Ismail decided to focus all his energy on leaving Iran, and we met during this time. Ismail explained to me that if he stayed in Iran, he would end up struggling to find and keep a job, earn enough money to buy a house, and make enough money to support a family of his own before even approaching the possibility of trying to reach his aspirations. Ismail sought a profession that would allow him to contribute something toward the betterment of society. He admitted, however, that Iran was "way worse than what we were thinking." He explained that "if it was not the regime who was suppressing you, society tried to constrain you to one specific path." This reality, coupled with the daily volatility of life in Iran where no two days were the same for Ismail (or for many of my participants), resulted in him completing his *sarbazi*, taking the TOEFL and GRE exams, and applying and gaining acceptance to an American university for his master's.

Karim

Karim grew up in a lower-middle-class family one hour outside of Tehran. His parents each had a modest education and held modest jobs. He spent his pre-university years in his hometown, where he attended public elementary school. After failing to be accepted into the middle school for the gifted, he continued his public-school education up until he graduated high school. Public schools in Iran are centrally operated and funded by the Islamic Republic and are free for students to attend. These schools are mostly considered of lower quality when compared to private schools (where Cyrus attended) and schools for the gifted (where Darius attended). Karim enjoyed competitive swimming as a teenager, though he abandoned it to focus on his studies because he greatly enjoyed learning and developing in many respects—philosophically, academically, psychologically, socially, and culturally. Despite limited opportunities and failing to reach the Science Olympiad, Karim was accepted into Sharif in industrial engineering. In addition to his studies during those five years, he also had a three-month volunteer job, a three-month internship, and a position as an officer in the student body committee where he was in charge of his department's graduation ceremony.

When Karim graduated in February of 2018, he enrolled in a career services program at Sharif. This was to improve his "soft skills" and "hard skills" as they related to the job market in order to increase his likelihood of getting hired. Simultaneously, he took the MBA *konkur* as a backup just in case so he could avoid the *sarbazi* for two more years. For close to a year, Karim searched and applied for jobs, posted his résumé on employment websites, and had one interview, but no offer, to show for it. Although he struggled and experienced moments of unemployment, he was reluctantly optimistic that he would reach his aspirations. And the more he experienced and learned, the more he realized that he wanted a profession where he could have a positive impact on the country.

In the midst of his unemployment, Karim was offered admission into Amirkabir University's MBA program. When we met during this time, he was deciding on whether to drop out of that program and apply to go abroad. In the seven months we were together, Karim was accepted to a university in the Netherlands and was preparing to leave when family and financial reasons forced him to postpone. He said that he still wanted to leave but would in the meantime continue with his MBA. He also acquired a job as a data analyst but was unhappy with his situation and felt he had not reached his aspirations yet. Although he was hopeful, he admitted that there were many obstacles inside Iran for young men like him, especially those who aspired for a profession that aimed at improving society. By the conclusion of my fieldwork, Karim admitted that he had yet to reach his aspirations but did not blame anyone or anything for his struggles. He strongly believed that he was in control of his destiny. He explained that his mentality was extremely different than what the country was teaching him and his peers. His evolution and progression out of that "one-dimensionality," as he called it, was not easy and needed work, but he believed he was on the right path.

Nader

Although a man of few words, Nader and I had conversations that were as equally fascinating as those I had with other participants. In some ways our discussions were perhaps more consequential because Nader hoped our interviews would help him finally discover what discipline he liked and what occupation to pursue. He noted that even if my research does not help him, he hoped it could help other people like him. What he meant by "other people like him" were students and graduates who were lost and confused about their academic and professional futures. Nader's sentiment was similar to Karim's point of trying to depart from the one-dimensionality that he felt the educational institutions and tentacles of the State were pushing them toward. Nader grew up in a lower-middle class family in a town seven hours away from Tehran. His mom was a housewife, his dad had a "simple job," and neither were well educated. He loved soccer and wished to pursue it professionally, but he abandoned it to focus on his studies. Every time Nader had to make such decisions, he did what he was told, whether that was giving up soccer, selecting his high school major, deciding which university to attend, figuring out what to major in at Sharif, or finding a job.

Unlike Karim, Nader had no trouble passing the gifted school exam. He attended a gifted middle school and a gifted high school. And unlike Cyrus, Nader had no trouble with the *konkur*, ranking as one of the highest among his fellow test takers. Throughout his academic life, Nader was one of the top students, if not the top. Schoolwork, exams, and standardized tests came easy to him. He never stressed about these significant moments and never felt the pressure of having to achieve high marks or attend top institutions of learning. However, his indifference toward school and work grew as the years passed. As a result of his intelligence, Nader felt neglected with no guidance, which resulted in his aimless ascension through the *konkur* and into Sharif. He attended Sharif and majored in mechanical engineering. He finished his bachelor's in four years (2017) but did not graduate until a year later. He would purposely fail his internship requirement to prolong his stay in Tehran, to evade the *sarbazi*, and to attempt to find a job. Similar to Karim, he took the MBA *konkur* to help him buy time.

Although he did not know what his aspirations were, Nader knew he wanted to work somewhere that provided a service in improving society and paid well enough to support an independent life and family of his own. Similar to Cyrus, Nader had job offers, but he declined most of them because they did not meet these requirements—he described them as "dead-end jobs" or "simple routine jobs." However, he did accept some offers to help him determine what profession he liked or disliked, but his indifference persisted, leaving him with no clear direction. As a result, he decided to accept the enrollment offer from Sharif to pursue his MBA. During his first semester was when we met. He enjoyed his program and was hopeful he would discover what career path he liked. He also searched for work, but was again troubled by the same shortcomings. Nader eventually accepted a job in digital marketing but hoped for more. He was working toward leaving Iran through higher education (to pursue his doctorate), and was saving up the money to do so. Although he thought he could accomplish his aspirations inside Iran, he was unsure how and had yet to do so.

Stakeholders

The most difficult yet rewarding part of my fieldwork was securing and interviewing stakeholders. It was difficult because of the risks of possibly getting caught by the regime, but rewarding because, in many respects, the curtain was pulled back. I initially reached out to ninety-six individuals with professions in government, higher education (professors, administrators, and counselors), high schools (teachers and counselors), human resources, career services, and civil society. Seventeen did not reply, four could not participate due to company policy (high school counselor, high school teacher, professor, and an employment website), and five professors were not interested in participating. I was able to speak with the remaining seventy individuals. After I fully explained the scope of the work and answered their questions, eight declined to participate: three cited company policies that forbade them (human resources, high school teacher, and an employment website), another three stopped returning my calls (Sharif University administrators), and two did not believe they would be helpful toward the research (Sharif professors). Of the remaining sixty-two that agreed to meet in person, I interviewed each of them individually. Appendix B provides the list of the sixty-two stakeholders along with some of their most notable comments. I have used pseudonyms and generalized most of their job titles in order to protect their identities.

The timing of these sixty-two interviews was carefully threaded throughout my forty-six participant interviews in order to create a debate between these two groups. Considering that under normal circumstances many of my participants would not converse with many of my stakeholders—due to ideological and/or security reasons—I found an opportunity to dig deeper into each side's talking points and challenge them beyond the counterarguments and rebuttals to possibly reach the root of the matter. Moreover, the significance of interviewing stakeholders is that the literature on Iran is limited—either outdated, biased, untrustworthy, or underresearched. Thus, I was able to gather additional data and context from stakeholders, my personal experiences, and local literature. In the end, after hundreds of hours of interviews, there were ten stakeholders in particular that offered valuable insight into aspects of Iran's government, education system, job market, and society.

Dr. Ali

A professor at Sharif University's Business School, Dr. Ali had expertise in economics and management. He received his PhD from an Ivy League school in the United States. He was a fairly young professor compared to his colleagues, and being Western educated, Dr. Ali saw his positionality as a unique perspective on youth struggles within Iran. As we conversed about *Sharifis* and their experiences in higher education and the job market, Dr. Ali confirmed most of the participants' experiences. He explained how the majority of MBA students at Sharif came in for the wrong reasons. For example, engineering students saw the influx of MBA students and just followed the trend—a situation almost identical to how high school graduates followed the crowd to major in engineering. He went on to explain how very little thought is put into planning and executing a strategy from both the institutional side and the youth side. Regarding the latter, considering the youths' naivete and their need for guidance and advice, the institutions around them do virtually nothing to aid them on their journey, so the youth are stuck making ill-informed decisions. Regarding the former, institutions do not seriously take into consideration the needs of the country or the youth in their decision-making process. He gave Sharif's MBA program as an example: "A bachelor's degree in business, management, or economics is not popular in Iran, so the quality of teaching and the programs are low. Therefore, an MBA program is also weak because its foundation is weak, and they're building an MBA program not out of necessity but because it's the latest trend and it'll make them a lot of money." Dr. Ali also attributed political and economic issues to the reason that many graduates were unemployed. For example, the Iranian government is excessively involved in the job market, and in most areas, meritocracy has been replaced with ideology.

Dr. Hossain

Another relatively young professor, Dr. Hossain taught in Sharif's Industrial Engineering Department. Although he did agree with many of the participants' criticisms of Sharif and the job market, Dr. Hossain had one counterargument that placed the onus back on the graduate. He explained that he felt that Sharif graduates had high expectations going into the job market. He described how the younger generations were not willing to work hard and incrementally excel in their profession—he even called them lazy in the course of conversation. When I challenged him on this point and provided examples from the participants who worked hard and lowered their expectations, only to end up un(der)employed, he admitted it was difficult to earn a high enough wage that could lead to a stable independent life, but it was not impossible. One of his central points throughout our interview was stressing the importance of agency with each graduate. He admitted there were obstacles in Iran, but he argued that obstacles existed in every country, and did not think that going abroad (as he believed 70 percent of Sharif graduates did) would increase one's chances of success. He asserted that if they worked hard, they could prosper. The dichotomy in Dr. Hossain's answers—where, on the one hand, he conceded that life in Iran was difficult, while on the other, he was convinced that the youth could still prosper—left me seeking more clarity, which he was unable to provide, as he offered no recommendations as to how the youth could prosper within this political, economic, and social environment.

Dr. Sajjad

According to *Sharifis* and professors, computer engineering was the most popular engineering department at Sharif because of its high graduate employment rate. Considering how this one department tells a very different story than others at Sharif, it became integral to interview at least one professor (I was able to interview two) to learn from their perspective. Dr. Sajjad was a much older gentleman than all the professors I had interviewed. He had been a professor at Sharif since 1991 and received all of his higher education degrees within Iran (he had never gone abroad). Similar to Dr. Hossain, Dr. Sajjad placed the burden on the graduates. However, unlike Dr. Hossain, Dr. Sajjad's recommendation was for students to strengthen their faith in Islam and in God. He quoted verses from the Quran, spoke of his youth, and explained how "my generation did not have such high expectations . . . we would get married and build a life with [our] spouse out of nothing." Dr. Sajjad blamed the younger generations for expecting to become successful overnight. He admitted that other departments at Sharif should provide more assistance to their students after graduation to help them prosper, but he defended his department and its strong ties with the job market. Their internship program was outstanding, and the majority of their graduates acquired jobs—I discovered this to be true based on what Cyrus and other *Sharifis* had said. He mentioned that they may dislike their first job, and the pay may be insufficient, but he insisted that with time and hard work they could excel. Considering this was the second time I heard this argument, it made me think of a proverb about how a fish that had never been caught on a fisherman's hook will never understand the pain of a fish that had. I explained this to Dr. Sajjad, and asked whether the generational difference, and the fact that he had never experienced unemployment, had made it difficult for him and his generation to understand the struggles of the younger generation. He did agree to an extent, though he countered by saying God has been and will always be helping regardless of the generation.

Dr. Baqir

Dr. Baqir had been a professor at Sharif's Aerospace Engineering Department since 2010. Much of what he explained echoed the perspective of his colleagues. He spoke of the barriers that limited students and graduates from realizing their professional aspirations and the one-dimensional mentality that felt pushed upon them. He went on to say that they were not given opportunities to learn about and discover other areas of study or career paths. Instead, they were told what to study and where to study, but there was no motivation. He recognized the struggles graduates face in the job market and attributed it to the volatility of Iran's domestic and international problems. Dr. Baqir also argued that graduates should not compare Iran to other countries because of the unique problems Iran has. On the one hand, he challenged the graduates to attempt to build a life within the barriers in Iran, yet on the other hand, he understood why most graduates leave the country. He gave the example of the aerospace industry and how this entire industry is controlled by the regime; as long as the Islamic Republic exists, aerospace will not be privatized, therefore employment in this field is heavily influenced by one's ideology rather than their credentials. He went on to say that while going abroad had its own struggles, at least there was some level of consistency from one day to the next; if you abided by rules and laws, you knew you could prosper with hard work. He added that the only consistency in Iran is inconsistency, so you cannot plan for the future.

Dr. Zaynab

One consistent problem discussed throughout my interviews was the lack of guidance and support students receive from the institutions and people in their lives. After listening to the professors defend their rationale as to why they could not assist their students more—either because (a) time did not permit it, (b) it was not their responsibility, or (c) it had not become a part of the culture yet—it became critical to hear from the university's guidance counselor to see what kind of support they were providing. Dr. Zaynab described how her office had incorporated a number of programs to acclimate incoming freshmen to life at Sharif. Her office also provided an open-door policy to all students who require assistance with the pressures of Sharif. Dr. Zaynab believed many of the problems her students faced at Sharif could be traced back to their upbringing prior to Sharif. Specifically, she pinpointed the pressures and competition of having to be the top student without knowing what they were interested in pursuing academically and professionally. She explained how the country's mindset has been fixed on the human capital belief of just ascending the levels of education without contemplating why, for what purpose, or to what end. She went on to say that by the time students walk into her office they are already lost, anxious, and confused about what they are doing and feel it is too late to change course. Therefore, the best help she can provide is offering a place where they can talk about their problems and figure out what kind of options they have. Dr. Zaynab continuously stressed the need to help these students at a younger age—preferably in middle school (grades 6, 7, and 8)—and not just push them down a single path.

Mr. Sadiq

Considering Dr. Zaynab's description about the lack of guidance and support students receive prior to their university years, it was important to interview a high school guidance counselor. And after months of difficulty, I was able to find one willing to speak with me. Mr. Sadiq was a recent graduate from Sharif (2019), and at the time of our interview (also in 2019) he was in his first semester of his master's program at Sharif. My preconceived notion of a high school counselor was influenced by my American understanding: an individual who wore many hats as a therapist, career counselor, and academic counselor, and who typically was employed full-time and had credentials in counseling. Mr. Sadiq's description, however, painted a very different picture. Not only was he not a full-time employee, but his role solely focused on the *konkur*. In other words, he provided counseling on the phone, through WhatsApp (an instant messaging service), or in person to students who were unclear about what university major to select based on their *konkur* ranking. He explained that the required qualification needed to become a high school counselor was ranking high on the *konkur* and graduating from a top university like Sharif—therefore, he was essentially a *konkur* counselor.

When I went back to my participants (and other stakeholders) with Mr. Sadiq's description, they all confirmed his story. Furthermore, the participants added how their counselors were too young, inexperienced, and indifferent to the students' problems. When I went back to Mr. Sadiq with this critique, he agreed for the most part and added his own student experience. He explained how he disliked his intended bachelor's major (mechanical engineering) and how no one assisted him in discovering what he liked during high school. The counselors during his time would just glance at a student's *konkur* ranking and tell them which major to select. Thus, when Mr. Sadiq became a counselor, he tried to do more in helping students. For example, he would challenge them to view the positives and negatives of every major they thought about selecting, encouraging them to do more research. As Mr. Sadiq and I discussed further, it became apparent that the younger generation of counselors were more (inter)active with their students to ensure the same mistakes were not repeated. However, Mr. Sadiq lamented the fact that a change in approach by a *konkur* counselor is just a trickle compared to the waterfall that is the government, society, and institutions still pushing the same one-dimensionality.

Mr. Kazim

Mr. Kazim was one of five stakeholders I interviewed from Sharif's Technology Services Complex, an equivalent to a career services center (operating since 2014) that houses many offices (internship/job assistance, résumé/cover letter workshops, career networking, entrepreneurship, and much more) all dedicated to a particular aspect of assisting *Sharifis* in the job market. This was the first of its kind at Sharif and what many called the pilot study that later influenced other universities to follow. Mr. Kazim worked at the Entrepreneur Center where they taught students about entrepreneurship and guided them on how to initiate their startup. One aspect of their work was protecting their students' ideas through nondisclosure agreements with investors. He admitted that Iran had weak laws and even weaker enforcement in this regard, but his organization diligently worked to strengthen protection for *Sharifis*. Another aspect of their work was supporting students in finding reliable and trustworthy investors, because *Sharifis* have historically had to relinquish up to 80 percent of their company to obtain funding. In most instances, those providing the funding and acquiring the stake in the startup were affiliated with the *khodi*. Other aspects of the Entrepreneur Center's work included an orientation class for incoming freshmen and weekly training courses taught by an expert in a particular field. Mr. Kazim acknowledged the struggles of the majority of *Sharifis*, including my participants, who have tried to prosper within the job market. He believed that conditions were improving because of organizations like his and Sharif's Technology Services Complex, which offer an alternative to *Sharifis* while most institutions neglect the youth.

Mr. Rida

Considering that many of my participants utilized the Sharif Career School, it was important to learn more about this career services center and its employees' experience with graduates in Iran's job market. The Career School was located at Sharif's Technology Services Complex. Scheduling an interview with the school's director was very difficult. After six weeks of persisting, I finally got through to his assistant, only to find out that the director left the organization to complete his *sarbazi*. His replacement was not willing to meet with me, so I asked a friend at the Complex if he could assist in scheduling an interview with someone at the Career School. After another three weeks, I was able to schedule a meeting with one of their managers, Mr. Rida. At the time of our interview (2019), Mr. Rida said that their organization had been operational since 2015, yet most *Sharifis* had not heard of them. Due to the small staff and limited funding, they could not assist everyone who entered their office. Therefore, they interviewed applicants and accepted those who were identified as serious job seekers—which for them were students in their final year or semester, and recent graduates. Our conversation often returned to the school's mentorship program because helping students without direction was the most pressing issue his office encountered. Mr. Rida described how "90 percent of *Sharifis* do not know what their interests, abilities, and skills are, and they feel lost." He also explained how *Sharifis* were unaware of what the job market was like and had unrealistic expectations as a result. Therefore, the Sharif Career School advised its students on these matters. The Career School also provided training and seminars, résumé and cover letter workshops, internship programs, and mock job interviews with real companies that sometimes evolved into real job offers.

Mr. Rida was somewhat optimistic about the future generations going through Sharif now that the university had established a career services center. However, he echoed an almost identical sentiment to that of high school *konkur* counselor, Mr. Sadiq: "While the positive change of having a career service center is promising, it will still take many years until we see if it is helpful since we are understaffed, underfunded, unable to help all those who need it, and working against a system that does not share our philosophy on how to help our youth." When I asked him what he meant by the system or to elaborate on the philosophical differences, he paused for a moment and said he could not tell me because of the risks if anyone found out. He then paused some more and said, "If you think about it, you know who I'm referring to." Such a comment—one that was critical of the regime, the *khodi*, and its tentacles of influence—was ubiquitous in my conversations.

Mr. Jawad

After learning about the positive changes from Mr. Sadiq and Mr. Rida, I wanted to see what employment organizations outside of Sharif were providing graduates in the job hunt. I met with Mr. Jawad, the co-founder of an employment website (I will refer to it as JobMatch) at his company's headquarters in Tehran. JobMatch's function was very similar to many employment websites like Indeed, Monster, or Glassdoor. Its online platform connects companies with university graduates. The companies (six thousand members) post job openings and search for individuals who match their needs. The graduates (fifteen thousand members) create a profile, develop their online résumé, and apply to posted jobs. JobMatch also has a résumé builder in case the graduate requires assistance. Mr. Jawad explained that JobMatch serves as a bridge between companies and graduates but does not provide person-to-person assistance. It does, however, provide sources and materials to assist members in evaluating themselves and discovering their strengths and weaknesses. It also sends newsletters and emails with updates on the job market.

One of the leading issues Mr. Jawad determined from the feedback he received was that a gap existed, or there was a disconnect, between companies and graduates. Companies required particular skills that graduates were not being taught in university, and graduates were searching for positions that were unrealistic given the job market climate—"Their expectations were too high" he said. He went on to say that some companies were starting to develop their own academies where they train their employees.

Mr. Jawad was not willing to share the success and failure rates of his members finding a job, but he did stress how more companies like his have been forming and how support groups in Telegram (an instant messaging service like WhatsApp) have also been successful in helping youth find jobs. Again, there was a caveat with this optimism: "The jobs that do exist are not careers. There's virtually no job growth with most companies. There are little to no promotions, and definitely no pay increase based off inflation. Your income is in Toman [Iran's currency] while your expenses are essentially in US Dollars . . . which means your salary is being held hostage by a mafia benefiting from the sanctions. Therefore, maintaining a standard of living to start a family is very difficult."

Dr. Mahdi

I met with Dr. Mahdi in person on three occasions throughout my fieldwork, and we also communicated periodically via WhatsApp. We built a close professional relationship and even discussed possibilities of collaborating (but we never did). Dr. Mahdi held a position at the Ministry of Education at the time, so he was well informed on many of the issues my participants detailed in our interviews. Having worked for the Iranian government for over twenty years, Dr. Mahdi had firsthand knowledge and experience to offer an insider's perspective to many of my participants' claims about the education system. While our first meeting was more of a trust-building conversation (for both of our sakes), by our third meeting Dr. Mahdi spoke more openly about some sensitive topics. One in particular was what the participants called the "mafia" of the education system. While Dr. Mahdi did not use that term to refer to them, he did explain how there are individuals within the regime that support, defend, and elevate specific policies and agendas that have more to do with them retaining power, control, and wealth, and less to do with helping the youth, society, or the country. He went on to say that "there is much resistance to change, and in most cases, they don't allow for change to happen." At the end of my time in Iran, Dr. Mahdi was thinking of leaving the government to start his own company to provide mentoring and counseling for high school students (this was one of the collaborations we had in mind). He argued that if you really want to help the youth, you have to start when they are younger, and it needs to be on a more personal, one-on-one level because policy changes are not going to happen. The curtain that was pulled back by Dr. Mahdi led me to realize that one of the criticisms the West has of the Islamic Republic—their mismanagement of the country—is inaccurate. There is a very deliberate, calculated, and orchestrated *dismanagement* of the country in order to benefit the *khodi* at the expense of the *ghayre-khodi*.

Local Literature

In addition to in-depth participant interviews and stakeholder interviews, I collected local literature (in Farsi). These documents contributed contextual, empirical, and evidentiary support for the lived experiences my participants described throughout their pre-university, within-university, and postgraduation journeys. I was unable, however, to obtain official and credible data on unemployment, transfer, and dropout rates in order to provide a backdrop to where my participants were situated. Detailing this backdrop was important considering the already convoluted situation most Iranians face, as detailed in chapter 2, without the added stress of transitioning from university to the job market and un(der)employment. Furthermore, with educational institutions and the media regulated and/or controlled by the Islamic Republic, unemployment numbers provided to the public have been criticized for being biased, incomplete, and/or unreliable.

Moreover, Iran does not have freedom of press like the United States or Europe does—or as one of my stakeholders said, "There is freedom of press, but there's no freedom afterward." Another government official I interviewed explained that such public data cannot be trusted. Also, as a policy, Sharif, its departments, and many of the entities and stakeholders were prohibited from sharing such information. Of all the organizations I visited and people I spoke with, only the Department of Statistical Research and Information Technology was willing to share some of the data from their 2016–2017 annual report—the synopsis of which is provided in figure 3.3. And even then, the data is on enrollment rates and distribution of students and faculty by program and province.

Since local data were either biased, incomplete, and/or unreliable, I created an informal database as I collected information throughout my eight and a half months of fieldwork. I collected data on unemployment from specific fields from specific universities, yet I was unable to find data on engineering majors from Sharif. Thus, the credible documents available on Sharif graduates were statistics on the university's brain drain. For example, one study from the class of 2012 showed that 31 percent of students left Iran directly after graduating while another 30 percent left Iran one year after graduating. In a smaller study, focusing on 2015 graduates of the Mechanical Engineering Department, 40 percent left the country after graduating, and an additional 18 percent was projected to have left. Regarding credible data provided by the government, what I acquired dated back to the pre-revolution years (before 1979), and what exists from the Islamic Republic is census data on higher education students, graduates, and professors. Nevertheless, I continuously searched, even joining twelve Telegram groups or channels (see table 3.1) that focused on an issue important to university students and recent graduates in the job market.

As a result, I was directed to at least 153 articles (each cited in the references) that discussed some of the issues my participants described throughout my interviews. However, the *khodi*-versus-*ghayre-khodi* tension was not found in local literature considering the regime controls the media. Nevertheless, these publications reveal that a public debate does exist in Iran, which highlights two suggestions. First, that my participants' experiences may not be unique to only them, and therefore broader research on this study could uncover a deeper understanding into the lived experiences of Iran's youth within the education system and job market that goes beyond just political and economic debates of corruption, inflation, sanctions, and dismanagement. And two, the resistance to change by the Islamic Republic may not be just an overtly confrontational resistance that we see in the public sphere vis-à-vis police crackdowns, stricter laws, arrests, detentions, and executions.

There may also be a covert resistance to change—which I will explore in this book—that the Islamic Republic has been implementing in its attempts

Figure 3.3. Department of Statistical Research and Information Technology: Statistics of Higher Education in Iran (a brief) 2016–2017.

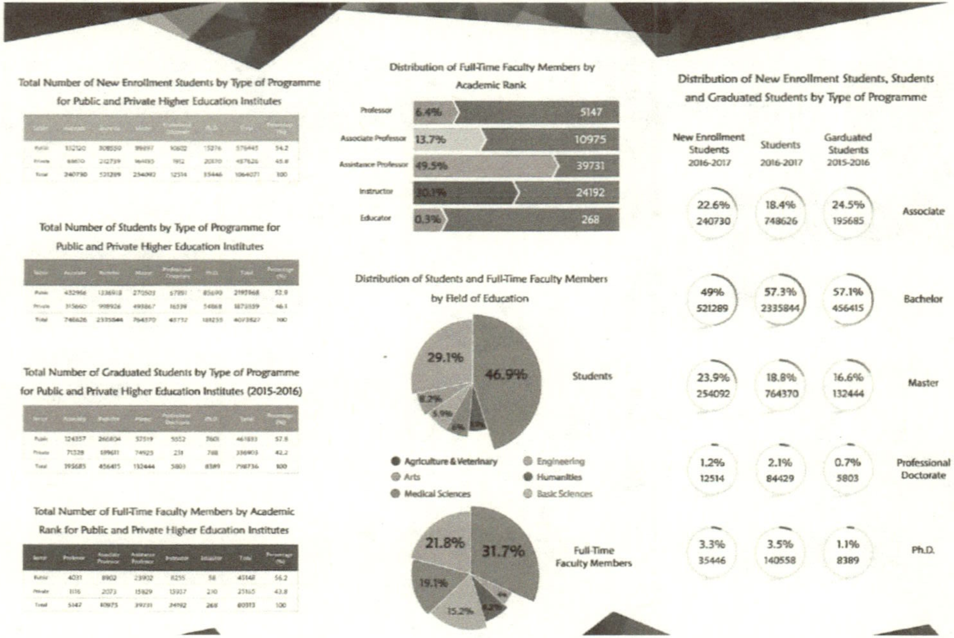

Figure 3.3. (*continued*).

Table 3.1. List of Telegram Groups and Channels Focusing on Issues Important to University Students and Recent Graduates

Telegram channel	*Description*	*Followers*
Military Service Deduction	An employment channel that helps young men find jobs that are accepted by the army to substitute for their *sarbazi.*	12,535
Sharif Club	A startup accelerator for *Sharifis*	5,224
Jobinja	An employment channel for job seekers	8,336
Sharif Job	An employment channel for *Sharifis*	5,449
Job Vision	An employment channel for job seekers	59,620
Sharif Daily	The Sharif newspaper	24,716
Career Counseling	A support counseling group for Sharif graduates seeking employment	1,928
Sharif University Tweets	A channel that posts tweets from *Sharifis* in Telegram	77,213
Economic Channel for Sharif Graduates	A channel for Sharif graduates who discuss economic topics and issues	910
Karboom	An employment channel for job seekers	7,388
Sharif Policy Research Institute	A think tank that provides policy proposals to the Iranian government	2,752
Iranian Migration Observatory	A think tank that provides policy proposals and reports on Iran's migration issues	2,219

to maintain the status quo and thwart any possible existential threats to the regime. For example, Dr. Mahdi helped me understand the concept of dis-management, where subtle and strategic measures were taken to limit the youth within specific academic and professional parameters with the aim of trying to stunt their maturation and potential. One strategy appears to be a reframing of the human capital investment, where the focus is directed toward a one-dimensional mindset of achieving short-term academic milestones while neglecting a mid- to long-term strategy that would potentially help the youth identify and actualize their aspirations. Therefore, as they grow up beyond high school, through university, and into the job market, the youth are unclear about what they want to do for a living and uncertain about how they will build a standard of living inside Iran. This sense of confusion and lack of purpose/direction leaves the youth struggling and (pre)occupied with their day-to-day challenges and thus less likely to be a threat against the regime.

This covert resistance is also significant because of those who have been profiting and benefiting from it. Institutions like the Sazman Sanjesh (or the education mafia), *khusulati* companies, and the IRGC, for example, which have monopolized vast sectors of the job market and economy, have too much to lose if generations of the country's youth—and in particular, the *ghayre-khodi*—were to accomplish great financial and professional success to the point where the balance of influence and power were to shift away from the regime. Thus, one's ability to shape and achieve one's own aspirations with the aim of realizing a better standard of living inside Iran may be limited within the parameters that have been established by the Islamic Republic. Thus, similar to Brown et al.'s (2010) argument of broken promises of human capital theory through globalization, it appears that the Islamic Republic has also broken a promise in the way it eventually limits returns on investment in accordance with the *khodi*'s expectations and job market stipulations.

CHAPTER 4

A One-Dimensionality to Human Capital During Pre-University: School, Family, and Society Postponing Living

Do you know that for a child in Iran who goes to school, they tell him that life starts after university? You should pass a routine process, after that you start living. They postpone living.
DARIUS

As illustrated in this comment from Darius, many of my participants felt that Iran's education system worked against them as they tried to explore their aspirations. Three topics in particular highlight their struggles with Iran's education system. First is the national entrance exam for schools for the gifted—an IQ exam administered during the transition period from elementary to middle school. The second is the National Science Olympiad exams, which typically are available to second-, third-, and fourth-year high school students. The third is the national higher education entrance exam (or *konkur*), which occurs during the pre-university year at the end of high school and is the sole deciding factor in admission into university. The participants described that instead of an environment where they could expand their minds and explore different disciplines, they were confronted by their school, their family, and society who minimized the importance of discovering their aspirations and interests while pushing them toward a one-dimensional human capital pathway. This push was seemingly aided by governmental entities that pursued a curriculum specific to the regime's policies, as well as constant reminders that the participants must listen to their school, teachers, and counselors.

The next section details how the participants believed the educational, governmental, and societal actors failed to help them in discovering their interests in order to determine what course of action to take regarding their academic trajectory and reaching their aspirations. Instead, the participants explained how they felt neglected or misguided by the people around them. The underdeveloped guidance infrastructure they detailed demonstrates an effectiveness in keeping the participants uncertain about their plans and future while pushing them down a one-dimensional path. Finally, I briefly discuss how the isolated nature of schools from universities added to the participants' difficulties in exploring not only their aspirations but also the major they wanted to pursue and the university they liked.

In the third section, the participants discussed their experiences of feeling pushed toward becoming one-dimensional. In other words, the participants believed their sole focus during this first stage was ranking high on the *konkur* and gaining acceptance into a top-tier university. They depicted growing up in a system where they could not think about anything beyond what was in front of them, and what was in front of them came with its own limitations and stipulations. Irrespective of their successes or failures, the participants still felt pushed toward a one-dimensional mentality. If they succeeded, they were labeled as gifted, pressured to major in a STEMM program and attend a university like Sharif, and neglected along the way because they were seen as smart enough to handle the journey on their own. If the participants failed, they were labeled as unintelligent and subsequently neglected because they were seen as hopeless cases. Either way, they felt discouraged in thinking about their future, thus remaining unaware about their aspirations. As a result, the participants' aspirations had yet to take shape. Instead of discussing options and debating scenarios about their future, the participants felt controlled in doing what they were told. The vignette below from my conversation with Darius highlights this:

> [Schools are] like a factory. The [regime] tells the schools what to do, and we all follow. This ancient, traditional system is problematic. They chastised a classmate for promoting Buddhism because he wore a T-shirt that said Budapest . . . Budapest! A capital of a country for crying out loud! This is terrifying! These closed-minded people are just following orders from higher up. They don't care . . . unless you riot . . . we had a dreadful Arabic teacher, so all his students stood outside the school refusing to go to class until he was fired.
>
> DARIUS

An Education System Working Against You

These scenes and interactions between the participants and their schools highlights a tension in this relationship where the former felt bombarded with obstacles that impeded their ability to (a) persevere into the next stage of their lives, a trajectory they were following because they were told to, and (b) explore their aspirations, which they did not know was possible. Instead, the participants felt that the school system, as well as family and society, were trying to keep them on a one-dimensional pathway. This appeared to be a distorted version of the human capital argument due to the (f)actors that influenced the participants' environment—i.e., the *khodi* and mafia. And the obstacles, impediments, and inabilities that manifested as a result were not felt by the participants until they later realized how unprepared they were for the future.

Another element that made participants feel stuck on the one-dimensional path was the faith-based disposition—which was also propagated by State-run media outlets—when the conversation about their aspirations and future would arise. The participants explained that instead of an environment where they could explore academic interests or discuss scenarios about their future, their schools, communities, and the regime's tentacles of influence would curb such contemplation and redirect them toward the short-sighted one-dimensional path by telling them to move forward one step at a time and not worry about the future because it is in God's hands. Darius explained that "there is an old saying that God controls everything in Iran, so no one takes responsibility for the problems of the country or how to remedy them."

This mentality that participants felt was being instilled in them led them to recognize three experiences that had happened in their lives. First, they felt that they were taught from a young age to believe in this one-dimensional path because it would lead to a guaranteed and successful future. However, some of the aspirations the participants did have during pre-university were later determined to not be their own but rather goals inculcated in them. Darius also explained that the education system had an ideologically tailored curriculum that taught them "this is good, this is bad, this is halal, this is haram, this kind of person is good, this kind of person is bad." What was troubling for the participants, however, was who was defining these terms of good and bad, halal and haram. While Cyrus's private school had some level of autonomy from the Islamic Republic, it had to use State-approved teaching materials. The schools for the gifted that Nader and Darius attended and the public schools that Karim and Ismail attended were under complete control of the regime. Thus, the way good and bad, halal and haram, were defined by the schools, and comments the participants heard (e.g., "They tell the schools what to do" and "They are following orders from higher up"), pointed to the *khodi*.

Second, the participants described a sense of ignorance regarding the influence of this one-dimensional attitude on the way they viewed their future throughout pre- and within-university. As Darius illustrated, "Society and school postponed living, and the students were unprepared to start their life after higher education because they were unable to imagine what that life could look like"; I will expound on this later in the chapter. Third, they described the struggles of accepting what society and their school system were telling them to do or not do and be or not be, and how they faced obstacles in opposing the one-dimensional mentality in order to pursue their own interests and explore and discover their own aspirations. When the participants spoke of their younger years and how they felt that school and society had pushed them down a one-dimensional pathway, they did not express negative emotions when reliving those moments because, as they explained, "that's the way it was for everyone. It happened and it's over . . . there's nothing we can do about it now, so why get upset?" The resolve in each of the participants was strong. With each story they told about a hardship, a setback, or an obstacle, it concluded with their declaration of moving forward, evolving, maturing, and adapting in order to reach their aspirations.

For example, Karim greatly desired acceptance, like Darius had attained, into a school for the gifted. He "did not have anyone to help" him prepare for the exam, so he studied on his own. Growing up in a town one hour outside of Tehran, Karim had a humble upbringing: his parents had a modest education, and his family could be considered lower middle class. After failing the gifted school exam and enrolling in public school, he experienced obstacles that accompanied his new label as unintelligent, or as he put it, "being stupid according to society." One example was when he wanted to participate in the Science Olympiad:

> I really liked Olympiad. Olympiad was always a level higher than the classes you had. I didn't have that confidence and my school didn't acknowledge Olympiad, and the people around me felt the same way, so I thought it's something difficult. It's impossible to go . . . the gifted schools bring people who have passed the [Olympiad] exam to teach, [the government] doesn't bring them to the public schools.
>
> KARIM

In addition to being labeled unintelligent, Karim was not provided with a top-caliber faculty at his school to help him down the path he perceived as the best way to reach his future. This insufficiency for Karim was disheartening as he recalled moments when he became increasingly hopeless toward his country's educational and societal assistance. At times, Karim also became hopeless about himself. One of his earliest aspirations was obtaining knowledge. Karim enjoyed learning and therefore desired to attend high-quality educational institutions. However, after failing to gain acceptance into the school for the gifted and not having the opportunity to apply for the Olympiad, he was convinced he would not rank high enough on the *konkur* to receive acceptance into a top university:

> There's an ideology in Iran that one of the ways to fulfill your dreams is through university, [and] society is dictating in a way that the *konkur* has become that goal somehow . . . it's . . . been forced by the society and dictated that success is in terms of . . . [the *konkur*]. . . . If you can in this, in this tournament . . . perform well, you'll be labeled as good. I didn't expect to pass [the *konkur*] at all. I thought [gifted students] are from a different world. They studied somewhere else, they are definitely better than me.
>
> KARIM

As he described the ideology on how to achieve aspirations, what those aspirations should be, and how those aspirations should be tied with the tournament-style culture of the *konkur*—where knowledge and aptitude are substituted for memorization and strategy—Karim went on to describe how school and society constantly pushed a one-dimensional mentality where he was fixated on the schools for the gifted, the Olympiad, and the *konkur*, which he felt prevented him from thinking beyond these goals and exemplifies how Karim's aspirations were being shaped for him. Nevertheless, and despite the lack of guidance and support from his public school and from society, Karim studied on his own, and from his success on a practice *konkur* exam, he was offered a scholarship to a private *konkur* class where his tutor was a teacher from a school for the gifted. As a result, his score was sufficient to gain him acceptance into Sharif, and Karim was one of two students of the eighty he graduated with who went to Sharif.

Cyrus was one of twelve students out of sixty from his private school to gain acceptance into Sharif. Unlike Karim, who was discouraged from believing he could make it to a top-tier university, Cyrus was overwhelmed with the pressures to outperform his classmates and score high on the *konkur*:

> Everyone told us to study, and you will ace it and be accepted in a good university like Sharif, your future is guaranteed, and you will have no worries

> and you will build your life. Or no, if you can't, you will destroy your future. And they put a lot of pressure that you should study and get accepted [in university] and be successful. And because of that we tolerated all the pressures . . . we tore ourselves to pieces . . . it's a negative feeling.
> CYRUS

Cyrus grew up in a very wealthy household in an upscale part of Tehran. His neighbors were politicians and doctors, and his classmates were their children. His grandfather made the family wealth, and his father increased it until he transitioned into real estate investment. Being able to afford private school provided Cyrus with remarkably advanced facilities and capabilities; he attended school twelve months out of the year and never thought about applying for the schools for the gifted or the Olympiad. However, despite his best efforts, Cyrus ranked seven thousandth on the *konkur*—Darius and Nader, for example, ranked eighty-ninth and thirteenth respectively. He described the atmosphere leading up to the exam:

> In high school, everyone said "just *konkur*." They made everyone's dreams just the *konkur*. "Take it, if you're accepted, everything will be fine." This that I am saying, I'm not exaggerating, if you talk to high school students, especially those who are in their pre-university year, *konkur* is like a monster for them, and their minds revolve around the monster of the *konkur* . . . several of my close friends got nervous tics. One of them fainted, the ambulance came to our school and took him away because the stress and pressure on us is so high. Well, one of them one week before the *konkur* was confined to a hospital bed . . . during high school my only concern was to reach the summit of the *konkur* and nothing else mattered. . . . I didn't have time to think about anything else.
> CYRUS

From these two passages, Cyrus further illustrates the ideology that Karim reported. The pressure of having to rank high enough on the *konkur* to have a future was too much for Cyrus to bear. Not only was his score unacceptable for Sharif, but no university in Tehran would accept him. Cyrus's admission into Sharif, therefore, came with the aid of a *khodi* member:

> **Cyrus:** . . . I wanted to say how high he is in the government. His son got in [because] a path opened up for him and I got into Sharif with him.
> **Reza:** When you say a path opened up for him . . .
> **Cyrus:** I mean a rule was created that said people like this could come to university, and this didn't exist before.

Reza: What do you mean by people like this?

Cyrus: Something called [redacted for confidentiality purposes] was added, which is over now. We got in but it's over. I mean they no longer can get into university like that.

Reza: Did they do this on purpose for his son?

Cyrus: Yes.

Stories like this were ubiquitous during my time in Iran, but they were always anecdotal. This was the first firsthand account I heard about the *khodi* performing such an act. Although Cyrus did not consider himself a *khodi*, he benefited from his close proximity to the *khodi* (through his family's wealth) in discovering the nonpublicized special rule to gain acceptance into university—or in his specific case, Sharif. Considering his acceptance had little to do with his private school, Cyrus was very critical of the way they mistreated their students to the point of becoming sick and used them to promote their image and recruit more students. While Karim's criticisms of public school were accompanied by admiration for gifted and private schools, Cyrus's criticism for his private school demonstrated that regardless of the type of high school, the one-dimensional distortion of human capital aspirations were inculcating their minds and averting them away from exploring, identifying, and pursuing their own aspirations.

Moreover, Cyrus learned to compete individually instead of work collaboratively. He explained how he and his classmates distrusted one another and were forced to be selfish in order to progress. Cyrus, along with the other participants, described how this individualistic mentality was not exclusive to school and how it existed in society where people were focused on themselves because of the daily struggles of trying to survive in Iran. Additionally, they reported that many people cheated and stole to make ends meet. The participants blamed society for this individualistic mindset that had turned people against one another (Ghanyatpishe, 2005; Mafi & Mafi, 1999). But they saw the Islamic Republic as the creator and enabler of this societal status quo to struggle in order to continuously keep the youth on the one-dimensional pathway, yet another example of the regime's covert resistance to change and a strategy to keep its citizens divided. When I asked Cyrus how he unlearned this mindset, he said, "I'm still unlearning it." He stressed the continuous difficulty in overcoming the "pressures to be like everyone else" because of its prevalence. He attributed why and how he was able to undertake the process of unlearning the one-dimensionality to human capital to his faith (Shia Islam), his mother (a psychologist), and his own will to persevere and succeed.

Ismail's upbringing was more comparable to Karim's. He grew up in a town one hour outside of Tehran. His parents had a modest education, his family was middle class, and he attended public school. Similar to Karim, Ismail experienced the expectations for an unintelligent public-school student, but in a different way. Ismail was unaware of the gifted school exam and the Olympiad exam. He explained that "there was very little information about these" where he grew up. He also never heard of Sharif University until high school. He was fully aware of the importance of the *konkur* exam, however hopeless in receiving assistance from his school and the people around him:

> Two weeks [into my pre-university year] I realized that there was a huge difference between what the teachers were teaching us and what we were supposed to know to take part in the *konkur*. It would have been impossible to get accepted based on what they were teaching us. When I told my math teacher about this, he said that he is not supposed to hold a "*konkur* class" here and he is just teaching based on the book provided by the [government]. Officially, what he said was true, but it just demotivated me.
> ISMAIL

Karim and Ismail felt that their public schools did very little to prepare them for the one goal they were told to accomplish if they wanted to guarantee a successful future. The two explained how their final, pre-university year of high school was supposed to include preparations for the *konkur* exam (Islamic Parliament Research Center of the Islamic Republic of Iran, 2006), but their teachers seemingly neglected the *konkur* aspect of their curriculum. As a result, Ismail decided to drop out and study for the *konkur* on his own. His school and parents were against this decision—his principal told him, "You are making the biggest mistake of your life"—but it did not change his mind. Moreover, public school for Karim and Ismail was devoid of any advanced facilities compared to Cyrus's private school. The quality of their teachers was also lower than those at Nader's and Darius's schools for the gifted. Ismail, for example, explained that although he was unsure what he aspired to be, he refused to believe that public school students were too dumb to rank high enough on the *konkur* and attend a university like Sharif. Thus, he dropped out of pre-university, and with hard work and determination, he was the only student from his graduating class of sixty to be accepted into Sharif.

Nader, on the other hand, was one of nine students from his graduating class of fifty at his school for the gifted to be admitted to Sharif. Unlike Karim and Cyrus, who studied for one and three years, respectively, for the *konkur*, Nader studied for eight months. School always came easily to Nader. He never felt the pressures of exams or schoolwork. He endured no hardships in earning acceptance into the school for the gifted or Sharif University. The Olympiad exam was of little interest to him, primarily due to his unfamiliarity with the subject areas and his uncertainty in what he wanted to pursue. This was Nader's primary struggle throughout his academic and professional life—he never discovered what his interests were. He admitted in our interviews, on more than one occasion, how he made mistakes in his decisions because there was no one to constructively guide him. Thus, he followed his peers when deciding on Sharif, but they were following what their school, families, and society were telling them to do. Then, when choosing his university major, he continued to search for valuable guidance, but to no avail:

> The [high] school counselor was only there to see when your grades are low and would come to you and ask why didn't you perform well and would plan for you to study. It was all related to studying . . . and because I didn't have any problems in studying the counselors didn't have much to do with me . . . there wasn't someone who would help me. . . . I mean, I used to go to them for help, but they would just say, "Choose electrical engineering" or "Choose mechanical engineering." . . . Somebody like me, who can choose any [STEM] major I want but doesn't know what to do or what I like . . . I don't know . . . like somebody has to do something to help us understand what each major is and what kind of jobs we can get.
>
> NADER

A parallel can be drawn here between the participants and how they felt a lack of support and guidance during their pre-university experience. Although their different experiences were intriguing (Darius having to postpone life; Karim and Ismail being labeled unintelligent; Cyrus's school being more interested in its own reputation, and Nader's uncertainty and indifference), perhaps the how and why of their neglect raises more questions.

The how can be partly attributed to the covert resistance to change by the regime and the *khodi*'s strategy in ensuring that the youth's aspirations are within the *khodi*'s acceptable status quo parameters—in other words, believing that high marks in school, top rankings on the *konkur*, and acceptance into a top university will guarantee a successful future. But students are then pushed down a one-dimensional pathway that is camouflaged within the human capital argument to accomplish these goals. However, as the participants followed this one-dimensional path, they felt neglected in their pursuit. Furthermore, the emphasis that schools, teachers, society, family, and classmates placed on the *konkur* was exacerbated by the mafia that ran it.

I was first introduced to the colloquial term *mafia* by Karim, but the participants explained it as a conglomeration of certain private, government, *khodi*, and *khusulati* organizations who were in the *konkur* business. The term *mafia*, however, is used throughout many sectors in Iran—most notably the water mafia, the oil/gas mafia, the banking mafia, the real estate mafia, the import/export mafia, and the education mafia. The three main organizations of the education mafia are the Sazman Sanjesh (or the National Organization for Educational Testing, the governmental body that administers the exam), the Gaj, and the Ghalamchi. It was speculated that the latter two are *khusulati* companies, but I was unable to verify those reports. The participants, and some of the stakeholders, reported that this mafia had become so influential over the decades that they had diversified into a multimillion-dollar industry with television programs, mobile phone applications, computer software, study materials, prep books, private classes, consulting firms, and tutoring workshops. The participants also reported that while members of parliament and local NGOs had submitted policy proposals to either alter or eliminate the *konkur* ("Rahkare hazf konkure," 2020; Sobhani & Shahidi, 2007), every attempt had failed due to the mafia's power and influence (Pouyan, 2016; "Tahre do foriti," 2020).

Thus, one part of the reason the participants felt neglected was the lucrative business of the *konkur*. Considering that this multimillion-dollar industry provided a steady stream of revenue to the *khodi*—especially at a time of crippling international sanctions—and that the mafia had monopolized the industry, it appeared highly unlikely that this aspect of Iran's education system would change. Another part of the reason connects back to the covert resistance mentioned earlier. Considering that the Islamic Republic has been weakened by regional conflicts with Israel as a result of the October 7, 2023, Hamas attacks, and has experienced domestic unrest since the death of Jina Mahsa Amini in 2022, the regime is focused on (a) holding on to power; (b) procuring and controlling major revenue streams to help them stay in power and circumvent economic sanctions; and (c) superimposing ideological, social, political, and religious norms in order to influence its citizens' thought processes and behavior to counteract threats to (a) and (b). As a result, the participants did not know (a) where this one-dimensional path would take them; (b) what was meant by a "guaranteed successful future"; (c) whether they had other options; and/or (d) whether the one-dimensional pathway was what they actually wanted; and then (e) what their own aspirations were.

Misguidance and Inaction

As the participants relived their pre-university stage during our conversations, they explained that for the first time, they were revisiting and reexamining a part of their life they had chosen to forget. In doing so, three (f)actors emerged that highlighted the participants' experiences of feeling misguided and neglected by their school, their family, and society, and the transition from high school to Sharif. In addition to the education system and society, the participants' counselors reinforced the one-dimensional pathway as well. This was another part of the reason why the participants felt neglected, with local documents showing a debate for the need for reform in the counseling apparatus (Islamic Parliament Research Center of the Islamic Republic of Iran, 2019a, 2019b, 2019c). But according to the participants and three of my stakeholders (Dr. Mahdi, Ms. Zaynab, and Mr. Sadiq), these debates have been ongoing for thirty years with no meaningful change (Islamic Parliament Research Center of the Islamic Republic of Iran, 2018). Each of the participants either experienced very little guidance or assistance in selecting their university major, or what they did experience they described as unhelpful. According to Mr. Sadiq and Dr. Mahdi, high school counselors were primarily university students. These individuals were one or two years older than the students they counseled, with no substantial experience in the job market and limited knowledge about their own discipline. They had no formal training in counseling, nor were they well informed on the several majors their students could choose from.

Mr. Sadiq, who was a high school counselor, echoed Nader's experience and described how most counselors were unqualified, having very limited experience in the job market. The counselors' qualifications were: (a) they graduated from the high school that hired them, (b) they ranked in the single or double digits on their *konkur* exam, and/or (c) they were attending a top-tier university like Sharif. He went on to describe how most counselors at private schools and the schools for the gifted were incentivized to push students toward Sharif in exchange for bonuses—either monetary or commodity gifts. The counselors I spoke with, including Mr. Sadiq, explained that their profession had no strict regulations or assessments; there were no courses or programs to take, nor any required experience. Mr. Asad (Isfahan University guidance counselor) told me, "Many talented and educated psychology graduates and trained counselors can't seem to get these jobs when they're the most qualified."

Mr. Sadiq recalled similar experiences when he was a student; so when he became a counselor, he promised himself he would help his students discover what discipline they wanted to major in and which university they wanted to attend. Interestingly, he did not challenge them on possibly pursuing a different path outside of that, which was explained earlier. Rather, he attempted to improve/alter the existing path for his students. In the five years he was a counselor, Mr. Sadiq advised approximately one hundred high school seniors, and around 60 percent struggled to identify what their aspirations were in order to pick the appropriate major. When I asked him why 60 percent had not identified a career they liked, he replied that they "never thought about it because they didn't know they could think about it."

A counselor like Mr. Sadiq did not exist for Nader—nor did it exist for the other participants. As a result, Nader was, again, left following what society, school, and his counselor were telling him to do:

> Our counselor did not know what's what. Perhaps this was the reason as to why they couldn't guide us well. I mean, maybe if they had brought in someone who was, for example, six years older than us . . . someone who had finished his education. Someone who was employed. Or someone who had gone after finding a job. Perhaps if I had someone to help me, I would not have chosen [mechanical engineering] . . . if I knew then that the job market is going to be better for, um, programmers, developers for example, perhaps I would have gone toward software [engineering].
>
> NADER

The inadequacy of guidance, or misguidance, from school, coupled with a focus on the *konkur* signified a systematic problem where the participants felt overwhelmed and preoccupied with these short-term aspirations. As I argued with Nader on why he did not try harder to find out what subject area, academic major, and/or career he liked (or did not like), he replied with bewilderment that he "just didn't know where and how to look" or what to look for. He also acknowledged his young age and ignorance, but he argued that he believed the people in his life at that time knew what was best for him, so he followed their instructions.

As a result, the participants' aspirations were being formed for them, and they remained dubious about their futures. The participants felt they did not have time to think about their mid- to long-term goals and aspirations, and when they moved on to the next phase of their young lives, they continued with no true purpose except to accomplish the next task:

> During that time you never realize that there was a wall because you were thinking that this is the only way and that's it. This [system] was established a long time ago. . . . In Iran, education is such that it has a specified pathway,

> and if there is another way it will not be successful. . . . I mean, just think about how this system was formed when you can only choose between math and science [as your major] and they're not allowing you to decide [on whatever major you want].
>
> DARIUS

Darius's mention of "this system" that "was established a long time ago" further highlights the *khodi*'s covert resistance to change. Much of the evidence provided in this section has been discussed at length in global debates—for example, the competition and focus on grades and standardized tests, or the neglect the participants experienced, as well as the one-dimensional expectation from family and society that often leads to an underdeveloped understanding of one's aspirations (e.g., in Japan [Aibao et al., 2007], Singapore [Ang et al., 2009], and Hong Kong [Ma et al., 2018]). However, two aspects that appear to explain the *ghayre-khodi* context a bit differently are the role of the State as an adversary and the resistance to change even after research and literature expose these issues and academics and politicians offer proposals—I will discuss this at length in chapter 7. As Dr. Mahdi, a government official, stated:

> In most cases [they] don't allow change to happen. . . . These conversations have been going on, and very little has changed. Comparisons between Iran and most other countries are good, but once you bring in the government, that's when you really see a difference.
>
> DR. MAHDI

Darius's quote about how he could only choose between math and science for his high school major was the experience of all students who attended a school for the gifted at that time. Public and private schools, on the other hand, offered five high school majors: math, science, humanities, art, and vocational training. Darius grew up in a town about twelve hours away from Tehran. His family had a modest life, considered to be middle class. After passing the gifted school exam and completing middle school and his first year of high school, Darius had to decide between two high school majors: math or science. However, Darius was as much an artist as he was a mathematician, and he often contemplated pursuing an art degree, though he never felt like it was a sensible option. In fact, his perception of a career in art was heavily influenced by school and society:

> The major of art . . . they said people who were very lazy chose art and they'd form cliques that were morally and behaviorally unhealthy . . . so after

> hearing this and seeing some of them . . . it caused me not to try in that field and not think about it, because it was presented as not a real option, because they made the conditions look so bad and difficult.
>
> DARIUS

This is another example of how the participants felt their aspirations were being formed for them by school and society while they were also being labeled as unintelligent, lazy, or gifted and then separated into different majors or cliques. I recall my conversations with Hamid and Mohamad, who both received their art degrees from Tehran University, and their stories of how they felt like it was "me against the world." Hamid explained that the example of non-STEMM individuals being viewed as "lazy" and unintelligent began from the 1979 Revolution and the regime propagating that the majority of artistic expressions were against the teachings of Islam, and therefore a sin, prohibited, and some were punishable by law (Agah, 2019; Ministry of Culture and Islamic Guidance, n.d.). To further this propagation, Hamid explained how societal discourse and the manifestation of that discourse, via media and entertainment outlets and mosques and religious centers, often appeared to assist the school system in teaching the youth that "a profession in art was immoral" and/or unsuccessful. For instance, Darius explained that "majoring in art in school was disapproved in society." They were taught that "intelligent and obedient students major in math and science, and later become successful in life." Thus, not only were the participants feeling pushed into certain majors, but they also felt pulled away from the humanities and social sciences. Darius recalled not feeling any negative emotion for not pursuing art for reasons similar to what Nader explained: immaturity, ignorance, and trusting the people around him. However, Darius did stress his indifference toward the majors he had to choose from:

> No one spoke to me and said, "Okay, imagine, what you like your job to be twenty years from now" [or] "in which activity you feel you are happy" or test me to find in which fields I work well. . . . there was no other solution.
>
> DARIUS

Ismail's recollection on that time of his life was quite poignant: "I regretted my past a bit . . . I told myself . . . that I could have lived differently or maybe everything didn't have to be about studying because you initially set the foundation for something and continue accordingly, but later on, when it changes, it . . . affects you." The change he was referring to was the guarantee of a successful life if he focused on the path he was told to follow, but later discovering that not only was that not the case, but he was also uncertain about what direction to take and how to remedy his situation. There has been much debate on expanding school curriculum by strengthening the humanities and social sciences, and providing more options, but these proposals have broadly been ignored ("Madares farhang," n.d.; "Ulume ensani," 2020). Mr. Sadiq also alluded to this problem when he said that the youth are pulled away from humanities and pushed toward the STEMM programs.

This pull away from humanities was an experience Nader very easily related to. Nader grew up in a town seven hours away from Tehran. His parents were not well educated, and he considered his to be a lower-middle-class upbringing. Nader was a talented soccer player yet was never encouraged to pursue it. He described following a one-dimensional path that pushed him toward math or science, and he was led to believe that anything counter to this was not an option or would not lead to a life of success:

> If we say the view of society, family, school, et cetera, et cetera, everybody thought that if you are a smart person, well then go study [math or science]. Especially the fact that humanities in Iran is really in a bad state. Like I said, this is the view from everybody. It's not like anyone says, "Which one do you like?" Even between math and science, they say, "These students are not good at math, so they should choose science." And [no one] suggested like, "Do you want to choose a vocational major?" They didn't even ask. . . . I think, the only time that I could and was able to try different things was then. And society, school, family should have allowed me to try music, soccer, or whatever, but this wasn't possible at all.
>
> NADER

One account, in particular, highlights these problems described by Nader where the participants illustrated a path they felt bound by without fully understanding why. Figure 4.1 illustrates the participants' perception of their one-dimensional path. Cyrus and Karim described it as a linear path, and Cyrus would argue with his school on "why everybody has to go down this path like sheep." Darius and Ismail described it as a road, and Darius explained how "everyone must race each other and try to get ahead." Nader likened his experience to a train track, and "once you are on it there is no getting off."

Karim identified another issue of the one-dimensional pathway: "Another shortcoming that we have in Iran is we don't have any idea about majors at all." In addition to the participants' experience of misguidance from school and society, and the covert resistance by the *khodi*, the participants' unfamiliarity about different university majors was also a result of the disconnect between

Figure 4.1. An illustration that serves as a metaphor for a student's life, where there is only one path to follow because everyone tells them where to go and what to do. *Direction*, by Marian Kamensky, 2010. https://www.toonpool.com/cartoons/Direction_97811 (in the public domain).

high schools (irrespective of type) and universities. During this time of their life, the participants depicted no university fairs, and there were no exchanges of information or programs where they could visit universities or speak with a representative from a university visiting their high school. Karim, for example, traveled to Sharif and stood outside the entrance for hours hoping to find a student willing to answer his questions. As Nader stated earlier, "I saw that everybody's trying to get in [Sharif], but not everyone can, so I thought something is going on there—even though I didn't know what—so I said sure, I'll go." Ismail never heard of the country's most popular and prestigious university until high school. Darius explained that "I too wanted to [attend Sharif] because all the things instilled into us [were] that Sharif is the best university of the country, when I haven't even seen Sharif!" He went on to describe the negligence of, in addition to the misguidance from, his school and society:

> No one spent time on a student who was disorderly to see what he's cable of offering despite his unorganized style, which is what I was. They just wanted to make everything regulated. This results in what? Someone who is a bit jumbled is labeled as unsuccessful in education. Using *their* criteria from *their* measurements, you will always come up short. The person who was weak became weaker and the one who is good became better. That is, no one tried to help those who are weak. The way they did help was they gave us a pamphlet [called] "education guidance" in which I answered [yes or no questions about different professions] to identify which [major] I like or don't like. But

> someone who doesn't know what accounting is, well, what does it mean to like it or not?
>
> DARIUS

Nader, on the other hand, who was always at the top of his class, felt abandoned by the people around him because "they saw [he] was getting good grades, so they said he knows what he is doing." However, Nader was perplexed when it came to figuring out what area of study he liked or disliked. Therefore, when the time came for him to choose his university major, he just "followed the crowd." He later realized he "made a mistake," but by then "it was too late" since he was already in Sharif, and changing his major would require dropping out, retaking the *konkur* in the discipline he wanted, and practically starting over again.

When the time came for Karim, he was accepted into industrial engineering. He described how fortunate he was, because although he knew very little about this field, he ended up liking his major—which he stressed was a rare outcome. Ismail, on the other hand, strived to make his own decision regarding his academic trajectory. While the path Ismail took was no different from that of his fellow classmates and the other participants, he found places along the one-dimensional pathway to best position himself for a successful career after Sharif. Since Ismail showed me the possibility of resisting the one-dimensional path for a so-called "dumb" student, I continued to press my other participants, like Nader and Darius, on why they did not resist their one-dimensional path in order to shape their own aspirations and pursue their own goals. Nader spoke of his apathy in making decisions throughout his academic journey. He followed his peers in obeying what school and society told them to do, and where to go, and later admitted the mistakes he made for not questioning the process and where it would lead him. Darius described his lack of self-confidence and motivation. He explained how he often required a push from friends and family to achieve many of his academic tasks, and therefore he followed his peers in obeying what school and society told them to do and where to go. Darius went on to argue that "finding ways to challenge the system doesn't change much because you're always in it . . . whether it's high school, university, the job market, society . . . it's always there in some capacity." I found this argument to be compelling considering how Nader admittedly followed the crowed like a sheep while Ismail disobeyed and dropped out of his final year of high school, yet both men ended up in the same predicament in the job market despite their best efforts to succeed.

Similar to Ismail, Cyrus did question the one-dimensional path and tried to defy it, but he was not strong enough to resist the educational and societal pressures from the people around him. Cyrus was the only participant who had the opportunity to enroll in different classes at his private school. With various programs running twelve months out of the year, he was able to discover what he liked and disliked. Although he admitted that none of his classes helped him make a decision, he did choose the university major he wanted (computer engineering) and not what his family tried to make him select (medicine). However, similar to the other participants, Cyrus detailed how his high school did not provide constructive counseling, guidance, or advice. Like Nader said, they did not ask him what he liked, they just told him what to major in. Mr. Sadiq had the same experience when he was a student, so when he later became a high school counselor, he developed an approach to better assist students in discovering what discipline they desired to major in.

> I help my students from three aspects. Look, it is a triangle, deciding about the future is a triangle. . . . [1] Your aptitude, meaning your capabilities. [2] Your interests, concerns, and aspirations. And [3] the circumstance, environmental conditions. Environmental conditions mean what the working conditions are like. Can you work within them or not? [These are] completely external factors. The other two are internal. When the external conditions are terrible or do not exist at all, an Iranian family—especially within this current economy—doesn't see any reason to send their kid to study [non-STEMM majors].
>
> MR. SADIQ

The third aspect that Mr. Sadiq described—"the circumstance, environmental conditions"—foreshadows the challenges participants faced later in life that will be discussed in the subsequent chapters of this book. It is worth noting here that one common thread throughout the participants' lived experiences is this tension of constraints and opportunities that balance on a tightrope of ideological conformity, on one side, and the ability to develop highly critical perspectives, on the other.

Creating the One-Dimensional Aspiration

The participants' apparent limited success in resisting the constraints and ideological conformity in order to explore their own aspirations and discover their own path suggests a type of mindset that goes beyond just the immaturity of a young teen. The participants truly believed the path they were told to aspire for was their best and only option. However, what if this path is bereft of continuity and plagued by uncertainty? Moreover, what if that discontinuity and uncertainty are hidden in plain sight within a deliberate concoction of projecting a sense of purpose through a human capital understanding? Meanwhile, the youth are actually limited within set parameters in order to suppress any possible threat to the *khodi*'s status quo, thereby also suppressing youth potential as a byproduct. In other words, this is a path with a disconnect between high school and university; misguidance or negligence from school, family, and society; and a pull away from non-STEMM disciplines, leaving the participants to make underdeveloped decisions for their short-term goals and no decisions for their long-term goals. All the while, students are being told that this is the best and only option to take. Nader's explanation of this is poignant:

> Nobody gave you any other option, they didn't suggest any other idea, they didn't say, "Other than this path, there is another path." Everybody was in agreement that you have to choose this path that, no, I didn't even doubt like perhaps this isn't right, I mean from school, school deputy, teachers, school principal, everybody at school had this view, at home everybody had this view, our relatives all had this view. I mean there was no place to doubt. I don't know, there was no place to even think about these. Everybody told me you will go to Sharif and after that you will either apply or there will be a good job for you. . . . We were on this path that we had to take the *konkur* and then go to university.
>
> NADER

Faced with thought processes like "nobody gave you any other option," "there was no place to doubt," "everybody is in agreement," "there was no place to even think," and "everybody told you," participants felt that the path they were told to take and the aspirations they were told to have created another tension with their own academic—and eventually professional—maturation. This struggle highlights the possible systemic issue where society and the education system manifested and perpetuated the *khodi*'s status quo while the Islamic Republic passively ignored calls for change and the *khodi* and mafia actively opposed change. The participants later determined that the mentality of only having a one-dimensional option of passing through the *konkur* and enrolling in a top university in order to secure a successful life set them up for failure because of two reasons. One, when they reached the end of their academic journey and started their life in the real world, they discovered that the successful life they were promised did not exist inside Iran. And two, during this journey, they were unable to think about their own aspirations, explore alternative avenues to success, discover their own interests or passions, or attempt to plan for the long-term future. Thus, when these two reasons occur at the same time, participants are plagued by uncertainty and compelled to rethink how they are going to actualize a successful life inside Iran.

With the exception, for example, of Cyrus and Ismail—who knew what discipline they wanted to major in (computer and chemical engineering) and what kind of career it should lead to—most of my participants felt uncertain about their academic decisions and the career it could lead to. Darius chose mechanical engineering through a process of negation. Karim was offered industrial engineering due to the rejections he received in electrical and mechanical engineering that he had at the top of his 150-major list. Nader followed the trend in selecting mechanical engineering. And many of my other participants, listed in appendix A, also followed the crowd. During a significant portion of their pre-university lives, the participants considered themselves multidimensional. However, they pushed these aspirations aside to focus on the *konkur*. The participants thought about nothing else because that is what they were told, and they eventually believed that disciplines such as art or sports would not lead them to a successful life. Karim explained:

> One of the things that pressured kids in childhood was . . . that in school they look at things one-dimensionally . . . [and] it won't be useful if you go to sports, "You are not a normal member of society" or "You are not accepted by us." [This] was implanted in my mind by family and the society.
>
> KARIM

Nader also mentioned on multiple occasions that he regretted not pursuing soccer, but he stressed that he did not dwell on it because there was nothing he could do to change it, and he had to focus on his future.

Although each of the participants described similar situations in their own way, it was Karim who first used the term "one-dimensional" when discussing his experiences after failing the gifted school exam and attending public school:

> You [are] somehow labeled in [high school]. They call it, هنگ شدن, or being controlled. You just focus on one thing and . . . you frame your mind and think you are not gifted; they tell you from the beginning that you have lost the game, from the very beginning. This is extremely bad, meaning it distances you from other opportunities . . . In my opinion, the ones around you are much more influential because a child . . . during middle school . . . the kid hasn't really formed a personality. However you are raised is how you

> will end up. I feel the push at this phase is a lot! . . . this one-dimensionality has become very embedded in society, specifically in education where families don't have any perspective. We even have a lot of proverbs in our culture, things like پاتو از گلیمت درازتر نکن [know your limits and do not exceed them]. I want to say that some subconscious thoughts are affecting us, okay? That we are not aware of. These are dictating some kind of one-dimensionality in us from childhood.
>
> KARIM

One aspect of Karim's story that was intriguing was his description that subconscious thoughts, of which he was unaware, were affecting him; thoughts that were "dictating some kind of one-dimensionality . . . from childhood." The participants described such an experience, as well as the moment in their lives (during within-university—which will be discussed in the next chapter) when they realized this one-dimensionality. What was fascinating was not only their ability to overcome their sense of despair after realizing that what they had been told their entire young lives was misleading or inaccurate, but also their self-awareness to not solely blame the institutions and people around them. The stakeholders I spoke with appreciated the criticisms the participants directed toward school, society, and the government; as Sharif professor Dr. Hossain (stakeholder) explained it, "If they had made these decisions themselves, they should bear the responsibility, but because it was others [saying] what to do, the [participants] become like a machine." Simultaneously, however, the stakeholders argued that if the participants truly wanted to realize their aspirations, they could do so if they tried hard enough. When I returned to the participants with these comments, they initially reacted by furiously and unconditionally blaming everyone and everything around them. However, after calming down, the participants did acknowledge their own shortcomings—which will be expounded upon in chapter 6.

Another aspect of the one-dimensionality the participants relived was the intense and unhealthy competition for the best grades, the best schools, the best *konkur* rankings, and the best universities. And while the participants were having these conversations, one missing aspect in their narratives was any discussion within society or at their school about life after university. As a result, three issues emerged that further complicated the participants' attempts at actualizing a successful life inside Iran. First, an individualist disposition emerged within them, which they later had to unlearn when trying to succeed in their jobs. Second, unhealthy competition reinforced the one-dimensional mentality that they were following the only path to a guaranteed successful life, and thus, they felt a deeper sense that their aspirations were being formed for them. Third, public school students like Karim and Ismail were essentially forgotten because they were seen as having already failed this competition. Interestingly, Darius felt a similar sense of being forgotten because of his disorderliness, and Nader also felt this way due to being labeled "too intelligent." Furthermore, the proverb Karim stated above (know your limits and do not exceed them) emphasized this exclusion. The same can be said for Cyrus, for when he had an opportunity to think outside of the one-dimensional path, he did not:

> **Cyrus:** I mean when you are at school, all the teachers tell you that you should study mathematics. Counselors tell you the same. Your family tells you the same. The society tells you the same. Your relatives tell you the same. They say, "Shouldn't you study mathematics?" Your friends tell you the same too. Everyone means literally everyone, with no exception.
>
> **Reza:** Did you discover anything about what you liked from your other courses?
>
> **Cyrus:** Yeah, but it wasn't like . . . I wouldn't choose my future job based on these. For example, I learned carpentry. I had this idea then that an engineer who knows carpentry is way better than an engineer who doesn't know carpentry. So let me learn it. An engineer who . . .
>
> **Reza:** In your high school?
>
> **Cyrus:** Yeah, in secondary school.
>
> **Reza:** During secondary school you thought about being an engineer?
>
> **Cyrus:** Yeah, I was thinking about it, there were no other options. We were supposed to be either engineers or doctors since the first grade of elementary school.

As a gifted student, Darius felt his one-dimensional path was also set:

> The path was set for me. They have made everything one-dimensional by limiting it to only one path. . . . What is taking place is that we in this [educational] framework were "good kids." "Good kids" are always expected to do the right thing. And what is the right thing? What [subject] are you good in? Your grade is best in which [subject]? You go there . . . then when you get to the konkur, when it gets to choosing the [university] major, this is repeated again. You got a good rank, so what is the right thing? Choosing this major. It is not good to choose another [major]. Even, for example, if somebody with my rank chooses another major, for example, management at University of Tehran, it is not good! He has made a mistake! As if this person has committed a deadly sin! Well, this is something that subconsciously occurs in

> our minds. We were not able to think about anything other than what they forced us to do . . . well . . . as long as we were going to school. I mean . . . we didn't see anything except konkur! I mean, you won't believe it, but when you enter pre-university level, everyone is studying for the konkur! You don't see one person who does something else and thinks about something else. This issue . . . this culture is so dominant that you are sure nothing is possible except with this [path] and that causes the minds to be limited. . . . The interesting point is that even if you do well in that aspect, you don't have a great chance of being successful. But a student is not allowed to explore otherwise.
> DARIUS

The frustration in Darius's voice as he recalled those moments was upsetting. He felt he grew up in a system where he could not think about anything beyond what was in front of him. And what was in front of him was a short-sighted one-dimensional version of a human capital understanding that had limitations and stipulations in accordance with the *khodi*'s status quo. As stated by the participants, and as Darius explained, school and society were only interested in keeping them on a one-dimensional path, and anything counter to this was a mistake, "a sin." It seemed it was of little concern to them what these young men's aspirations were, or if this pathway was what they wanted. This further raises questions of the possible covert resistance to change by the *khodi* and the Islamic Republic enabling these socially accepted norms to persist throughout schools despite calls for reform.

This covert resistance appeared to be further compounded by a cultural manifestation of the *khodi*'s status quo that reminded the participants of the one-dimensional aspiration and uncertainty about their own long-term future and aspirations. Cyrus spoke about this culture:

> The school did something to us that we weren't friends anymore, I mean I didn't consider my classmates as friends, I saw them as competitors—the school did this—so much emphasis was put on our scores and ratings, I mean I killed myself to get better scores than my friends and this didn't make us sympathetic and empathetic, this made us competitors. And if I knew something, I wouldn't help my friend. I said, what if he learns it and gets ahead of me? Let me keep this to myself so I can stay ahead of him. That was awful! I mean it was one of the most ridiculous things in school, and this wasn't just us, most schools were like this. The culture and common sense are so low that if you want to do teamwork you will face hostility and competition, I mean it is the culture . . . they teach you the wrong culture.
> CYRUS

This "wrong culture" with a low common sense, according to Cyrus, also illustrates the resistance to change that Karim spoke of regarding the professor who was forced to retire after challenging Sharif's president, or an example Darius gave about Dr. Kaveh Madani, a former Imperial College professor invited to advise (and later became the deputy head of) the Department of Environment regarding the country's water crisis, who left Iran after being harassed because of the changes he aimed to implement. Another is Dr. Mahdi, a Ministry of Education official, who admitted that there was significant resistance to change from those in power in both the government and the *khodi*. Also, Dr. Babak, a professor at Tehran University who had lived through every major event in Iran since the 1950s, explained that "you either have to become like them or quietly live your life." He elaborated that the *khodi*—primarily consisting of individuals within or devoted to the Islamic Republic—had built a system it did not want to change, nor did it want to give up power. Therefore, it only allowed people to enter its domain, or make changes, who thought the way they did and believed in what they did—essentially having the same ideology—while everyone else should just live a "quiet life" and not disrupt this system. Darius's further depiction of this culture and quiet life—where he previously described "committing a sin" if you do not follow the prescribed path—began with the completion of a to-do list: "If you don't check these boxes, your life will not start. . . . I just knew that the reason for getting good grades is to be in a good place in that competition so I can move on and check the next box."

A prime example of the participants' inability to aspire for the future is how Ismail exercised his agency to that pursuit in a dichotomous way, simultaneously effective and frail. While the other participants, like Darius, "were not able to think about anything other than what they forced us to do," Ismail broke away from that by dropping out of his final year of high school to prepare for the *konkur*. However, he continued down the same one-dimensional path as the other participants in trying to rank high on the exam and gain admission into a top-tier university. Simultaneously, Ismail never planned or thought about his long-term future or aspirations. On the one hand, he understood the magnitude of his decision, which was scorned by the people around him, but he was not prudent in his long-term strategy. He explained that, at the time, he chose to wait until university to decide about his future but later regretted not exploring his options.

Nader also did not think about his future or aspirations, but not because he chose to; rather, he was unaware of what he was interested in. He followed what society and school told him to do and fell into the one-dimensional pathway. After checking every box on his to-do list in order to reach that successful life he was promised, Nader was still searching for his aspirations while confused about his future. While Nader was achieving short-term success, he felt the inadequate support structure—which could have helped him determine what disciplines he liked or disliked—simply push him, unable to aspire for his future. During our interviews, he sometimes reached certain realizations and admitted he made mistakes, and he once said he hoped our conversations would "help me discover what I like, but if not, at least your research can help future students like me."

While Karim and Ismail experienced neglect because they were labeled as unintelligent, and Nader was neglected because he was too intelligent, Darius was neglected for his "sloppiness," as he put it. However, he made it through this first stage on his own, despite his school labeling him irresponsible. Considering how he was neglected, I asked him if there was ever something he preferred to do but faced pushback from those around him. His answer was the quote at the beginning of this chapter, that they postpone living, and thus anything contrary to the "routine process" encountered pushback. Darius's lived experience of this routine process where life was postponed until after university, thus resulting in an unimagined future, highlights the participants' struggles in being able to explore their aspirations and how they continued down the one-dimensional pathway couched within the human capital argument. Karim described his interpretation differently and proposed a way out:

> You have to take control of your life, the dictation of society and the mind barriers that it instills in you and the labels that are given to you won't be important to you anymore. But when you are not aware, those mind barriers are always there, you won't ever become an initiator, you'll always be waiting for others to tell you what to do, so you are a puppet in others' hands. . . . You have to have courage to not become like everybody else . . . courage to get out of that comfort zone, and embrace punishment, embrace the punishment from society and family. . . . You have to embrace the punishment, be strong to think long-term that I'll show them in four years that my path was right.
> KARIM

While Karim's assessment was consequential not only to his but also the other participants' ability to overcome such mind barriers, dictations, and labels, his final thought at the end—"I'll show them in four years"—further highlights how ingrained these mind barriers were. As Karim relived these memories, he admitted in a later interview that he had more barriers to overcome if he was only thinking four years ahead instead of eight or ten or more.

Thus, like Ismail, Karim also exhibited a dichotomous proclivity toward his effectiveness and frailty in exercising his agency. It appeared that with Ismail and Karim, they at least had a rudimentary awareness of their own abilities—which may be accredited to their public school experience and being labeled unintelligent and subsequently neglected, and thus left to persevere on their own. However, throughout that journey, they were unable to aspire for the future.

Conclusion

During my participants' pre-university journey, school, family, and society seemingly obstructed the exploration of their own individual aspirations by forcing them down a one-dimensional path camouflaged within a human capital understanding. With barriers that mislabeled, misguided, and neglected the participants, this pathway was established for them to focus on standardized tests, schools for the gifted, *konkur* rankings, top-tier universities, and STEMM degrees. As a result, the participants reported experiencing their aspirations being formed for them. While these accounts are no different from many youth experiences throughout the world—for example, in Japan, Hong Kong, and South Korea, as well as in parts of Europe and North America—there appears to be at least one difference in how these countries' respective governments participate in their citizens' pursuit of aspirational attainment toward a successful life. In this regard, Iran's government is more comparable to Russia, China, and North Korea. In other words, while public debates on these problems were prevalent within Iran and reform proposals offered, the Islamic Republic was identified as ostensibly enabling the existence of barriers to such reform through what appears to be a covert resistance to change. The *khodi* (which includes the mafia), on the other hand, exercises a more overt resistance. Such resistance to change ensures (a) that the *khodi* holds on to power; (b) that the *khodi* procures and controls major revenue streams to help them stay in power and circumvent economic sanctions; and (c) the superimposition of ideological, social, political, and religious norms in order to influence its citizens' thought processes and behavior to counteract threats to (a) and (b).

The following vignettes from Karim and Nader succinctly illustrate the participants' state of mind throughout their pre-university experience. With Karim's vignette, there is a strong sense of determination and purpose on his part that was constantly circumscribed by the people around him and led to his subsequent complacence. With Nader's vignette, there is a strong sense of uncertainty coupled with unsure regret.

I want . . .	
I want to take the gifted exam!	"You failed, you're stupid, go to this school."
Okay. I want to take the Olympiad exam!	"No. You're at this school, take these classes."
Okay. I want to compete in swimming!	"It's irrelevant, it's a waste, focus on studying."
Okay. I want to take the *konkur*!	"You can't . . . You passed!? Go to this university."
Okay. I want to study this subject!	"What's your score? Study *this* subject."
Okay. What future will this give me?	"Don't worry about it."
Okay . . .	

KARIM

What if . . .		
What if I knew what to do?	"Do this."	I mean, what if I knew what *I* liked?
What if I knew where to go?	"Go here."	I mean, what if I knew where to find *my* way?
What if I knew who to ask?	"Ask us."	I mean, what if I knew who could help *me*?
What if *I* could do it all over again?		
What if . . .		

NADER

The tension between the participants and their school systems was evident in the way they narrated how their aspirations were shaped for them by their teachers and counselors. This tension is juxtaposed with the participants also trying to contemplate alternative ideas of their aspirations that eventually became worn away by the societal discourse and the participants' tension with the manifestation of that discourse—that is, the people in their lives, and the regime's tentacles of influence (media and entertainment outlets, the *konkur/education* mafia, and the *khodi)*. Thus, what resides in place of their underdeveloped aspirational agency is an internalized manifestation of the one-dimensional pathway that is camouflaged within the human capital argument. As a result, the differentiation between *khodi* expectations and individual aspirations becomes blurred. And the participants continued down the one-dimensional pathway, remaining uncertain about their future. They wondered why they had to follow this one-dimensional path, where it would lead them, if it would be as successful as they were promised, if they even wanted to move in this direction, and why there were no other paths to take.

CHAPTER 5

A Tense Realization Within University: A Feeling of Isolation and Ejection

A scary number of people expect you to apply and leave Iran . . . the youth and even more from society, they kept saying, "Why don't you go? Why don't you go? Why don't you go?" It is very bad, maybe you like to stay here! I mean, constantly . . . if they find out you are a Sharifi they ask you, "Why you don't leave?"
KARIM

One direction the participants quickly found the people in their lives pushing them in was an exit from Iran because of the participants' association with Sharif. Even if they did not want to, the pressure for them to leave was often so great that they were unable to think about anything else. Parallel to this and occurring simultaneously was their perception and slow realization that Sharif offered them very little alternative to this push. Thus, in this chapter I first detail the participants' tension with the higher education system, which they felt was working against them. I then present the participants' narrative surrounding a concept that illustrates how and why the one-dimensional pathway continued to persist from pre-university into within-university. This concept is *khodi* versus *ghayre-khodi*. In short, the *khodi* constitutes any individual/entity who has any kind of affiliation, directly or indirectly, with the Islamic Republic—e.g., Sharif University, which is owned by the regime. And the *ghayre-khodi* is everyone else—particularly the participants. The participants described five experiences as a result of their tension with the *khodi*: (1) a sense of hopelessness toward society and the institutions they had to navigate; (2) the pressure to leave Iran; (3) an inaction from the top down and bottom up for change; (4) misguidance from the people in their lives as they tried to navigate the parameters they felt were limiting their academic and professional maturation; and (5) a disconnect between Sharif and the job market. In the second section, I detail how the participants' uncertainty about their future was compounded by their struggles to distance themselves from the one-dimensional pathway while simultaneously trying to identify their own aspirations and find ways to manifest their agency and employability to an extent where they have an increased likelihood in realizing their aspirations inside the limited parameters of Iran. I close the chapter by briefly highlighting two additional issues—the *sarbazi* (or conscription) and the economy—that added to the participants' struggles in shaping their own aspirations and increased the tension with the Islamic Republic and *khodi* as they transitioned into the job market.

Tensions with Sharif University

The participants were mindful of being fair in telling their story, often stressing their avoidance of categorical statements and acknowledging alternative views and exceptions to their examples. I did notice, however, that their emotions got the best of them at times, and their tone became more accusatory toward Sharif, society, the government, and even their families. In those moments, I gave the participants the opportunity to speak freely and uninterrupted because I believed there was truth within their stories, even if they were biased at times. Also, the participants' ability to speak for one hour straight exemplified their suppressed anger, I believe, because of the limited outlets afforded to them in expressing their frustrations. The example of Sharif's popularity and high rank resulting from its students rather than its professors was one of those frustrations. As the conversations progressed, however, I discovered that the participants' view on this matter was not isolated squarely on the argument that students, not professors, made Sharif elite or popular. There was a compilation of issues on how Sharif operated that continued to limit the parameters in which they could academically mature, which subsequently continued to shape their aspirations.

Each of my *Sharifi* participants (see appendix A) recounted many issues regarding their university, four of which were commonly shared among all twenty-three participants. First, professors focused more on publishing than teaching. Elam (2018 Sharif graduate), for example, talked about how some professors publish an article every two weeks: "Some of the professors have become an article-submitting factory. And then these articles provide no help to our country, our industries, our people . . . nothing." He went on to say that universities in Iran should not be competing with American or European universities but should rather work to help our country. This connected with the second issue: professors were disinterested in engaging with their industry and preferred to focus on the academics of their discipline. Hafez (2019 Sharif graduate) recalled professors explicitly stating that they did not care about the job market. Third, professors taught outdated material and/or simply reused previous semesters' syllabi. One example that was ubiquitous throughout the interviews was that the teachings were heavy on theory—another example of a disconnect with industry needs. Fourth, professors had no interest in helping their students, either academically, professionally, or personally, even when they were assigned as advisors. For example, Nader and Karim remembered how professors "did not reply to our hellos," and "they did not see us as humans." Nader recounted having to track down his advisor somewhere off campus to have him sign his class schedule and how his advisor did not care what classes he was taking.

Because the participants were careful in being fair in telling their stories, they also provided favorable examples as well. Interestingly, the paradoxical nature of their criticism of the institutions that still helped them to advance in life was not lost on the participants. Some mentioned experiences with academic departments and/or professors that were more judicious in helping and preparing their students throughout their bachelor's program and beyond. Cyrus mentioned how his department (computer engineering) had strong connections with the industry, which led to high employment rates for its graduates. His department's internship program was the envy of other departments because (a) "the students actually learned something," and (b) there was a stronger possibility of getting hired afterward. Nader skipped over his bachelor's (mechanical engineering) and spoke of his MBA department (at Sharif) hiring practitioners with firsthand knowledge they acquired from their work experience. He also spoke of his department being well connected with the industry and providing ample opportunities for employment. Darius and Karim, who later pursued their MBAs at another university, did not share the same sentiment. However, Karim did recall one semester when his department (industrial engineering) hosted a visiting professor from Canada, whose teaching style extremely motivated him in spite of his department's disconnect with the industry.

Even as the participants provided these positive examples, they still gravitated back to the negative side—which did monopolize their overall narrative. Thus, even the positive examples came with caveats, primarily that positive change within Sharif was very difficult to achieve. Karim detailed an example:

> One of the physics lecturers . . . one of the decorated professors of Sharif. . . . He studied at Berkeley. He himself at his own expense had bought and

> brought books, meaning not on behalf of the government, *himself* had purchased all the books from abroad, *himself* . . . then had so much criticism that . . . (laughs) . . . no I'll say it, there's no problem, they gave him mandatory retirement . . . he was invited to a discussion regarding university policies, and which way the university is headed. He challenged the vice chancellor in a debate. And a month later . . . he is retired all of a sudden. It's pretty clear. I mean you can see the one-dimensionality even on the highest levels of Sharif still exists. Instead of learning from our failures and using them . . . we don't learn from failure at all, it's as if someone who criticizes us wants to replace us, he wants to undermine our position. Instead of using the criticism, which is genuinely compassionate, one of the best professors of Sharif, in the world, he is extremely good, but he has been chastised.
>
> KARIM

This example—as well as the ones provided above—confirmed for the participants that Sharif University was not only working against them but also working against anyone whose academic/professional intentions went counter to their socially accepted norms. In other words, the participants did not feel alone in their pursuit of manifesting their agency while simultaneously discovering the extent to which they were allowed to enact that agency. The participants explained that if certain professors were denied opportunities to accomplish their aspirations—particularly in what they felt was a professor-centered university—then their own chances of realizing their aspirations were even more bleak.

Therefore, the participants' within-university stories of lacking significant support structures for their maturation as higher education students within and throughout the academic environment, or as transitionary graduates in pursuit of identifying their aspirations, illustrated how they were left to navigate this journey on their own. As the years passed, the participants increasingly felt the need to become self-reliant and sought assistance elsewhere in their pursuit of identifying and realizing their aspirations inside Iran. On the one hand, the participants felt abandoned and discouraged because of the broken promises they received of reaching a successful life if they followed the path to Sharif. On the other hand, they continued to strategize ways to attain that successful life. Hence, they experienced a continued tension of constraints and opportunities, balancing on a tightrope of ideological conformity, on one side, and the ability to develop highly critical perspectives, on the other.

The participants increasingly realized that they had to stay within a set of constraints in order to achieve a certain level of success. This also coincided with their experience of the one-dimensional pathway. In addition to feeling frustration from such a realization, they discovered one added issue during their within-university time that was troubling: leaving their country just to get out. This sentiment seemed to prove truer than ever in the aftermath of the 2025–2026 protests. But even during my time with the participants, we experienced the 2019–2020 protests, and the participants calculated that the degree of success they would be able to accomplish inside Iran by staying within the parameters was considerably incomplete, unethical, or illegal when compared to the degree of success they could potentially achieve in a country not plagued with such troubles. The participants did not plan to leave Iran, nor did they want to, during the within-university stage of their lives. They also recognized that going abroad came with its own complications. However, traveling abroad appeared to offer much greater opportunities than those they perceived inside Iran, thus making it worth the risk.

One key architect of the tension the participants felt and the one-dimensional path they continued to be pushed down was the *khodi* within Sharif. This has particular relevance because Sharif belongs to the Islamic Republic, which means its employees are essentially hired by different branches of the government—or individuals within the *khodi*. Therefore, this tension between the *khodi* and *ghayre-khodi* was visible in the relationship not only between participants and Sharif and its faculty and staff, but also between the faculty. The participants referred to the *khodi* as the "mafia" when discussing the individuals who benefited from societal norms, Sharif's status quo, and resistance to change:

> Most [professors] have created a monopoly in different departments. I mean, they have created a kind of mafia that won't allow other professors to do anything. . . . In the Mechanical Engineering Department . . . there is something like a mafia that doesn't allow new professors to work easily unless they are accepted in their group based on the existing regulations . . . a professor came there and he taught us for one semester, and I took his class. He said that he couldn't . . . I mean, with those conditions and the mafia that existed there, he said that he couldn't finish [teaching] and he went to University of Tehran and became a professor there.
>
> DARIUS

I asked Darius what those "existing regulations" were. For example, I wondered if seniority or age played a factor, if the professor had to abide by a particular curriculum, if he had to pay his dues, so to speak, or if his ideological beliefs aligned with the Islamic Republic since Sharif belonged to it.

Although Darius could not speak to the specifics, what he did know was fascinating:

> Our problem is that with the current educational system that exists here, we don't gain many sources of knowledge in order to make change happen. Because, for example, the universities here are old in some ways . . . they are outdated. Most professors who are here are not that good. They are the people who have been developed in this system and now are back in the same system. I mean, it is a chain linked to its own end, and so it's declining rather than improving.
>
> DARIUS

The system that Darius refers to initially had its roots in the Islamic Republic. As detailed in chapter 3, the Islamic Republic closed all universities in 1980 in order to change textbooks, subject matter, curriculum, and faculty to align with the regime's ideology (Mahdi, 1999). However, the culture of that system was eventually inculcated by the newly appointed professors and administrators of Sharif, who years later came to embody the mafia or *khodi* that the participants had experienced. Because Sharif is a part of the Islamic Republic, "the people who have been developed in this system and are now back in the same system," as Darius explained, had gone through some form of a vetting process and had agreed to certain regulations. And any professors considered as *ghayre-khodi* found it difficult to enact any scenarios contrary to the status quo.

The point the participants were trying to make was a counterargument to those stakeholders—like Dr. Amir, Dr. Bahar, Dr. Bahram, Mr. Hadi, Dr. Hossain, and Dr. Sajjad—who told them that their ability (or inability) to identify and realize their aspirations had practically nothing to do with what kind of university Sharif was or should have been. Rather, it depended on the individual, their agency, and their use of capital. However, when professors leave Sharif and their vacancies are filled with "people who have been developed in this system," then the status quo continues to persist. The Islamic Republic subsequently and passively enables this, along with the existence of the mafia. Thus, a tension has been created between the participants and Sharif because, as the participants continued to navigate through these parameters, they felt pressured into continuing on the one-dimensional pathway from pre-university.

I discussed this point by the participants with seven Sharif professors: Dr. Ali, Dr. Baqir, Dr. Esmail, Dr. Hassan, Dr. Hossain, Dr. Khosrow, and Dr. Sajjad. Six of them (not Dr. Sajjad) confirmed that there were professors who made it difficult to achieve change and help their students, which essentially was "setting them up for failure," as they put it. They referred to these professors as the "revolution generation" (of 1979). Dr. Sajjad was from that generation and disagreed with the participants' depiction of the *khodi* and *ghayre-khodi*, and their tension within Sharif. He went on to explain that while difficulties and challenges may exist, one's ability to provide a sustainable livelihood for a family is achievable if you know where and how to navigate the job market. In order to avoid any possible risk to my safety, I did not push back against Dr. Sajjad's argument too much since he was a part of the system. Nevertheless, it became clear that certain parameters were in place to limit the *ghayre-khodi*.

Moreover, Dr. Mahdi, a Ministry of Education official, explained that for the most part, Sharif University (as well as Iran's higher education system) was working against most of the youth, either actively through the mafia's resistance to change or covertly through other governmental bodies' disregard of calls for change:

> These entities work very slowly and are resistant to change, and in most cases don't allow change to happen. . . . A top-down approach will not lead to change and will only be frustrating and disappointing. Take me as an example, I've learned the hard way that going through the government is fruitless or difficult.
>
> DR. MAHDI

Thus, similar to the pre-university experiences of my participants, they described how the people in Sharif and society would tell them what choices to make, what paths to take, and what to worry about (or not). The participants believed it was of no interest to those around them what their own aspirations were. This tension between the participants and the people around them, in particular the *khodi*, intensified during their within-university time as they matured and slowly identified their own aspirations, manifesting in four ways: hopelessness, the push to leave Iran, inaction, and misguidance.

Starting with hopelessness, the participants began to construct from their experiences that there was a set of parameters regarding the extent to which a *Sharifi*—specifically a *ghayre-khodi Sharifi*—is able to exert his agency. Also, according to stories they told about some of their professors, there appeared to be repercussions if one attempted to go beyond the *khodi*-defined parameters. The participants explained how "you can only try so much before you hit a ceiling." Thus, the participants felt that if certain professors were unable to accomplish their aspirations because of this tension, then what hope was there for them? The existence of this tension for the participants removed the hope for the possibility that Sharif could have made improvements to potentially help them as they moved into the job market—especially considering the volatility of the country's economy due to sanctions, corruption, inflation, and dismanagement.

This sense of hopelessness demonstrated that if you are part of the system and have relationships with the *khodi*, you can acquire certain advantages. Therefore, a new understanding was emerging where human capital—and even religious, social, and cultural capital—did not appear to be enough to actualize a successful life inside Iran. There is also an ideological capital that one should, and perhaps must, invest in to attain a standard of living inside Iran that is conducive to, for example, home ownership, a family, and a career that can provide and sustain such things. According to the participants, if one subscribed to anything contrary to this ideological capital, they could find themselves continuing to follow the one-dimensional pathway, thus perpetuating the tension and eliciting hopelessness. Frustration with this sense of hopelessness toward Sharif manifested even more in Cyrus than it did in the other participants. He explained that the hopelessness was not just because of the resistance and/or inaction from the top down—vis-à-vis policy proposals, education reform, amendments to laws, and institutional changes—but also because bottom-up change did not occur because people chose to leave Iran rather than stay and try to improve living standards.

> We are basically producing students and giving them to America, and this is the height of catastrophe. Everybody comes here and studies, and basically we don't use them in this country. Like I said, most of the students who were studying computer with me are not in Iran, they are all in America. We are practically training a workforce for America. The best, the most elite, and the most educated, we prepare them and give them to America. This is the *catastrophe* of Sharif! I *detest* it.
>
> CYRUS

Nevertheless, the participants rejected the feeling of hopelessness and quickly adapted to their environment, finding extracurricular activities and motivation to accomplish different goals in different environments. However, in addition to facing the limitations on enacting their agency and fighting off feelings of hopelessness, participants faced the second manifestation of whether or not to leave their country.

A small number of my participants—like Cyrus, Nader, Karim, Darius, and Ismail—were initially uninterested in leaving Iran during their time at

Sharif. They aspired to contribute toward the betterment of society but were unclear on how to identify what that would be and how to realize it. Not only did they feel that Sharif left them ill-prepared for life after graduation, they also believed that it cultivated an atmosphere where *Sharifis* were dominated by this obligation that they had to leave because they were only allowed to navigate within the limiting parameters imposed by the *khodi*. The participants were advised by people throughout society and Sharif—at times even bombarded by them—to leave Iran, which adversely occupied their thoughts.

> Of the fifty who entered the university with me in the same year, just two people stayed in Iran. That is because there are no foundations to help each other, and everyone leaves. All are seeking to leave, all are thinking about leaving, madly . . . and it causes those who stay to even feel connected with the purpose of leaving, so we get entangled, that is, you cannot do anything . . . it's a very strange place to be.
>
> DARIUS

Darius struggled the most with whether he should leave. He even haphazardly applied to foreign universities in his final year at Sharif because he saw the people around him were applying, but he was not accepted. He mentioned on numerous occasions that because "everyone leaves, you feel indebted to yourself if you don't go." Then, when he initially decided to stay, he worked to transition a class project into a startup. When the startup failed, he reconsidered leaving. This constant back-and-forth for Darius left him idle for over a year.

> We kept seeing that salvation is in applying . . . the atmosphere in the university . . . all the students . . . they all said that this is probably the way to salvation, which means that you don't have any better options . . . but I wanted to stay and make a difference here.
>
> DARIUS

Thus, not only did Darius experience difficulty in identifying his aspirations, but he also struggled with distinguishing which aspirations were his own (contributing toward the betterment of society) and which aspirations were societal or State constructs (going abroad). For Cyrus, the constant push to leave was more of a nuisance than a bewilderment or indecision. He was steadfast in his desire to stay in Iran and help his people. Ismail and Karim also found it to be a nuisance when people insisted that leaving Iran was the best choice, as quoted in the beginning of this chapter. The participants recalled conversations with their professors who advised them to leave Iran. When "everyone tells me to leave," the participants emphasized, they meant literally everyone. Cyrus's response was that he wanted to stay in Iran and attain a profession where he could help "move our society forward." Karim expressed frustration with wanting to stay in Iran but also feeling like he should leave. The majority of the stakeholders agreed with the participants' comments about leaving Iran, and Dr. Hossain (a Sharif professor) added that 70 to 80 percent leave because they heard about or saw others like them who went abroad and entered a university that offered many options of support and guidance, which later led to a successful postgraduation life.

What was interesting about Cyrus's comment that everybody went to Sharif to leave Iran was that it suggested a premeditated strategy of taking this path in order to leave, which could mean some of Cyrus's peers were not necessarily hopeless, like he was, as a result of their experience. The participants argued that the one-dimensionality of studying and aiming for top grades, high GPAs, and top projects was a deliberate plan by most *Sharifis* to gain admission into a master's or doctorate program outside of Iran so they could leave the country. This would then suggest that the other students had a comparatively less-distressed mental/emotional/psychological state than my participants did. Where the participants became hopeless through experience and then upset—and sometimes depressed—from that revelation, most of their peers were using this opportunity to leave. Moreover, this premeditated strategy further highlights the bottom-up neglect of not striving for change inside Iran.

Another point to highlight was the advantage students had of being able to leave Iran if they wanted because of their degree from Sharif. The participants explained how many of the country's youth wanted to leave Iran but could not, primarily because they did not have the means to do so. Thus, while there was a positive aspect of graduating from Sharif, the participants (less Cyrus) saw their exodus as a failure. In other words, the impetus to leave Iran was a push from within rather an external pull from another country, because the extent of their agency inside Iran was bounded within the parameters described thus far, which limited how and where they could manifest their agency and employability—ultimately capping success and their standard of living.

The third manifestation of the participants' within-university tension was inaction. While the first manifestation of this tension was hopelessness, caused by struggles for change between the *khodi* and *ghayre-khodi*, it also created the second manifestation of this tension: an atmosphere where participants felt pressured into leaving the country. This gave the impression that very little attention would be given toward making internal improvements, thus perpetuating the socially accepted norms within Iran/Sharif and the idea that no matter what one did, the status quo would remain—the result: inaction. Darius explained that "no one," including the *ghayre-khodi* professors, "was interested in improving Sharif because they had one eye on leaving":

> Professors are faced with similar challenges as these students. The pay is low, usually a professor makes five to six million Toman [roughly $450 USD in 2019] a month, which is considered under the poverty line if you are married with two kids. And the negative atmosphere of society takes a toll on your own mind so you cannot focus as much on the students. And on top of all that, if you studied in a foreign country but came back to Iran, a part of you is regretful that you didn't stay there because you compare yourself with your classmates and see how much more successful they are, making more money, having a more relaxed life, and you think to yourself that you wish you wouldn't have come back to Iran.
>
> DR. HASSAN

Dr. Hassan went on to say that as a consequence of many Sharif graduates and professors leaving, Iran's job market was scarcely populated with *Sharifis* who may have been inclined to hire a fellow *Sharifi*.

Ismail provided an example of how the inaction from Sharif resulted in poor-quality education that could have otherwise inspired him to pursue his major professionally, considering he enjoyed chemical engineering:

> The facilities of the university are very poor. The labs for example . . . you think that it's a high school not a [university] department. Its building is just like a school. It's really bad . . . as I was looking at one of the labels on one of the [pieces of] lab equipment, [I noticed] it was made . . . in the year 1966 . . . that means before the Revolution. 1966! How long ago is that!? . . . isn't this terrible!? It's because it's a part of the State, because it's the State, because it is the State . . . they can make [the lab equipment] in Iran, but they won't do it.
>
> ISMAIL

Darius explained that he forgot more than he learned during his four years in Sharif because the material he was taught at the Science Olympiad was on a "much higher level." One example Darius gave was how certain courses and their corresponding lab classes did not even occur in the same semester (he experienced a four-semester gap between one course and its lab). He expressed how proper knowledge was lost with such a gap, and "that is a weakness that bothered me very much." Darius went on to point out that these gaps had more of an impact on the students' psyches rather than their intelligence, because if we looked at the students who scored the highest on the *konkur*—he claimed the top eight hundred (which was out of millions)—they were already intelligent to begin with. Ismail explained this further by saying that if you removed the students from Sharif and kept everything else the same, the university "would not be among the top ten in the country."

Many of my other participants also explained that most professors use students to write their articles and then use the Sharif name to help publish in order to advance their own careers—similar to how students use the Sharif name to help them apply to foreign universities. Therefore, no one was interested in improving the conditions at Sharif. When I challenged the participants on what they were doing in spite of the shortcomings of outdated laboratories, ineffective evaluations, disengaged professors, a disinterest in change, and inadequate services, they unequivocally responded with, "I can only rely on myself." The participants understood that they had to work that much harder to overcome these shortcomings. However, the extent of their agency could only take them so far when considering how the parameters within which their agency could be manifested were limited by the *khodi*.

The fourth way that the tension between the *khodi* and *ghayre-khodi* manifested for the participants was through misguidance. As explained above, professors were preoccupied with their own problems, which prevented them from fully advising, guiding, and/or mentoring their students. Moreover, the participants also experienced a faculty who "did not care about us"—as Nader and Karim put it. They explained how the majority of professors they encountered held similar views as Dr. Sajjad, who argued that "Sharif's mission is advancing the borders of knowledge" and that students need to "lower their expectations of life inside Iran and work harder to make a living." And while professors were giving this advice, Karim and many of my participants were experiencing the following:

> Professors actually don't consider you a human. They often don't respond to your hello. Students don't dare to speak unless spoken to . . . it's not the way you think like we comfortably converse with them, no, not like this at all! It's a *very* top-to-bottom look.
>
> KARIM

This stark contrast between what professors were advising and how they were allegedly acting highlighted two problems for the participants. First, the professors' perspective was empirically detached from the world the participants were experiencing outside of Sharif. Second, and perhaps most importantly, the professors' advice to work harder and lower expectations was void of any alternative practical recommendations that the participants could implement during their transition into the job market.

During their pre-university time, the participants were told to work hard for the best grades, the best schools, the best *konkur* rankings, and the best universities. Now within-university, they were told to work hard for the best grades, the best professors, the best projects, and the best letters of recommendation. As a result, the participants explained that not only did they learn very little regarding knowledge and positive attributes to help them beyond Sharif, but they were instead taught negative qualities in order to progress along the one-dimensional pathway. This, they explained, was part and parcel of the inaction and misguidance from Sharif, which opened the way for unhealthy or extreme competition, as they called it, and immoral and unethical behaviors inside Sharif.

Darius explained how his experience with the misguidance at Sharif was a microcosm of a larger issue that highlighted the *khodi*-versus-*ghayre-khodi* tension:

> Competition means that everyone should have equal access to the procedures and everything and everyone should be aware of what is going on. But I believe that Sharif has an unhealthy competition because one might have some information which is not shared with others and in fact doesn't want them to enter the competition.
>
> DARIUS

As a result, Darius shifted toward photography and basketball to distance himself from the Sharif environment. Similarly, Ismail disassociated with the circles he frequented at Sharif by the end of his second year and gravitated toward philosophy in search of a deeper meaning and clearer understanding about what he was doing with his life (he also exercised more and played volleyball). Nader never encountered the struggles that Ismail and Darius experienced. He did not experience these negative behaviors, nor was he greatly affected by the Sharif environment. However, similar to pre-university, Nader aimlessly ascended through Sharif while feeling neglected and misguided. The one-dimensional path for Nader was affecting him, even though he did not fully realize it until the end of his final year at Sharif. Karim, however, had similar experiences as Darius and Ismail. As a result, Karim refocused his learning toward online classes from universities such as Stanford and Harvard. Cyrus was more comparable to Nader in the sense that he focused on his classes while also working throughout his time in undergrad.

Considering how the majority of my participants struggled at Sharif, and how some even withdrew from it, I asked them if they had regretted going to Sharif. And without hesitation, they all said no, highlighting two advantages of being a *Sharifi*. First, they were better off than non-*Sharifis,* who struggled worse than they did inside Iran. Second, the label of *Sharifi* provided them with a path out of Iran since Sharif was an internationally recognized institution. Nevertheless, Ismail went on to express his frustrations with what he felt were broken promises, that if one were to follow the one-dimensional human capital path, one would have a successful life:

> You try so hard to achieve something . . . you try really hard . . . and the university doesn't provide anything for you. It's a fact . . . nor does society. In fact, they tan your hide, and you don't get anywhere at the end. You try and you get nowhere.
>
> ISMAIL

Some of my participants admitted in making mistakes with some of their choices but later clarified that they were not so much choices but a path they were told to follow. Nevertheless, those participants, like Rumi, believed that "there was no changing what had happened in the past, so there was no point in dwelling on it." They also discovered that the whys and hows of these shortcomings, obstacles, and tensions they had experienced were no longer important to them. The participants accepted that this is how things are. As a result, they maneuvered through higher education alone. Doing so meant having to unlearn the misguidance and look elsewhere for help.

Similar to how schools were disconnected from universities, most of Sharif was disconnected from the job market. One example the participants provided was the absence of a department or office serving as a career services center. The participants could not believe—and at times were frustrated by the fact—that Sharif University developed a careers services center, called the Sharif Career School, in 2015 to help its students transition into the job market. It was absurd to the participants that it took so long for such a university to create a career services center considering that Sharif was globally ranked 646th at that time (according to *U.S. News & World Report*, 2021), with an engineering program ranked 127th, was the MIT of Iran, and had graduates like Maryam Mirzakhani (winner of the 2014 Fields Medal). Cyrus and Karim were at Sharif when the career school was operational, so they were able to capitalize on its services in helping them develop into multidimensional, well-rounded individuals who had acquired enough capital, strengthened their employability, and enabled them to succeed in Iran's job market.

Also, Hezekiah (2019 computer engineering) and Cyrus's Computer Engineering Department was viewed as helpful to its students. They spoke highly of most of their professors as well as the job fairs, co-ops, and internships their department featured that led to employment for the majority of its graduates. This was not the case for the other participants, however, which further disappointed them in the hopes of trying to figure out what they could do after leaving Sharif. The participants argued that the anomaly of the Computer Engineering Department having a strong connection with the job market had less to do with the department's interest in building bridges to its industry and more to do with the demand of the nation and the world, vis-à-vis mobile apps, website development, IT services, and tech companies. Furthermore, the participants, as well as my stakeholders, explained how the *khodi* professors—or the mafia, as *Sharifis* called them—had established ties with their respected industries and prevented *ghayre-khodi* professors from either entering the industry or connecting with the companies the *khodi* already had relationships with—which were primarily State or *khusulati* companies. Due to the gap between Sharif and the job market, Karim, for example, decided to help his fellow peers in their final year by building a consortium consisting of students and professors from his department (industrial engineering) and companies within their industry. He realized that if his department and/or university would not take an active role in building bridges with the job market, then he would be the one to initiate the process:

> I had this plan so our department can be linked to the industry and . . . no surprise, the industry side was much more eager. I was in charge of our graduation ceremony . . . so I'd go to different companies to see if they could be our sponsor . . . they were ecstatic to do so even though there wasn't any profit in it [for them], they just wanted to initiate contact so they would be able to collaborate with the university in the future, which would enable them to benefit by using the elite students in that major. But a student made this connection, not the university . . . it's very discouraging . . . universities do this stuff, but not ours. After I graduated, no one continued with these relationships, and it ended.
>
> KARIM

The majority of my participants, however, experienced a complete disconnect. Aram (2019 mechanical engineering) explained how easy it is for his professors and department to build connections with their industry, but they do not pursue this path. Darius added that the Mechanical Engineering Department was "very much involved in mafia stuff." He went on to add that "the mafia professors would simply say something and it would happen," but they rarely said anything about building ties with their industry. Eight of my participants pursued an MBA program either at Sharif or Amirkabir, and they all had positive stories of how well-connected their programs were with their industry. Even with his many criticisms of the regime and society, Elkanah (2019 electrical engineering and 2021 MBA) described how major businesses would send their managers and directors to Sharif's MBA program to strengthen networking between the companies and Sharif, which sometimes resulted in internship opportunities.

Elkanah's story further highlights Karim's point regarding the enthusiasm that companies had in wanting to connect with Sharif, whereas Sharif showed a lack of interest or initiative to do so. The participants also referenced other newly formed companies that had greatly developed as a result of US sanctions—since American companies could not enter the Iran market, Iranians created their own version of Netflix and Uber. Such companies had the potential for a mutually beneficial relationship with Sharif but had yet to link with the university: Snapp (Iran's equivalent to Uber), Tap30 (Lyft), Namava (Netflix), and Divar (eBay). Karim went on to explain what he learned from his brief, and failed, attempt at trying to build this relationship:

> Sharif doesn't have a relationship with good companies, especially the very good companies that can have good internships or bring projects. They have official relationships with some companies . . . those connected with the government.
>
> KARIM

As a result, Karim described Sharif as an island. On the one hand, the university was isolated from schools and the job market. On the other hand, students were isolated from the faculty and department. Figure 5.1 illustrates how many of my other participants' perceived this sense of isolation between Sharif and the job market. They described a landscape that was built for success but was being destroyed on purpose to keep people within the *khodi* parameters.

Ismail pointed out that the full name of Sharif is دانشگاه صنعتی شریف, which literally translates to the Industrial University of Sharif, and he argued:

> I think the word "industrial" should be taken out. I haven't seen anything like this from professors. They don't have many relationships with their students or the industry. To be successful in the job market requires other factors. But

Figure 5.1. An illustration of a Sharif graduate trying to transition into Iran's job market. The image showing "No Hiring" is from Dave Granlund. Copyright 2020 by Dave Granlund. The bridge is from iStock. Copyright 2023 by erhui1979. The rest of the image is from People Matters. Copyright 2017 by Arunima Shrivastava.

> we look at it in a linear way, if you get this GPA from a very good university, you should certainly be successful in your job, but you aren't. You need other skills . . . not merely the knowledge. Working requires skills that you don't have.
> ISMAIL

As the participants neared the end of their time at Sharif, they began realizing the limits to their agency and employability and how far these could take them within the *khodi* parameters of Iran's education system and job market. The complex tension between the *khodi* and *ghayre-khodi*—of which the participants found themselves a part during their within-university experience—further confirmed for them that they were left alone to navigate their way into the job market while still facing uncertainty about their future.

Tensions with the One-Dimensionality to Human Capital

The participants' uncertainty was compounded by their struggles to distance themselves from the one-dimensional human capital pathway while simultaneously trying to identify and realize their own aspirations within the limited *khodi* parameters inside Iran. As participants remained disconnected from the job market and continued to face the aforementioned obstacles and shortcomings, the one-dimensional focus of "study, study, study," as Cyrus put it, continued to dominate the environment in which the participants were navigating. Figure 5.2 illustrates this one-dimensional focus of studying and was a heavily circulated graphic throughout multiple Sharif social media channels. The participants considered it an accurate depiction not just of their four-year experience at Sharif but also of their transition out of Sharif. This continued tension according to Darius was "completely negative . . . the fact that we never see the things which are supposed to be intermingled with our life is very frightening." Darius went on to explain that "this is a structure which is imposed on you in a top-down manner . . . and you have to run in this straight line. This reality is very sad, and you can't get along with it." There was much to unpack with this comment, and as we spoke further, terms such as "imposed" and "top-down" helped paint a picture similar to the participants' experience in having to "run in a straight line" during pre-university. The difference this time, however, was how that experience manifested and how the participants responded.

Nader, for example, who endured the least amount of hardship, comparatively, during his within-university experience, realized later in life—and identified during our interviews in particular—that the people around him in Sharif and in society pushed the one-dimensional pathway that led to his uncertainties about his aspirations. He explained how human capital was the only focus and that no one placed importance on things like social capital or becoming well rounded. Karim's description of this pathway further illustrated the one-dimensionality to human capital, the short-sightedness in goal-setting, and the adverse effects it had on their lives after Sharif:

Figure 5.2. A graphic used in Iran depicting an undergraduate student's educational experience at Sharif. By unknown artist. https://www.michaelkaechele.com/remote-community-partnerships-in-pbl/ (in the public domain).

> This path has been made beforehand . . . study . . . get into university, not just Sharif, get into university, get married, have kids, the end . . . as if you are done with one thing you are doing, it is finished, let's go to the next one. Many of the Sharifis! They are *many* . . . are one dimensional. They study *extensively*, and they don't care about other skills. . . . The individual fails in many aspects of their lives . . . soft skills haven't developed . . . we don't learn anything else . . . we don't [learn] these other aspects. We're essentially exam-taking—or studying—machines.
>
> KARIM

Considering Hezekiah and Cyrus's experience with their Computer Engineering Department was an exception to the rule compared to the departmental experiences of their fellow participants, including higher employment rates for graduates and better internship programs that often led to employment, I asked if their department had a different/alternative approach to the one-dimensional path. Hezekiah explained that it was still one-dimensional, and the anomaly of his department had more to do with the popularity and demand of the tech industry that forced his department to become more cooperative. Cyrus's frustration was palpable:

> They say just sit down—like an ass—and study, study, study, take the exam, go higher—study, study, study—and they don't know anything about the fact that life is multidimensional. Many people at Sharif have the problem of being one-dimensional. I really tried to break this [one-dimensionality] because I said to myself, I am not an original Sharif student, so I did a bunch of things alongside it.
>
> CYRUS

Similarly, Darius no longer wanted to remain one-dimensional or to have Sharif tell him what his future should look like.

> If you start with the wrong idea in your mind, it is more difficult to change rather than learning something correctly from the beginning. So now you have to cut those wrong roots. And I went toward photography, computers, basketball. But some people have those wrong roots too deep . . . so for them if you don't check these boxes, your life will not start.
>
> DARIUS

Ismail also took a similar approach, and he gravitated toward philosophy, languages, and volleyball. The experiences that Karim, Cyrus, Darius, and Ismail detailed highlight moments in their lives when their individual agency and individual aspirations took shape while remaining in contention with the educational system's continued reinforcement of the one-dimensionality of the human capital path. As a result, the participants actively pursued the aspects of themselves that were iteratively worn away by Sharif and society or that they had pushed aside to this point in their academic lives. This break from the one-dimensional pathway helped them forge their own path and identify their own aspirations. Karim and Cyrus focused on personal growth and strengthening their employability through the Sharif Career School. Darius spent less time at Sharif and more time at the University of Tehran, where he took up photography and athletics. He described how he wanted to change his environment in the hopes of discovering more about himself as well as his likes and dislikes. Ismail showed a quasi-arrogant attitude that he believed helped him overcome the barriers of the *khodi*. He described how he identified the one-dimensional problem and then broadened his approach in order to have a more holistic view while overcoming feelings of depression.

The Sharif Career School that some of my participants attended began in 2015 and initially served as a pilot career services office. By 2019 (during the second trip of my fieldwork) it developed into a well-established career services center that provided much of the help *Sharifis* needed to transition into the job market. I interviewed Mr. Rida—one of my stakeholders, and an employee at the career school—who detailed an average of 700 to 800 applicants every term, with approximately 125 accepted as members and 30 of those as active participants in the school's programs. The school conducted workshops and seminars to help its members/participants learn and strengthen soft skills, résumé building, cover letter writing, participating in interviews, networking, and more. Out of my 46 participants, 23 earned a bachelor's degree from Sharif, and of those 23, 12 did not participate in the Sharif Career School because either it was not fully operational during their time at Sharif or they did not know it existed. Seven others also did not participate for varying reasons: Elam (2018) was trying to leave Iran; Elkanah (2019) and Ziba (2019) pursued their MBAs; Farzan (2021) and Talmai (2019) enlisted in the *sarbazi*; Hafez (2019) pursued his master's; and Jahleel (2019) was too jaded, angry, and disinterested in anything Sharif had to offer. Jahleel could not wait to leave Sharif, but his anger clouded his judgment, so he did not have a plan for after graduation. After engaging him in a long and difficult conversation, I finally got him to a point where he calmed down and told me that he just needs a break, that he felt burned out. Cyrus (2017) and Karim (2018) praised the Sharif Career School for helping them with their employability, and Aram (2019) and Tooraj (2019) were grateful that Sharif assisted them with their startups.

Most of the twelve participants who missed the Sharif Career School believed they could have benefited from it, and many wished they could go back and enroll. However, there were some who held the pessimistic view that even with the help of the career school, they would not be able to change the overall struggles between the *khodi* and the *ghayre-khodi*. As a result, they were focused on leaving Iran, and even Nader, one of the twelve, was considering it since he still did not know where his degree (mechanical engineering) could take him in Iran's job market, even after four years at Sharif:

> One of the reasons they said choose electrical or mechanical engineering was that applying to foreign universities was relatively easier with these two majors. Most of the people who chose mechanical and electrical engineering have left by now. Maybe that was one of the reasons why I chose it . . . I don't know . . . I remember people use to tell me, they said people who go to Sharif either leave Iran or will have so many job opportunities in Iran . . . but still there is nothing.
>
> NADER

Nader admitted to many of his shortcomings and faults, including his apathetic attitude toward strengthening his employability and his incomplete decision-making based on misguided information. Unlike Karim, Nader was not active in searching for alternative paths like the career school. His continued aimless ascent from pre-university to within-university hindered his academic and professional growth. This resulted in his uncertainty about his future and inability to identify his aspirations. However, even though Nader's approach, journey, and mindset differed from Karim's, their experiences within the job market were not so different.

On the one hand, Karim believed that his time at the Sharif Career School helped him develop into a multidimensional and well-rounded individual who had acquired the capital and soft skills, as he put it, and strengthened his employability to the point where he had a greater chance of realizing his aspirations. On the other hand, he started at the same point as Nader during the final semester at Sharif. In other words, they still did not know what their own aspirations were, how they were going to achieve them, where they needed to start from, and who could potentially help them. Karim mentioned on multiple occasions how this thought process should have begun much earlier in his life rather than at age twenty-one, right before he entered the "real world." Cyrus, on the other hand, developed his entrepreneurial mindset after attending the Sharif Career School, so he had a business plan to turn to after Sharif. In addition to the *khodi* parameters the participants tried to overcome as they transitioned into the job market, there were two issues that further complicated their journey and transition. The first was their mandatory military service, or *sarbazi* in Farsi. And the second was the economy—the participants' initial introduction to the economy presented a more direct interaction with the *khodi*, and this interaction brought a tension that would escalate for the remainder of their time in Iran.

In Iran, every able-bodied male of sound mind must complete two years of *sarbazi* after finishing their formal education. For the participants, they had to do this after completing their bachelor's degree; however, some individuals enlist directly after high school, while others wait until after they finish their master's or doctorate. *Sarbazi* service will be expounded upon in the next chapter, but it is worth mentioning that this "box that needed to be checked," as Darius put it, was as much a burden as the stress of ranking high on the *konkur*. The attention the *sarbazi* demanded from the participants further stunted their ability in developing their own aspirations and distancing themselves from the one-dimensional human capital pathway. The participants' explanations revolved around two points. First, the knowledge and skills they were to acquire during the two-year *sarbazi* were not related to their degree, let alone their aspirations, and therefore did not prepare them for the job market. Second, after completing the *sarbazi*, they would be two years behind the job market, any advancements and changes within their industry, and their fellow job hunters. Furthermore, their professional, geographic, and financial mobility was contingent upon the completion of their *sarbazi*.

For example, during my time with him, Ismail completed his *sarbazi* in order to be granted his passport and his official bachelor's degree so he could apply to foreign universities and leave the country. He described how his peers initially ridiculed him for enlisting but later commended him because he "was now free to do whatever" he wanted. The job offers Cyrus and Karim received through the career school were reneged on shortly after when the employer discovered they did not complete their *sarbazi*. Thus, they spent the majority of their final months at Sharif, as well as the subsequent months after graduation, trying to navigate, and possibly resolve, the *sarbazi* obstacle.

Nader, on the other hand, tried a different approach. He purposely failed his internship requirement to postpone graduation in order to find a resolution to his *sarbazi*. I asked him if he only used the internship for that purpose or if he also used it to help find employment. After contemplating for a couple of minutes, Nader admitted he never thought about using the time to find employment. He went on to explain that internships from his department (mechanical engineering) did not lead to employment, so he was not hopeful in attaining his aspirations through this program. However, Nader did see the internship program as an opportunity to postpone his *sarbazi* while he looked for a job in Tehran. Cyrus and Karim similarly explained that they attempted to avoid their *sarbazi* by applying for a master's program while also trying to find a job. Darius, on the other hand, was exempt because of a medical reason. Nevertheless, portions of the participants' time and attention that could have been spent on their professional maturation and transition into the job market were allocated toward their attempts to avoid or resolve their *sarbazi*.

The second problem facing participants that further complicated their transition into the job market was the volatility of the nation's economy. Cyrus described how the feeling of impossibility in planning for the future and the uncertainties of life in Iran overshadowed his aspirations:

> After I passed the *konkur* everything got worse. The stress got *really* worse, the pressure got worse, competition got worse . . . in Sharif all these things became more acute, and things get simply worse than in school. And . . . none of the problems were resolved, and everything got worse. My aspiration . . . at that time . . . was to set up a computer company based on my ideas. These things were on my mind at that time. . . . Look, the only awful thing about this country is that . . . the right thing to do is one should have a plan for the next five, ten, fifteen, or twenty years. I always had these plans. I knew where I wanted to be at thirty years old; what I'll be doing at thirty-five, where I'll be at forty. However, you sleep and wake up, and you see the country has an unstable situation and everything is messed up and everything is destroyed, and you should begin from scratch. This volatility destroys you, and in some places you can do nothing, and you are easily irritated and want to fight with everyone, and you don't have the patience for anyone.
> CYRUS

As a result of the economic volatility and uncertainty, Nader, for example, did not pursue computer engineering for his master's:

> I thought that if I go start learning it until I become an expert, then perhaps the job market would no longer be good, they would no longer have a good salary . . . or maybe I made a mistake. If I had gone and I studied computer . . . yeah . . . well, I made a mistake. If I had gone, by now, it would still have a good job market. . . . If I go back, I would probably choose computer.
> NADER

My conversation with Nader about the economy was fascinating because in this quote you can see how, in real time, he discovered he made a mistake.

We went on to discuss how computer engineering (or science), or related fields—for example, digital currency, smart devices, software applications, and artificial intelligence—continues, even twenty years later, to be one of the dominant industries in the job market. I asked him how and why he did not see it this way, to which he explained that "in Iran the economy is so broken [that] even a guarantee as the tech industry is not immune." He gave the example of how every major tech company in Iran is in the hands of the regime and is a *khusulati* company. He also noted that the regime controls the internet, including its accessibility and speed, and the Islamic Republic is working on rolling out their intranet (a State-run internet for the entire country) and no longer allowing access to the internet.

Interestingly, Darius also did not pursue a degree in computers for the same reason as Nader: "It is better . . . and that is just for now . . . no one knows what will take place tomorrow." Darius grew up with, and greatly enjoyed, computers; he even taught himself coding and software and hardware applications. But he still did not seriously consider pursuing a degree in this field out of fear of not knowing "what will take place tomorrow." Even when I raised the same point from my conversation with Nader, about how the job market for computer-related careers had remained strong for at least twenty years, Darius also did not believe that applied to Iran.

Conclusion

During the participants' within-university time was when they began to realize the strength of their agency and their ability to push back even harder against the *khodi* parameters and one-dimensional human capital pathway. As a result, the tension between the participants and their surrounding structures also increased. The participants were older, smarter, and capable enough to analyze which aspects of their lives needed alteration in order for them to shape their own aspirations rather than having their aspirations shaped for them. However, the participants' resistance was counterbalanced by an equal resistance from the *khodi*, the mafia, and the regime's tentacles of influence, which continued to covertly and overtly resist change to ensure the *khodi*'s status quo would not be compromised.

One aspect of the increasing strength was the *khodi*-versus-*ghayre-khodi* dynamic, which positioned the participants at odds with the very institution—i.e., Sharif University—they were told to attend and trust in order to attain a guaranteed successful life. As a result, the participants' tension with their own aspirations also sharpened because they felt the efforts they made in strengthening and improving their employability in order to increase their chances of reaching their professional aspirations inside Iran were not being reflected in the trajectory of the path they were on. In other words, the participants' changed their environment, pursued extracurricular activities, became multidimensional in their interests, strengthened their mental health, and became self-critical, but they only seemed able to navigate within the *khodi*-limited parameters.

The following vignettes from Darius and Ismail summarize the participants' experiences and perceptions during their within-university journey. The shaping of the participants' aspirations during this time was one of tension and conflict, both internally and externally.

> I knew my self-confidence was weak. I knew my aloofness was overpowering. So, I worked on them. My friends became depressed, my sister passed away, my grades were dropping. I got a sports injury! I had to move!! I'm falLING BEHIND! I AM RUNNING IN PLACE! BUT!! (ahem) . . . but . . . I adapted, I adjusted, I evolved. I did what I had to do to make it . . . but what about you?
>
> I have to think about that . . . let's come back to that one.
>
> I found my interests. I found some hobbies. I found a new spot that gave me good vibes. I changed it up! I got good grades. I finished my senior project. I checked the boxes you [the *khodi*] wanted. I jumped through the hoops you wanted. I listened. I obeyed. I "learned," I waited. I searched. I assessed. I unlearned . . . (sigh) . . . but what about you?
>
> You . . . you gave me an easy path to leave my country, even though I didn't want to.
>
> DARIUS

> Look. I get it. I'm a realist. Funding is low, wages are low, sanctions are suffocating, competition is insane, brain drain is high, corruption, nepotism, cheating, stealing, lying, blah, blah-blah, blah-blah.
>
> Look. I get it. I was a bit unrealistic . . . when I was younger, inexperienced. They make sure you do things a certain way. They watch over you. They can get things you can't, they have more access, different rules, better connections, more power, more control, blah, blah, blah.
>
> Look. I get it. I'm not naive. You don't care . . . or, you don't have the time to. You have your own problems. You have your own regrets. But when you're the ones we're looking to . . . no . . . when you're the only ones out here that know better than us, that know more than us, that have gone through this

journey, that are "molding" and "shaping" and "guiding" and blah, blah-blah, blah-blah . . .

Wait. I get it. If *you* have been going through this, for this long, then what the hell am I going to do?

ISMAIL

As the participants increasingly became self-critical in acknowledging their own shortcomings, while also internalizing their focus to strengthen their employability and become multidimensional with the aim of finding their own aspirations and forge their own pathway, they still felt the inequities of the one-dimensional pathway. They were still uncertain what their own aspirations were, how to identify them, and/or how to realize them inside Iran. As we move forward into the participants' postgraduation time, we will see how the human capital argument became deflated for them, thus leading to a sense of broken promises on human capital return vis-à-vis State expectations, and to the continued struggles and obstacles the participants faced despite their efforts in enacting their agency and employability to navigate the job market.

CHAPTER 6

A Clash of Ideologies in Postgraduation: A *Khodi*-Versus-*Ghayre-Khodi* Tension

It's like that one government employee told you . . . it's only difficult for the first forty days (laughs) and then we get used to it . . . because we grew up in this environment, we know that there is no need to compare khodi versus ghayre-khodi. He is talking about one thing over there and over here it is something completely different . . . there's no relationship . . . we are disconnected from each other.

DARIUS

While there may be no perceived positive relationship between the *khodi* and *ghayre-khodi*, there is a negative relationship. In this chapter, therefore, I further expand on the ways participants enhanced their employability in order to avoid the negative relationship of feeling pushed down a one-dimensional pathway. I also detail the moments when the participants realized that the guarantees they were reassured, if they followed the one-dimensional human capital path, were not accurate reflections of the postgraduation life they were experiencing. The (f)actors in this third stage of the participants' lives were, in particular, the *khodi* and *khusulati,* and manifestations of society's discourse through the regime's tentacles of influence.

There were, however, two significant changes in this third stage that distinguish it from the previous two stages. First, the concept of *khodi* and *ghayre-khodi* became increasingly tactile for the participants as they reported direct involvement by the *khodi*—i.e., the Islamic Republic's tentacles of influence—in counteracting their attempts to realize their aspirations inside Iran. Their reports highlight an issue that has mostly been colloquial and the subject of hearsay. What the participants explained illustrates the *khodi* as being afforded certain privileges, concessions, and preferences—depending on the extent of their connection to the Islamic Republic—that *ghayre-khodi* individuals do not receive. This leads to the second significant change: unlike their pre- and within-university experiences, where the participants believed they could eventually realize their own aspirations inside Iran, at this stage they believed they were confronted with a ceiling that denied their attempts to realize their aspirations and therefore ended that belief or hope in Iran. This resulted in the participants either (a) lowering their aspirations, accepting their current state of affairs, and reverting to the one-dimensional path, or (b) leaving the country. Cyrus offered his account of these two significant changes when discussing his former boss:

> He owes a lot of people a lot of money. Collectors track the poor man down every day with legal threats. And some promise to kick his ass! A good man, who could easily earn money a thousand different ways . . . he had very lucrative offers from foreign companies to help their child education programs, but he said, "I want to stay in my country!" . . . "I want to serve my people." What was the outcome? He's miserable! He sacrificed his own life and his family . . . the regime doesn't want people like him to improve society. They don't allow you to grow in this society. They beat the hell out of you . . . if you want to raise your head just a little, they hit you back down. Either shut up and live in this society . . . or else.
>
> CYRUS

Tension with the Job Market

The participants aspired to contribute toward the betterment of society through their professions. However, they reported encountering resistance in their efforts in trying to realize this inside Iran. Darius, for example, planned to go to a developed country but return to Iran and try to implement what he learned within the context of Iranian society/culture; he admitted, however, that it would be difficult with "many obstacles deterring you from succeeding since they're standing in your way." As the participants navigated Iran's job market, it became evident to them that certain industries or areas were denied or restricted to them despite having made what they believed to be their best efforts to enter those industries. Similar to how Darius experienced the *khodi* standing in his way, the other participants also explained how, historically, this resistance could be seen since the beginning of the Islamic Republic. Many of the individuals who went missing, fled the country, or were imprisoned or murdered during the rise of the Islamic Republic were individuals whose profession aimed to make changes within society—through academia, civil society, social work, human rights, and political engagement (Bayat, 2009). These were individuals that the *khodi* considered an existential threat to the socially accepted norms they had established and wielded into power and control. Karim gave an example of a Sharif professor who was forced into retirement because he "criticized the university's condition" and had ideas about improvements. Darius also gave an example of a ministry advisor who fled the country because of the severe opposition he faced to implementing changes (Tamman, 2021).

The participants went on to explain that when they were navigating Iran's job market, the parameters within which they had to operate appeared to have more limits than what they (a) were promised growing up and (b) experienced during their pre- and within-university time. As Ismail put it, "If one were to work for or own a company that sells/provides goods/services, they would be left alone and could potentially live a comfortable life." Thus, participants felt that particular business ventures (e.g., owning a retail store or restaurant) or employment opportunities (e.g., working for a company) were regularly insisted upon them by society and reinforced by the *khodi*. Moreover, there were large portions of Iran's job market that were either impossible to enter or extremely difficult to succeed in, often requiring compromises that the participants found ethically, professionally, and/or legally questionable. As a result, the participants described a sense of rebuff in their pursuits of realizing their own aspirations inside Iran if their aspirations did not comply with the *khodi*'s one-dimensional focus. They developed further tension with the job market when, on the one hand, the human capital argument deflated from the ambiguous promises of a guaranteed successful life to specific types of professions within specific types of industries. Thus, the participants' ability to realize their own aspirations inside Iran increasingly appeared elusive. Moreover, two issues added to this elusiveness and further complicated the participants' navigation of the job market: the monopolization of the job market and an unhealthy environment.

Monopolization of the job market by the *khodi* was one of those issues that the participants perceived as a limitation and barrier to realizing their aspirations inside Iran. For the participants, if it was not the push to pursue their one-dimensional aspiration, it was the restrictions on either entering the job market or trying to excel in certain industries within it. As Darius stated earlier, the *khodi* stand in your way, or as Cyrus described, "If you want to raise your head just a little, they hit you back down." Figure 6.1 illustrates the participants' perception of how a *ghayre-khodi* job seeker experiences

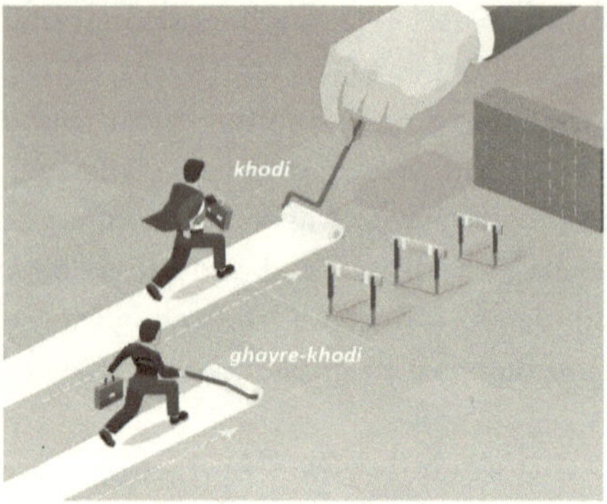

Figure 6.1. An illustration of the *khodi*-versus-*ghayre-khodi* tension within Iran's job market. Shutterstock. https://www.shutterstock.com/image-vector/vector-businesswoman-painting-her-own-career-1505570924 (in the public domain).

Iran's job market compared to a *khodi* job seeker. Interestingly, Karim believed this figure demonstrates the limitations and barriers in regard to government-related professions. However, Nader and Ismail believed this figure demonstrates the overall job market as well as the cultural and religious obstacles of Iran—in other words, if you are not a Shia Muslim and a Persian-Iranian, you have additional barriers to overcome inside Iran. Darius explained that although the term *khodi* was used to exclusively signify a specific group of ideologues within the regime's military and government, members of this group have now increasingly populated areas like education and the job market (along with real estate, trade, finance, tech, banking, and commerce) as well.

Moreover, the participants believed that this monopolization was also an attempt to curb the existential threats the *khodi* saw with individuals and/or entities aiming to engender any kind of change that could potentially weaken or challenge the *khodi*'s control and revenue. The protests/riots I witnessed in 2019–2020, the Women, Life, Freedom protests in 2022, and the 2025–2026 protests were emblematic of this existential threat. One example the participants gave was the one-dimensional push toward STEMM disciplines throughout pre- and within-university that continued during postgraduation in order to limit the exploration of non-STEMM fields—such as civil society, art, music, or politics—because these professions were seen as having a higher likelihood of producing workers who could disrupt the *khodi*'s status quo. The participants cited the *khodi*'s oversight of popular artists and musicians, allowing only those whose works are accepted by the *khodi* to publicly perform within Iran. On the other hand, underground artists and musicians who defied the *khodi*'s status quo either ended up being censored, imprisoned, sentenced to death, disappeared, or worse, or they could flee the country. Similarly, the participants felt their own professional maturation was stymied in order to keep them beneath the ceiling of acceptable social norms. They particularly felt limited by this throughout school and partly during their time at Sharif, as well as postgraduation where those parameters and limitations variegated to bar their ability to navigate the job market.

Many of my participants and stakeholders also mentioned the economic element of this monopolization as the *khodi*'s way of controlling the means of wealth. Two reasons emerged as to why the *khodi* did this. First, considering that sanctions had crippled the economy for over four decades, what limited streams of revenue remained needed to be monopolized in order to fund and sustain the *khodi*'s control, power, and influence over the country. Second, exercising such control ensured that competition, and potential threats, remained weak or nonexistent. From an employer perspective, Dr. Mahdi (Ministry of Education) described how private companies struggle to win projects and work: "Solely private companies in Iran do not get big projects. There is always a link back to the State. You need to give up a percentage of your company to the regime to grow past a certain point." He went on to explain how this adversely affected companies' hiring potential, quality of work, and employee growth within the company. Ismail elaborated on this notion that stores and restaurants who sell/provide goods/services had relatively more latitude to grow and prosper:

> I think it has become a fact in Iran . . . if you get involved in producing . . . the production of sneakers, bags, to computer software, electrical things, mechanics, for example, designing and stuff like that . . . most probably, you will go bankrupt . . . it can be anything, it doesn't matter. But if you get involved in providing services, you can make money . . . like if you run a restaurant, bakery, coffee shop, a corner store or retail store, it would be okay, you can be successful.
>
> ISMAIL

From an employee perspective, the participants explained how the available jobs from either the private, *khusulati*, or government sectors were routine or dead-end for different reasons. With private companies there was a lack of funds and projects, so the work required was repetitive and minimal. And in most cases these companies had a skeleton crew since there was little work to do. With *khusulati* companies, there was a dichotomous tension where, on the one hand, funding, projects, and job growth were more common because the *khodi* was involved, but, on the other, there was a ceiling on the participants' professional ascension due to their classification as *ghayre-khodi*.

With government companies the *khodi* was solely in charge; Karim provided a prime example of how the *khodi* kept tight control over Iran's auto industry and why that control exacerbated job market problems:

> Iran Khodro, the auto industry . . . it's owned by the State and it's a monopoly. Auto production has become monopolized, the State has the power, whatever they say, they can raise the price, lower the price, they can do whatever they want. But if someone else started producing better cars, then Iran Khodro would be forced to start research and development, improve themselves. But this doesn't exist. Now it's been so many years and their [Saipa] Pride car, I think it's being produced for thirty years now, and it's still the same, what kind of company is this? Because our country does not grow, does not develop . . . many fields cannot develop . . . it's an economic and ideological debate.
>
> KARIM

When Nader interned at Iran Khodro, he described how the engineers and employees barely worked, and if they did it was minimal and repetitive work. They explained to him how little they produced, that every day was the same, and there was limited professional growth.

Ismail described his experience with these economic problems and the monopolization of an industry he and his two friends tried to enter with their startup.

> The [company] that I told you my friends and I started . . . if you don't have a connection in the regime, it won't succeed. Because this [industry] is only with the government. There are no private companies in this [industry]. We learned that everything is in the hands of the regime. Because it's not open, in my opinion, they don't give just anyone permission to work [in this industry]. You can't enter the market and make the changes that you like; it's not like that.
>
> ISMAIL

Ismail added later on that they continued with the work, and his two friends persisted further after he left the startup, but they were unable to obtain funding because the major sponsors were also a part of the *khodi*. A couple years after Ismail's startup failed, a *khusulati* company formed to offer the exact same service (and it became a multimillion-dollar company).

Ismail's criticisms were echoed by the other participants, as well as by my stakeholders. Dr. Hassan (a Sharif professor), in particular, added that the disconnect between universities and the job market was partly due to the monopolization by the *khodi*:

> Ninety percent of major companies are in the hands of the State, so there is no competition and therefore production is low, R&D is low, the overall quality of these companies' output is low. Therefore, in Iran the mismatch between university and industry is enormous, and these big companies do not need graduates from Sharif but rather a simple engineer who fixes machines. The industry blames universities for not preparing their students for Iran's real world, and universities blame the industry for not lifting itself to the standards of the rest of the world.
>
> DR. HASSAN

Thus, on the one hand, the participants experienced a disconnect between Sharif and the job market because of what they described as a disinterest from the university side. On the other hand, however, the same disinterest existed from the industry side. This reciprocal disinterest left the participants feeling alone as they navigated the job market, which continually led them to the routine, dead-end, unmeaningful, and unthreatening jobs they had been trying to avoid. In other words, even though the participants tried to identify their own aspirations, they still pursued these routine jobs because their experiences and perceptions proved to them that these were the dominant positions available in the job market. Moreover, society and family were also pushing them toward these positions, but now the participants' rationale was different from before. During pre- and within-university, they were told to trust in God, and the pathway they were on would lead them to a guaranteed successful future. Now that they had arrived at that future, they were told to "just get a job, start working, start a family, and that's it."

Alternatively, there was the possibility of working for the government. However, none of the participants were interested in doing so, for the reasons provided above. Nader, for example, had a job interview with a government company and described how its focus was more on ideology than the work. Karim had a similar experience, and what he added was both fascinating and troubling:

> **Karim:** [Working for the government] can't be done, you know why? Now it's ideological. Like maybe we have someone competent who studied economics but doesn't agree with the system ideologically, so he can't work for the government. It's not necessarily a meritocracy or expertise . . . other factors are there, and that's their priority, the ideology, I'm saying things that . . . (chuckles)

Reza: Do you want me to stop recording?
Karim: Hmm, I don't know.
Reza: It's okay, if you want you don't have to say it.
Karim: Yeah, can you stop recording? The things I'm saying will cost me.

Karim's nervousness about criticizing the Islamic Republic was not a surprise because the other participants had the same concern. After I stopped recording, Karim went on to describe how the government's job interview process was more about its ideological and religious beliefs than the qualifications or expertise of the applicants—similar to what Nader experienced—which was followed by a grooming process to ensure employees think the way the regime wants them to. This is a prime example of how investing in one's ideological capital could lead to a successful/lucrative career within the government. But for a *ghayre-khodi* who opposes the regime, such an investment would go against their principles. Cyrus's criticism of the regime grew with such anger that it overpowered his fear, and he did not want me to stop recording and, in fact, made it a point to stress that it would be good if they found out about these things, because they should know how private companies "put their whole life in their job and have many employees and they became miserable" because of them.

For Cyrus, why and how the *khodi* monopolized the job market was a problem that went beyond the debates of meritocracy versus nepotism, competition versus monopolization, or ideology versus economy. Cyrus's lived experiences will show how his professional efforts in attempting to help Iranian society were repeatedly met with resistance, obstacles, and struggles due to what he believed to be the *khodi*'s fear of a private company amassing enough wealth and/or influence to possibly challenge a portion of the *khodi*'s revenue and control. The first company Cyrus worked for was unable to sell its product because "governmental organizations . . . bothered us, in various ways," and the company eventually went bankrupt. It was the first of four companies that he either worked for (one) or started (three) that eventually failed because of encounters with the *khodi*. Cyrus explained with much frustration that because of the *khodi*'s monopolization throughout the job market, his aspirations were denied, and over a span of five years (2014–2019) he fluctuated between employment and unemployment, and entrepreneurship and bankruptcy—I will go into greater detail about Cyrus's experiences in the next section.

Nader also encountered the *khodi*'s monopolization of his industry (mechanical engineering), but not through the denial of building a company; rather, he faced limitations on job opportunities:

> When I wanted to work in the field of mechanical engineering, I saw that there are very few positions available. One company was under the auspices of the Revolutionary Guard Corps. . . . This bothered me a little because I have heard that if you work for the Revolutionary Guard Corps, you would not be able to apply later and go to the US . . . one reason was this and also the day I went for the interview they said here everybody prays and fasts, and, I didn't tell you something, I'm not a Muslim and the fact that they said that, well, that bothered me too.
>
> NADER

I debated with the participants on why they would not start with these unmeaningful, unthreatening, routine dead-end jobs to gain experience, network, move on to something better, and make it, step by step, to the profession they desire. While Cyrus laughed at me and said, "Live here for twenty-five years and you'll see why it won't work," Jahleel offered a more compelling argument:

> I would love to start at a lower position with a lower salary if there was even a glimpse of hope to progress . . . there's no job growth or salary increase. You cannot progress . . . well you can progress to a certain extent. There's a ceiling and if you want to go past that ceiling you will need some other factors that are not ethical and may compromise your values.
>
> JAHLEEL

Unpacking Jahleel's comment highlights again the issue with investing in one's ideological capital. Many of my participants described this when trying to realize their aspirations inside Iran but not wanting to compromise on their beliefs. And as they navigated alternative options of employment other than working for the government, the participants initially grappled with, and later struggled to reconcile, certain aspects of the job market—aspects which, to them, appeared to contain prerequisites to a comparatively more feasible path to (a) earning enough money to buy a house, get married, and have kids, and/or (b) ascending in their career to possibly realize their aspirations. Those prerequisites, according to the participants, entailed morally—and at times, legally—questionable decisions.

Ismail echoed Jahleel's assessment when he said, "You can make progress only to a certain extent," and, "You will need some other factors that are not ethical." He gave examples of nepotism, deception, and unhealthy competition. I challenged Ismail's opposition to these "not ethical factors," as he put it, and argued that lesser versions of them—i.e., networking, embellishment, and competition—were common practices within the job market.

He agreed and stressed that he applied these methods, but he went on to explain that,

> Overall, maybe we can say don't be black or white. Be gray. But if you want to stay in Iran and make progress, you should move toward being black (laughs). In my view, this is my personal opinion, of course, but . . . when you enter a thought system, you have to accept it . . . you have to accept certain things. Now, if you don't observe some things in that thought system, it's okay but you won't [progress]. But now, I have some problems with that thought system, you know. . . . It's not really aimed at goodness, and it's not right, I think. It's not like it will be reformed and become better later on.
>
> ISMAIL

The "thought system" Ismail referred to is the unethical mentality that he believed individuals already had or needed to adopt, postgraduation, in order to achieve their professional goals within the framework of the job market and society, which have been greatly influenced by the *khodi*. He went on to argue that an unhealthy environment developed in Iran's job market as a result of the *khodi*'s monopolization and the void it created where immoral or illegal practices became the norm.

One of my stakeholders, Dr. Ali (a Sharif professor), who had a close proximity to Iran's job market because of his expertise, added a fascinating point to Ismail's argument:

> Most of the industries belong to the State. There aren't many powerful, wealthy, and big companies that are private . . . most of their success is not linked to their productivity or good management. What is it related to? To how much kickback they can give, to how close they are to political forces. Well, when this is the case, naturally many companies do not need an expert workforce.
>
> DR. ALI

The participants also believed that many individuals who were able to (a) earn enough money to buy a house, get married, and have kids, and/or (b) ascend in their career accepted the thought system and prevailed within the framework that the participants viewed as morally questionable. The example they provided was in reference to *dalal* work. The word *dalal* literally translates to "broker," but it means much more than the standard definition. The participants explained that this profession is stigmatized in Iran, carrying labels of thievery, chicanery, and immorality. Thus, while the participants complained of the parameters within which they had to navigate, none of them saw a *dalal* profession as as an option—even though there was a lot of money in it. The participants' aspirations primarily revolved around finding a career that provided a service and would improve society and raise the standard of living. They were not willing to compromise their beliefs or values for quick money, as they called it.

> When it comes to morality, society tells me to "get lost." (laughs) . . . It doesn't matter at all. Society doesn't care about morality . . . No, no . . . society . . . society cares about how much money you make and how you can get your work done through whatever means . . . violence even.
>
> ISMAIL

While the participants reported hearing about, witnessing, and often experiencing these unethical factors throughout the job market and society, none of them were willing to move toward being "black" let alone "gray," as Ismail put it. As a result, they felt this was another reason why the job market was working against them, pushing them down the one-dimensional pathway of a routine job and toward a quiet life.

Thus, the tension that developed for the participants between navigating these parameters, trying to depart from the one-dimensional path, and trying to realize their own aspirations left them with four options: (1) become an employee of a company that was either wholly or partly owned by the *khodi*, (2) become an employee of a private company, (3) start their own company, or (4) leave Iran. Regarding options 2 and 3, if the participants and their employers/companies remained within the parameters of the *khodi*'s one-dimensional pathway, they would make enough money to live a quiet life and be left alone. However, depending on what the company did, how lucrative it became, and/or how popular/influential it became, there was an increased likelihood that they would (a) be pressured to become partly or wholly owned by the *khodi* or (b) risk failing and going bankrupt if they refused to cooperate with the *khodi*. This, the participants described, was a part of what they perceived as keeping them boxed within certain parameters, so they could not challenge or threaten the *khodi* and its power, wealth, and influence throughout the country. The following section will expound on these four options in more detail, but in short, the participants did not see a fifth option where they could realize their aspirations inside Iran. Thus, twenty-two of my participants—out of forty-six—worked on their exit strategy. I challenged my participants again to think about why it was inconceivable for them to find a job in Iran, start a family, for example, and work toward their aspirations in other ways. Their response was that leaving Iran had a higher rate of success as long as the environment was healthy—irrespective of the country—where the laws were implemented and the parameters within which their agency could be manifested were comparatively less limited than what they had experienced with the *khodi*, the mafia (education system), *khusulati* companies (the IRGC, for example), and the Islamic Republic's other tentacles of influence (the media, for example).

Interestingly, the participants' ability to identify and oppose these monopolizations and unhealthy environments, at the postgraduation level, could be viewed as a product of their upbringing within a similar framework during pre- and within-university. The institutions and people holding the participants back appeared to have also enabled them to think critically about this thought system and position the participants outside it. Thus, again, we see a tension of constraints and opportunities that balances on a tightrope with ideological conformity on one side and the ability to develop highly critical perspectives on the other. As we further discussed the realization that the framework they rejected was, to a certain extent, the same framework that provided them opportunities, the participants detailed three points. First, while they were able to enact their agency and somewhat detach themselves from portions of the regime's status quo and tentacles of influence, it was the *khodi*'s parameters and *khusulati*'s monopolization that were more difficult to reconcile and ultimately navigate. Second, if my *Sharifi* participants had to start over again, they would still pursue the same path because when they compared themselves to my non-*Sharifi* participants, it was clear they were in a better position even within these parameters. All but three (Tehran University) of the twenty-two participants who were working to leave Iran graduated from Sharif. Even my non-*Sharifi* participants expressed a feeling of jealousy since their path to leaving Iran was exponentially more difficult without the Sharif name. Third, the participants did not believe that the ease in which one could leave Iran negated their criticism of the struggles they encountered when trying to realize their aspirations inside Iran. In fact, most of the twenty-two participants working to leave Iran saw their intent to migrate as a failure in not being able to realize their aspirations inside Iran and help their country.

A *Khodi*-Versus-*Ghayre-Khodi* Tension in the Job Market

The significance of the concepts *khodi* and *ghayre-khodi* was introduced in the previous two chapters regarding the *konkur* mafia during pre-university and Sharif's mafia maintaining the status quo within the university. It was also briefly mentioned in the prior section in relation to the participants' perception of the *khodi*'s monopolization of the job market. However, given that the extent to which the participants struggled in realizing their own aspirations inside Iran was influenced by their tension with the *khodi*, further examination is required. According to the participants, the *khodi* primarily consisted of individuals who had some sort of affiliation—either directly or indirectly through employment, family, partnership, or allegiance—with the Islamic Republic. The *ghayre-khodi* was everyone else—including my participants. The lived experiences from Karim's job interview with a *khusulati* company or Nader's interview with an IRGC company exemplified this *khodi*-versus-*ghayre-khodi* tension. Darius also had an interesting perspective:

> I might have felt that I am one of the *ghayre-khodi* because the decisions that were being made at the low and high levels of society are by the State . . . my needs were never realized. No one has paid any attention that such a person has the right to exist and live . . . (laughs) . . . Everything is unstable here, and it is not clear at all if something is going to happen or not. Therefore, these things . . . give off a bad feeling throughout society, all the time. Just like what they did a few weeks ago by disconnecting the internet for a week after the protests started. A person who belonged to the *khodi* group might have been on Twitter during that time, (laughs) . . . so he might have been connected to the internet.
>
> DARIUS

Thus, at this point in their life, the participants were convinced that the *khodi* opposed, and at times blocked, their attempts at realizing their aspirations inside Iran. As a result, they believed that their occupational options were limited within a set framework that was pushing them back toward the one-dimensional path. In other words, they had to graduate from higher education, complete their *sarbazi*, find an acceptable job within the *khodi*'s parameters, buy a house, get married, have kids, and live a quiet life. The end. According to the participants, certain parts of this path did not pertain to members of the *khodi*, however. Similar to Cyrus's example in chapter 4 on how a fellow *konkur* test-taker was accepted into Sharif because his father was a member of the *khodi*, those who want to avoid the *sarbazi* can simply pay to be exempt.

Therefore, the participants felt that there was a wall at the end of the one-dimensional path beyond which they were unable to ascend. Cyrus provided a firsthand account featuring one of his employers and three of his own failed startups that highlighted the tension with the *khodi* and the ceiling that capped his professional growth:

> **Cyrus:** Working in [redacted for safety reasons] needs ten years working at least, and that's if the State doesn't get you down and give you a rough time and if they don't pull the rug out from under you; including many ministries and other organizations, I mean Ministry of Culture and Islamic Guidance, Supreme Council of the Cultural Revolution, State newspapers bothered us, and State TV and radio bothered us, they gave us all kinds of nonsense, first, they stigmatized us as Israeli, they stigmatized us that "you want to [redacted] and you want to [redacted]." They did everything to make our [company]—which is private—fail, and boost the other [companies] that belong to the State so we cannot sell our [product] so they can seize the market, because when we had our [product] many of the [State's companies] were not selling well . . . I've told you every name, don't release these names . . .
>
> **Reza:** No. If you want, I'll delete them?
>
> **Cyrus:** No, it's not that important . . . it will be good if they find out some things about this stuff, because they should know private companies that put their whole life in their job and have many employees and they became miserable, it is their fault. We all killed ourselves to serve our country, and again you don't want us to work in our country.

After the company he worked for went bankrupt, Cyrus took some time to personally recover. He decided to pursue a master's in IT management in order to learn and grow, "so I can at least better handle the problems our CEO faced . . . so I can learn the business aspect and also marketing, management, accounting, economy . . . I wanted to be well rounded, so I don't fail as easily." Toward the end of his master's program he began his first startup:

> Once our work got a little famous and had good sales, the municipality came and made our lives a living hell. The Ministry of Culture and Islamic Guidance came and stopped us. [Redacted] [Department] prevented our products from being distributed. They came and said, "If you want to work, it is ok, you have to give us a bribe, and this much of your profits you have to give to us."

> We gave them some of our profits, but it kept increasing, they wanted more, they wanted more, and we couldn't . . . they were State-owned organizations. The municipality, Ministry of Health and Medical Education, all of them belonged to the State.
> CYRUS

After his first startup went bankrupt, Cyrus had an idea for a smartphone application:

> I worked on [a phone app] for a while . . . nothing. We went a little forward, the Ministry of Health [said], "No, you don't have permission, you have no right to do this, we won't permit you to do such a thing. We will stop you if you want to do it. You have no right to . . ." I told him, "Sir, it's okay if there's a financial profit, I'll give you a percentage." "Forget about it, this is a monopoly, and we won't let you." And that's why he rejected me.
> CYRUS

It was interesting to hear Cyrus tell these stories and learn how his perspective shifted from one where he reluctantly gave money to the government during his first startup to one where he volunteered a percentage of his profits during his second startup. And despite his best efforts to adapt to the *khodi* parameters and try to succeed, he was again denied the access and permission to build and commercialize his phone app.

While Cyrus was provided the space to explore his entrepreneurial ambitions, he experienced certain parameters and stipulations he felt he had to abide by in order to ensure the longevity of his startup. These entailed: (a) morally questionable actions—like bribery—that he was not willing to commit; or (b) the forfeiture of a percentage stake in his company, which he was willing to do but was either taken advantage of or rejected. The tension between Cyrus striving to achieve his aspirations inside Iran and the tentacles of the State—i.e., the *khodi* and *khusulati*—trying to either control or terminate his startup(s) reshaped his aspirations and pointed him back toward the one-dimensional path that was pushed on him since his pre-university time.

Similarly, Aram, Jahan, Tooraj, and Zechariah (all Sharif graduates) also, like Cyrus, experienced failed startups. Their voices, filled with frustration and exhaustion as they described failed attempts at realizing their aspirations inside Iran, took on further levels of aggravation when they each spoke of other startups that turned into lucrative companies: Snapp (Iran's equivalent to Uber), Tap30 (Lyft), Digikala (Amazon), Namava (Netflix), Divar (eBay), and Café Bazaar (Apple's App Store). They believed that these organizations succeeded while they failed was due to the companies' intentions. Aside from the fact that these companies eventually ended up in the hands of the *khodi* because they were growing in popularity and profit, they also offered a service, like ride-hailing, online shopping, or streaming, to their customers. Cyrus's startups, for example, either had a humanitarian element or competed in a market monopolized by the *khodi*. His experiences were similar to Ismail's, who said that "if one were to work for or own a company that sells/provides goods/services, they would be left alone and could potentially live a comfortable life." Although Ismail was referring to brick-and-mortar establishments, Cyrus's startups were the tech equivalents. When I asked the participants why they chose not to pursue a career where "they would be left alone," they replied, "That is where I ended up now."

What resulted from this tension between the participants and the *khodi* was the perception that if they wanted to start a company, there were preconditions they had to agree to. First, their company's mission statement had to be focused on selling/providing a product/service for the purpose of making a monetary profit. Mr. Hadi, a stakeholder who graduated from Sharif and owns a successful human resources company that he started, argued this very point and continuously stated that my participants "need to be realistic within this country we live [in]." Second, the participants discovered that they should not enter a market/industry that the *khodi* controlled—in other words, the monopolized sectors mentioned above. Third, if their company had the potential to be or become lucrative or influential, and/or to grow/expand into a larger company, they should expect the *khodi*'s involvement in some capacity—either through profit sharing or a minority/majority ownership. The successful companies mentioned above are prime examples of aligning with these preconditions.

One outcome that could result from the *khodi*'s involvement in a company was its transformation into a *khusulati* company. This term is mostly colloquial and is ubiquitous in Iran. The word *khusulati* is a combination of two Persian words: *khususi* (private) and *dolati* (government). *Khusulati* organizations primarily consist of the *dolati* portion: current, former, and/or retired officials of the Islamic Republic; members of their family; their friends; and/or their associates. And the *khususi* portion consists of some individual(s) with no ties to the Islamic Republic—usually the individuals who started the company. My participants also explained that the reshaping of ownership to include the *khodi*, and thus transforming into a *khusulati* organization, transpired for two primary reasons: financial security and national security. Cyrus gave an example that he lived through:

> Either you go to them for financial help because there was no one else with as much capital to help you, or they find you and make you join them. And if you don't [join them], they do whatever they can so you don't succeed, or they take your idea for themselves.
>
> CYRUS

Moreover, because of international sanctions against Iran, the financial aspect of starting a company was often tied with national security, so the *khodi* could continue to maintain control over the country. For example, Darius explained how "Snapp and Tap30 could have easily been shut down by the government when taxi drivers protested." However, because they use GPS tracking, and their American counterparts (Uber and Lyft) are multibillion-dollar companies, Snapp and Tap30 were seen by the government as a steady stream of revenue and a security advantage in monitoring its citizens.

Karim, for example, ended up working for one of the aforementioned companies as a data analyst, but he did not believe it was *khusulati* because, as he put it, it was publicly traded on Iran's stock market. I made the counterargument that Iran Khodro, the State-owned automotive company, was also a publicly traded company, to which he replied with uncertainty that he heard rumors that the government was involved but Karim was unconcerned by it. Cyrus briefly worked as a project manager (a higher position than Karim's) for the same company, and his response was interesting:

> [It is not private], no, it is another company that the Revolutionary Guard Corps interferes in. These [companies] that are so large have like a million [US dollar] per day sales record, those [companies] are definitely connected [to the State].
>
> CYRUS

I asked Karim if he believed he had a future at this company. He admitted there was most likely a "limit to how high" he could go but added that he intended to move on to a better job, if there was one, or leave the country. The more experience the participants gained within the job market, the better they understood the parameters within which they could navigate and exert their agency to try to realize their aspirations inside Iran—including that they were unlikely to discover their own individual aspirations inside Iran. Nevertheless, the participants understood the limits—especially as *ghayre-khodi* individuals who were unwilling to compromise on their principles and morals—and still tried to maximize the allowable opportunities in order to achieve their aspirations inside Iran.

One outcome for the participants within the *khodi*-versus-*ghayre-khodi* tension of the job market was the continued push toward the one-dimensional. Darius explained his lived experiences with the one-dimensional path and the broken promises of the human capital argument:

> There aren't many places for people who are multidimensional. The job market wants people who are able to work on one thing. . . . There were some people . . . I saw them . . . who would do certain repeated tasks and are in the same position doing the same job for fifteen years! I used to think that when I have gained experience in different areas, it is going to be an advantage for me, but it is the opposite here because they expect you to continue in a straight line. . . . In most places . . . I am not saying it is like this everywhere, but in most places it is like this . . . this one-dimensionality starts from elementary school and continues . . . until the end. . . . Everyone wants you to be one-dimensional because they are limiting the environment every day.
> DARIUS

Therefore, the participants felt there was a dismissive sentiment from society that the youth "just complains too much and wants everything handed to them without putting in the work." For example, the participants would hear the people around them say, "You're not going to become rich overnight," "Don't expect someone to hire you to a senior-level position just because you graduated from Sharif," or "Just get in and work your way up." The tension that resided within these scoldings for the participants was not that they objected to starting at the bottom, working hard, and ascending in their career; rather, it was that they did not experience the outcome they were told would take place if they pursued such an approach. What the participants reported experiencing entailed the stipulations and conditions mentioned above, which they were not willing to participate in. The participants' frustration while detailing their stories with the hopes of me understanding their experiences reminded me of a famous saying: It is difficult for a free fish to understand what is happening to a hooked fish (Menninger, 1930).

The experiences of a hooked fish were never more palpable for my participants than with Cyrus, whose entrepreneurial endeavors routinely seemed plagued with complications:

> They won't let you . . . this is generally their goal. Either be a good-for-nothing, ordinary person and live in this society, or you have to go abroad. I said that most of my friends had applied, and none of them stayed in Iran. If you even have a little ability, go abroad. Don't stay in Iran. Why stay? You're

> not going to do anything special here. Either you become an ordinary person, making ends meet, minding your own business, having a dead-end job, and they have nothing to do with you. If you want to do something important, go abroad, this is not the place for such a thing, or they will knock you down.
> CYRUS

Eventually Cyrus settled for a job so he could start his life, i.e., get married, buy a house, have children. He did not categorize it as a dead-end job, and while he did enjoy it, Cyrus admitted that he was unhappy with where his professional career had ended up. Even after struggling and ultimately settling for the one-dimensional path, he did not want to leave Iran. He was adamant about helping his fellow citizens and loathed the idea of going to another country, only to help the people there prosper while there were still so many problems to remedy inside Iran. At the end of our time together, I asked Cyrus if he ever thought about starting another company that did fall within the *khodi* parameters of the job market—something similar to what Mr. Hadi had done (human resources company). He thought about it, but the negative experiences he had coupled with his weariness in possibly having to confront similar limitations again left him unsure:

> How long can one put up with this? In my case, I put up with it for a while, then I couldn't. It's not possible anymore. Forget about it. I don't want it anymore. And no one wants you to have it either. And no one values what you can bring [to society]. No one respects you. You can't live in this. I can't take it anymore. Bye! Let it go! I don't care about whatever is going to happen. I'll do what I want to do. Forget about serving our nation and that stuff. I used to be very determined, and I wanted to serve, but we're all ending up in failure and no one wants it anyway. . . . They don't allow it. They always stall you. No one lets you grow. There is a reason for this, too. If *you* become powerful, *they* make a loss.
> CYRUS

This defeatist mentality expressed by Cyrus is, according to almost everyone I spoke with, one of the objectives of the *khodi*. The *khodi*'s covert and overt resistance to change and their push to maintain the one-dimensional human capital path are tactics they use in order to break individuals like Cyrus into accepting a subordinate life where they settle into a nonthreatening relationship vis-à-vis the *khodi*. In other words, one will not conduct any action, overt or otherwise (e.g., civic engagement through protesting, or professional aspirations that challenge the regime's revenue stream), that could be interpreted as a threat to the existence of the Islamic Republic and its subsidiaries (the IRGC, *khusulati* companies, the *khodi*, the mafia); in return, the Islamic Republic will not bother said individual. And if one is unable to agree to this relationship, they can either leave Iran or continue to struggle—I will go into great detail about this struggle and relationship in the next chapter.

Like many of the twenty-two participants who worked on leaving Iran, Ismail was unwilling to acquiesce to a submissive life, and as a result he became uncompromising in his decision to leave Iran. What was notable about many of my participants who wanted to leave Iran was while they distanced themselves from the one-dimensional path, they were still following the *khodi* parameters. In other words, individuals like Ismail, Darius, and Karim who initially intended to engender constructive change through their profession felt (a) inhibited from realizing that aspiration and (b) encouraged to leave Iran. The encouragement to leave was in the best interests of the *khodi* if the individuals were not willing to live a subordinate life inside Iran that correlated with the *khodi*'s monopolization of certain industries within the job market and their formation of *khusulati* companies. Either way, the potential threat from individuals who seek to change Iranian society is diminished because they have either left the country or are living a quiet life, thus allowing the *khodi* to hold on to power and influence.

While this appears to be the strategy of the regime, there are clear signs of how the active *ghayre-khodi* are continuing to resist. There are many instances of mobilized protests (2009 Green Movement), massive uprisings (Women, Life, Freedom), and even violent protests in 2019 and 2025; however, history and firsthand accounts by my participants and stakeholders have shown that such movements rarely result in systemic change. I was in Tehran during the 2019 Bloody November protests when gas prices literally increased overnight and people took to the streets. Gas stations and other commercial properties were set on fire, and streets were blocked off with protesters. But the government quickly responded by sending in the riot police, turning off the internet for a week, and severely cracking down on protesters or any group of people gathered in public. A protest sequence in Iran can be likened to that of an earthquake and its subsequent diminishing aftershocks. So, a week after the uprising, people went back to their daily routines and the internet was turned back on, and while there were aftershocks of protests, they did not result in a significant improvement in people's standard of living.

The same can be said about the 2025–2026 protests. Even after reports surfaced of tens of thousands of citizens being killed by the regime, the people went back to their daily lives. And with the Women, Life, Freedom movement, there was no systemic change that answered the calls of the protestors. In fact, one could argue that if there was systemic change, it was to strengthen the continued tactics of the regime to maintain the *khodi*'s status quo. Therefore, even if Iran's highly educated youth, like my participants and members of other disenfranchised demographics, could form the basis of these movements, there is little empirical evidence to suggest that their efforts would bear fruit.

My participants tell me that most protests have increasingly become a medium for citizens to unburden their frustrations in a public way. But they argue that most people find ways to protest the regime individually—as a passive *ghayre-khodi*—through their daily lives. One example is how women have found ways to bypass the State's gender segregation (Shahrokni, 2019), or how more women are not wearing the hijab in public. This and other arguments and examples contributed to my ideological-employability scale (table 7.1), which I will discuss in the next chapter. It is worth mentioning here, however, that the *khodi*-versus-*ghayre-khodi* tension is very complex with a gradation of constraints and opportunities that balance on a tightrope, with ideological conformity on one side and the ability to develop highly critical perspectives on the other. And while many citizens inside Iran may be able to find ways to individually protest the State or resist the *khodi*'s status quo as a passive *ghayre-khodi*, some of my participants continued to struggle in finding a path where they could actualize their own aspirations inside Iran. Nader, for example, was uncertain about his future, so he continued to follow what others were doing and stayed on the one-dimensional path to pursue his MBA.

For almost two decades of Nader's life he navigated within the one-dimensional human capital path, and by age twenty-five he struggled to break free from this mindset. Karim, however, was able to change his mindset, but he stressed how difficult it is to do so after nearly twenty years:

> When I started at Sharif, I can say I almost had no understanding of myself. I didn't know my values, it was just a broad concept . . . I didn't know who I was, I wasn't my real self, the self that I liked, because this force has always been present, it is present now, if you look around, its examples are even in the master's. . . . If you ask MBAers, they don't even know what they want from their future, what they are going to do in the future, what are their aspirations, we don't have introspection at all, what are our values, they don't give us a chance to think.
>
> KARIM

Karim's point about continuously feeling the "force" of following a one-dimensional path that led to uncertainties about the future, aspirations, and the self was experienced by the participants to varying degrees. The participants felt that the more time they spent in the job market, the more difficult it was to believe that they were in control of shaping their future. Cyrus, for example, described how after graduating from Sharif he enrolled in the Sharif Career School, where he participated in personality tests to "uncover what my interests were, and what my abilities were." During his postgraduation time, he intensified and diversified his efforts:

> **Cyrus:** I also attended BLS, which is a business program in Sharif University. Bootstrapped Lean Start-ups. It was for startup businesses. I have attended many programs. For example, I attended MBA programs, and by the end I was teaching some of the business programs myself . . . also, making résumés. . . . We had these classes in the career school. For example, three or four sessions we allocated to learning how to write a résumé. And . . . I have attended many personality programs in which you work on yourself. Classes in which they would teach us how to recognize different personality types. Although my mom was a psychologist, I attended many psychology classes . . . many of them. I have always been doing something. [Networking] with my friends who know a company or . . . Job Vision . . . do you know it?
>
> **Reza:** They help you find a job?
>
> **Cyrus:** Yeah, it's similar to Iran Talent. I have posted my résumé there. I have posted my résumé everywhere. In LinkedIn, Iran Talent. My résumé is everywhere. There is a job fair in Sharif University every year and I used to go to all the stations to fill in the forms.

The extent to which Cyrus multitasked his efforts during his postgraduation time in order to increase his chances to either realize his aspirations, at the most, or find a job, at the least, cannot be overstated. At any given moment he was engaged in at least three endeavors. Nader, on the other hand, simply applied for a few jobs on the social media channels of Iran Talent and Job Vision. Among my participants, no two individuals were as different as Cyrus and Nader, from their socioeconomic status and work ethic to their outlook on life and aspirations. However, none of that seemed to matter as they both ended up with the same result: working at a company just to make a living and start the next stage of their life, and not spending any more time on what they felt was the losing end of a battle against the manifestations of societal discourse vis-à-vis the *khodi* and *khusulati*. One difference, however, was Nader's intention to leave Iran.

Darius grew up with low confidence and low self-esteem. His mood and attitude would be greatly influenced by the people around him, and he often required reassurance and motivation from friends and family. But despite all this, he was still able to progress in life due to his intellect. For example, his fellow Science Olympians insulted and excluded him, but he ranked higher (silver medal) than most of them. But when he reached his postgraduation time, Darius had strengthened his self-confidence and was applying himself more in areas where he previously might not have.

> I think that I have some advantages in interacting with people in comparison to others. When I see the people around me, I feel that I am more patient and can get along with others better. I am not saying that I am the [laughs] master of soft skills, no . . . but I try to improve them every day, if possible. And if my self-confidence starts to decrease again, I change my environment because I have learned how to adapt . . . to work with different people and in different environments
>
> DARIUS

Interestingly, Ismail had a surplus of confidence since his pre-university time. One example he constantly gave was how he arrogantly and confidently dropped out of pre-university high school at age seventeen to study for the *konkur* on his own. He also pushed himself further than the other participants by taking master-level courses during his undergrad years to better understand what path to take in order to realize his aspirations. He then attended job fairs, conferences, and exhibitions. I asked him to describe that experience:

> When I went to job interviews . . . after some time, I realized that there were some other things that . . . as I said, there are some other factors that you should know, be familiar with, learn. . . . I searched for some of them on the internet or if there was a course that was useful, I would have taken it. And I think . . . I think that I made enough efforts. But as I said, I always consider ten percent for my weaknesses . . . like procrastination, laziness, lack of motivation. For example, there are some people who would try again even if they got rejected from ten places, twenty places, one hundred places. They try so hard until they succeed, maybe I wasn't like this, but I have tried enough, I think.
>
> ISMAIL

Darius was one of those people. He recalled applying for or sending his résumé to two hundred job openings. He attended job fairs and conferences while seeking advice from his former professors and peers. He also participated in a training-ship program (sponsored by the Sharif Career School)—he described it as one level below an internship where the company "prepares you for entering the work environment"—but was not hired afterward for the company's internship program. He explained how discouraged he got: "I really felt that I cannot find what I want here . . . and no one wants me for any job." Although Ismail was ahead of Darius regarding his agency, and Darius was more persistent in strengthening his employability, the two ended up in the same place: confronted with the barriers, limitations, and difficulties of navigating the uncertain job market of Iran and deciding to leave their country.

While Karim was also making plans to leave the country, he initially tried to achieve his aspirations inside Iran:

> **Karim:** I get upset, not because someone else became successful but why haven't I . . . we were almost in the same situation.
>
> **Reza:** What happens after you get upset?
>
> **Karim:** I decide that, tomorrow, with strength, I will sit and work harder. I don't let it get me down.
>
> **Reza:** Why do you think [others have] reached whatever it is they wanted sooner than you?
>
> **Karim:** Like I said, people's background is really important, but you shouldn't compare this part with yourself. You must compare . . . efficiency, I compared myself to myself and was like, maybe my efficiency is low, maybe my problem-solving is low, my attention is low. This comparison causes me to see these in myself . . . I analyze myself, not others.

He gave the example of his job as a data analyst, which was offered to him on his second application. After his first rejection, Karim identified his weaknesses and worked harder to strengthen his hard and soft skills to maximize his employability. During this time, Karim was also discovering that his professional future may not be in Iran. His explanation showed an internalized struggle between determination to improve his situation within the job market and uncertainty about his future and whether he could achieve his aspirations inside Iran:

> In Iran . . . if I say no . . . it actually isn't . . . the ceiling . . . it depends . . . on the person. I myself . . . don't think so . . . I don't think . . . with this . . . not that I don't think, but it is a bit far away and it is a bit difficult.
>
> KARIM

The confusion in how he answered the question about the possibility of realizing his aspirations inside Iran signified the struggle that many of my participants experienced. If I were to fill in the blanks using other parts of the conversation with Karim, his answer could read like this:

> In Iran . . . if I say no [it is because] it actually isn't [possible because of] the ceiling [in place preventing you, but] it depends . . . on the person. I myself . . . don't think so . . . I don't think . . . with this [environment I can reach my aspirations] . . . not that I don't think, but it is a bit far away and it is a bit difficult.

The ceiling Karim mentioned refers to the barriers and obstacles he experienced throughout his life that he believed denied him the realization of his aspirations. Cyrus spoke of it as "they hit you on the head" if you want to try to succeed past a certain point or within a certain industry. Ismail also called it a ceiling and referenced it when describing the limit placed on wages—the next section will discuss this further. Darius called it a wall and explained that by the time you realize it exists, it is too late because you are too old (i.e., toward the end of the bachelor's program) to make the necessary adjustments (like choose a different university, major, and/or path). As a result of Nader's aimless ascension, dispassionate pursuits, and subsequent uncertainty during his postgraduation time, he did not experience this ceiling like the other participants but did explain that "the ceiling would be invisible, like not everybody can see it, only when you get there you see that, okay, for this reason I cannot prosper anymore."

In addition to the aforementioned barriers, the participants also discussed their own shortcomings and failures in how and why they felt unable to realize their aspirations inside Iran. Nader described how his soft-spoken and introverted demeanor and his apathy toward most disciplines were detrimental to his initial professional pursuits. Similarly, Karim blamed himself more than anyone else and detailed the steps he took to strengthen his weaknesses, as well as how he articulated the struggles he endured and eventually overcame:

> Back during pre-university and within-university, I thought things were out of my hands, but it was internal . . . an inner control that I had, but I thought it was from the outside that was affecting me. If I want to talk about it now, many in our university think the situation in the country is because of external problems, there's no job, there's threat of war and so forth, well this . . .

> and the media is constantly sending negativity . . . this can't be controlled. You can't control these at all and since you don't have control you feel helpless. When I think back, I see I've changed so much. I mean I completely changed. But we see how the developed countries are teaching to look inward at a younger age, I mean it's extremely effective if you know these things from childhood. But in Iran I can say sixty percent of people don't know this or learn it in their twenties.
>
> KARIM

Karim was the only participant to identify, understand, conceptualize, and explain his situation using such terms. However, the conclusions he reached about his future in Iran did not greatly differ from those of the other participants—even if the other participants did not devote the same level of research or shoulder the same level of responsibility as Karim. Ismail, for example, felt the least responsible, standing in stark contrast to Karim.

> Reza, imagine . . . imagine that you want to . . . there is a road that turns right and left. The left side . . . your friends, not just one person, not just me . . . ten, twenty, thirty, one hundred people keep telling you, Reza, don't go this way. It has some problems. The road has some problems. I don't know. It doesn't have any lights. The road is not good. You might have an accident. You can't see anywhere. There are potholes. Then they say that the path on the right is clear, smooth, and brighter . . . we have taken this road. And even some say that we have reached the end of this road. Do this. This is a good road. Which path would you take? Why should I spend five years of my life in Iran?
>
> ISMAIL

This was Ismail's answer after I continuously challenged him on why he, like Darius, did not apply to more jobs or, like Cyrus, participate in personality and psychological tests or, like Karim, internalize his failures in search of a deeper understanding. Interestingly, whenever Ismail would say my name—like he did in the quote above—that meant he was emphasizing a point that he believed was a certainty for those living in Iran and an aspect of their lives that I needed to understand. Nevertheless, while Ismail took a different approach than Karim did, these two participants ended up reaching the same conclusion: In order to increase the probability of realizing their aspirations, they would need to leave Iran.

Unable to Obtain Their Future Inside Iran

Darius had an interesting analysis of why he felt about 15 percent responsible for not achieving his aspirations inside Iran: "When you can't imagine your future, how can you plan for it?" Darius's somber perspective of an unimaginable future further demonstrates the *khodi*-constructed ceiling, which they believed prevented them from realizing their aspirations inside Iran despite their efforts in strengthening their weaknesses and enhancing their employability. Furthermore, Darius and other participants provided an example illustrating how and why uncertainties about their futures continued to harden. This example was an experience I shared with them, when in November 2019 the government raised gas prices overnight with only a day's notice:

> Our government . . . one night in Iran, they announced that fuel prices will go up [the following day]. That same night, people lined up in front of gas stations from downtown and uptown. That night—it was interesting—I left my house, searching Tehran for an hour and a half, everywhere was full, people lining up . . . the government [does this] . . . I mean . . . they even line up to buy chicken.
>
> DARIUS

> On Thursday, I went to put gas in my car, I was running low on gas, there was a long line, I said, it's okay, I'll do it on Friday. The same gas that I wanted to put in on Thursday for 40,000 Toman, I did the next day for 120,000 Toman, the same gas, I am paying three times as much for the same thing, I couldn't believe it, what an awful country!
>
> CYRUS

As a result, protests ensued, along with riots, burning of gas stations, and shutting down of major roadways. That was followed by the Revolutionary Guard Corps—the military arm of the State—policing the streets and cracking down on protestors, and the government shut down the internet for one week.

> Oh, that one week when there was an internet blackout? At that time . . . when there was an internet blackout . . . I wanted to register for the GRE, and I couldn't . . . [laughs] I couldn't even register for a test . . . and after [that week] I worried about my [university] application process. . . . I thought that they would disconnect the internet again.
>
> ISMAIL

> Our living standards are much worse than abroad with respect to welfare, with respect to income, but for example, my [former] roommate, who is in Canada now, he has a car and a house of his own. He is not worried . . . about his life expenses. But I, who stayed here . . . forget about buying a car or house. They cut the internet connection one day, then something else happens . . . you're in a constant state of heightened uncertainty.
>
> NADER

I shared these real-time lived experiences with the participants, so I understood how they exemplified the argument that "you cannot make long-term plans in Iran or hope for the future because you sleep and wake up and everything is changed." Thus, after experiencing and witnessing the Bloody November protests, my counterarguments to their criticisms of the job market and society seemed insignificant. I remember when protests broke out and the riot police cracked down; then the internet was shut off, and I had to use a landline to call my family and friends overseas to assure them of my safety. I tried connecting to the internet, but the names of the only available networks had the word "basij" within them (the Basij is the paramilitary volunteer militia within the IRGC; its armed, plain-clothed members drive around on motorcycles and use any method they want to suppress the uprising).

With the accumulation of the aforementioned barriers and obstacles, some participants acquiesced to the limitations inside Iran and lowered their aspirations in order to move on to the next stage of their lives.

> I didn't get to my aspirations. I lowered them *a lot*! I'm very upset. So now I have chosen another path. I said no to my dreams. Look, my top wishes were that I will make it, a house, a car, a wonderful life. Now, not at all . . . my aspirations . . . they came down. Like I said, I am a simple employee, I want to solve my *sarbazi* issue, I'd like to get married and make a normal living. I am happy with it at this point. I am like, well this is good. Because I see that many people don't even have this. I see that many of my friends are getting fired from their work, cannot even have this life. They cannot even make it to this level. So, I see that if I can have this, that would be good. Because I know that the condition that I am in is what many people want.
>
> CYRUS

Cyrus had aspirations of contributing toward the betterment of society—as did many of my participants. He did not demand or expect outcomes like having his own startup grow into something like Amazon or Apple, nor did he expect to reach such heights overnight. However, at the very least, he hoped that the ideas he had and the startups he built would be allowed to run their course—success or failure. He understood the small likelihood of succeeding, but he took the steps he felt were necessary to strategically position himself to have the best possibility for success. However, when he was made to feel inconsequential about his investments in himself (Sharif Career School, MBA, personality and psychological tests, startup workshops) because of the resistance and denial from the *khodi*, Cyrus lowered his aspirations, and he eventually capitulated to a "normal life" as a "simple employee," as he put it. As a passive *khodi*, Dr. Mahdi (Ministry of Education official) offered his insight into this resistance:

> There is a ceiling . . . even for a government official . . . unless he tries to work on the side to try to make more money, but even then, there are complications in the work environment. The State does not support such business. Conducting business in Iran is complicated, it's difficult, you're not protected, laws change, you can't make long-term plans, there are problems. There is not much support here. There is very high potential in Iran for work. For example, we have created our own version of Uber with Snapp, or Amazon with Digikala. But because of the limitations, barriers, and problems that exist, it's almost impossible to do it. I mean that supportive environment does not really exist.
>
> DR. MAHDI

One example of the lack of support or, as Dr. Mahdi said, the "complications in the work environment" was low wages. Ismail made an interesting argument:

> **Ismail:** You can't make any progress . . . you can have an ordinary life. You can be an employee in a company who does his duties very well, and [you can] earn a relatively good salary. This is achievable even now.
>
> **Reza:** A relatively good salary, what is that, 2, 2.5 million [Toman per month]?
>
> **Ismail:** Yeah, if your performance is good, it might go up to 4 [million Toman], for example, yeah. So one could let go of their dreams, but what should you really do with the salary? Okay, okay, I accepted this. I accepted to be an average person . . . but how am I going to live?!

I feel the need to provide a contextual explanation using my own experience living in Tehran in 2019 in order to fully explain the significance of Ismail's comments in relation to Dr. Mahdi's statement. According to the participants, the best-case-scenario monthly income was 5 million Toman (or $416 in 2019 during my fieldwork, or $31 as I write this sentence in 2026), while the more common wage was approximately 3 million per month. In addition to infrequent promotions and raises, the price of real estate property had increased by 100 percent from year to year, and by 2019 one square meter cost 10 million Toman. Thus, for example, the apartment I was renting for 3 million Toman a month was roughly one hundred square meters—a sufficient size for a family of three—worth approximately 1 billion Toman. Also, conventional mortgage loans do not exist in Iran, and the government loans have high interest rates, so almost everyone buys such apartments with cash. That means, if all conditions and variables were held constant with zero expenses, it would take seventeen years to be able to buy an apartment with a monthly income of 5 million Toman. Furthermore, while wages increase by the Toman, expenses increase by the US dollar. The currency exchange rate for one US dollar in November 2019 (toward the end of my fieldwork) equaled approximately 12,000 Toman. As I write this sentence in 2026, the exchange rate for one dollar is roughly 161,000 Toman. The average monthly expenses, according to the participants and stakeholders, was 6 million Toman in 2019.

Therefore, the participants would say, setting aside their aspirations, it was extremely difficult and often impossible to own a home, get married, have kids, and save enough money at the end of each month to plan for the future when: (a) your income was considered under the poverty line; (b) you were unable to obtain a (mortgage) loan; (c) your wages did not increase or were not adjusted based on labor laws, performance, profit, and inflation; (d) you did not have job security or job growth; (e) the socially accepted norms and the job market parameters were greatly influenced by the *khodi*; and (f) the cost of living and monthly expenses drastically fluctuated on a daily basis. Thus, even if the participants lowered their aspirations in order to live within the *khodi* parameters of Iran's society, they still faced these additional obstacles.

Local research argued that this process and eventual outcome—i.e., having its citizens constantly struggling to make ends meet, which kept them (pre) occupied with their own problems so they did not have the time, energy, and resources to try to change the status quo and/or confront the *khodi* with their grievances—was preferred by the *khodi*. Cyrus reached this outcome by the end of my seven months with him:

> I can't take it anymore. Now . . . now I have reached a stage where I say (laughs) the hell with it! I don't want to help my country. I should make money and live my life. When no one cares about the country, no one cares

> about others, and everyone beats you up and doesn't let you work, it means they don't want change. So, forget about it.
>
> CYRUS

The other participants believed they faced fewer risks by leaving their country in pursuit of their aspirations than staying in Iran. Karim and Nader were employed, similarly to Cyrus, but they intended to leave. Darius received his university acceptance letter (from abroad) but still had a dilemma:

> When I leave Iran, I don't want to do it with the intension to stay there . . . but I'm not sure because my situation is not the same two days in a row; I mean, because there is no trust in the future here, you cannot even have a long-term plan.
>
> DARIUS

Ismail was at a point where he had only to make his travel arrangements before he could leave, but he saw his departure from Iran as a failure to reach his aspirations inside Iran. On numerous occasions he argued about what was causing him to leave Iran, whether he was being pulled from another country or pushed from within, and he strongly felt that he was being pushed to leave his country instead of being enticed by a foreign nation. Karim had an interesting perspective of how one can overcome this push to leave Iran:

> You are under attack constantly. . . . You have to vaccinate [your mind, metaphorically,] because [you're] always under attack from the one-dimensional frontlines of society, news, media, Twitter, WhatsApp, Telegram, they constantly . . . surround you and the person should vaccinate their mind . . . because . . . especially in Iran it's pretty common (laughs) its economic stability is pretty low. This negativity is being constantly injected in you that you can't do anything, it's out of your hands. But I can change myself, as much as I can, I can academically bring myself up so I can change myself, maybe.
>
> KARIM

As the participants moved through these moments in their lives, painting a grim future inside Iran, I asked them how so many Iranians were able to financially sustain a livelihood with home ownership (or renting a place), and a family. The participants' explanations revolved around four points. First, one's financial, professional, and domestic securities were realized through their family's wealth if it was built prior to the 1979 revolution and secured thereafter (Cyrus was an example of this). Certain stipulations accompanied this situation, however. Primarily those families whose assets were procured independent of the monarchy were able to hold on to their wealth. If the family was close to the Pahlavi dynasty or in opposition to the new regime, either their assets would have been confiscated by the Islamic Republic, leaving them impoverished, or they would have gone missing, fled the country, been imprisoned, or worse.

Second, "those who are a part of the system are well off," the participants would say. The three prime examples they gave were *khusulati* entities, the mafia, and the *khodi*-versus-*ghayre-khodi* dynamic. This meant that if you had close ties with the Islamic Republic, whether through employment, marriage, blood relation, or business venture, you were financially comfortable—in some instances, the land and assets taken from the families mentioned in the first point were allocated to the families with close ties to the Islamic Republic. The participants went on to say that although these families were financially comfortable, they were not necessarily professionally successful, because employment in and through the *khodi*-operated companies was based on ideology, nepotism, favoritism, and *khodi* affiliation.

Third, many of the individuals who went missing, fled the country, or were imprisoned during the rise of the Islamic Republic were employed in professions—e.g., academia, civil society, social work, human rights, law, and political engagement—aimed at improving society (Bayat, 2009). Therefore, such sectors of the job market were essentially desolate. Although the participants viewed the idea of improving society through a scientific lens, they all faced the same obstacles to realizing their aspirations. The sectors of the job market that were lucrative were professions in medicine, dentistry, real estate, and *dalal* work. However, since students know this, there has increasingly been a saturation of doctors and dentists to the point where jobs are few and pay is low.

The participants' fourth point stressed that the vast majority of Iranians were struggling to sustain an independent livelihood, let alone one with a spouse and kid(s). The participants explained that if you do not fall under any of the above categories specified in the first three points, then "you live hand-to-mouth," either as an employee for a company or as a small-business owner (such companies typically sell consumer goods or services to customers in the retail industry). The participants did acknowledge that these four points cannot explain the entire country in a general sense. However, as we have seen protests continue on an almost annual basis—with the 2025–2026 uprising spanning across two hundred cities in thirty-one provinces—the active *ghayre-khodi* are the people living hand-to-mouth.

This resulted in their choice to leave Iran. The participants accepted the argument that there were problems everywhere in the world, and certain notions that were once guarantees—such as job security, job growth, and wage increases—were no longer the norms in any job market. However, the participants compared themselves to Iranians who had left the country and become more financially comfortable, professionally successful, and able to sustain a livelihood for a wife and kid(s). The difference for the participants resided in the institutions they had to navigate. The participants' argument was, although problems exist everywhere in the world, a country like America has a more sophisticated legal and judicial system that supports workers' rights when compared to Iran. There are freedoms in America that allow one to prosper as long as they work hard and obey the law. According to the participants, the extent of such freedoms within Iran was mostly available to a small portion of society like the *khodi*. In developed democracies—e.g., those in Western Europe or North America—where the government's relationship with its citizenry is relatively more amenable, an individual can enact their agency in a recursive relationship with the institutions they navigate. Within the *ghayre-khodi* context, however, the participants seem to have a tense relationship with unamenable institutions that are mostly linked to the *khodi*. The participants argued that the American notion of "you can become anything you want as long as you work hard" is instilled in American children from a young age, which assists them in their academic and professional maturation and taking ownership of their agency. This is in opposition to the message in Iran, where participants are told to not worry about their future, that God will provide, and to focus on their short-term goals, which are camouflaged within a distorted version of the human capital argument.

Conclusion

The participants detailed an unhealthy job market that opposed their pursuits in realizing their aspirations inside Iran, despite their best efforts in strengthening their weaknesses and enhancing their employability. The participants also illustrated a temporal significance regarding a social context that continued to push the one-dimensional path on them. One way this push was effective was due to the *khodi*-versus-*ghayre-khodi* tension. For example, business opportunities through *khusulati* companies were reported to more easily garner investments, licenses, and support and approval by the *khodi*. Moreover, the participants' lived experiences throughout their postgraduation time also demonstrated a complex dichotomy where they tried to realize their aspirations inside Iran while also trying to avoid the one-dimensional path.

According to the participants, as *ghayre-khodi*, the time and effort they placed on enhancing their employability would eventually be counteracted by the ceiling that would either lead the participants to a job with very limited professional or financial growth or prompt them to leave the country. The following vignette from Cyrus summarizes these postgraduation experiences:

> I don't believe you! A good idea, a profitable idea, a humanitarian idea will grow roots. Why wouldn't it work here if the people need it? You must've done something wrong. I'll show you!!
>
> I'm depressed . . . I try, and I try, and I try . . . (sigh) . . . and I try . . . I'm tired. You tell me, "Cyrus, don't fret. Your time will come, just keep working hard. You'll get there." I have! Believe me, I have. I don't know anymore . . . (sigh) . . . I don't know.
>
> My life is shit! Don't tell me, "Cyrus, be grateful for what you have." I am! Believe me, I am. But when you scour the bowels of this country in pursuit of alleviating mechanisms to stimulate your advancements only to end up where you started . . . well . . . then I guess I'm grateful that my predicament is less shitty than the next guy's.
>
> I stop trying; you call it compromising. I've erased my aspirations; you call it being realistic. I point out the problems we have; you call it whining. How can we change things if you don't believe me?
>
> CYRUS

As the participants accepted a certain level of blame for not achieving their aspirations inside Iran, they realized as they matured that although they have more power and control over their lives than they initially thought, there were limits inside Iran to which they could manifest their agency and employability and be in control of shaping and realizing their desired future.

CHAPTER 7

The Role of the State and Ideological Capital

The Islamic Republic forces you down a one-dimensional path of obedience to the State or they push you to leave. Why? Because you are not a member of the establishment. Because you don't think like us. Your ideology is different. It is you who go to the streets and protest, so it's better that you leave. So, we'll lie to you during your youth and say yes, human capital is good, invest in yourself, but we won't tell you that is a lie. Then when you find out and it's too late, what do you do? You acquiesce to a submissive life, or you leave.
MAJID

I offered this epigraph in the preface as a way to lay the foundation on which this book would be built. Now that you have read the book, I offer it again here, at the end, to see if your interpretation of this quote has changed. As you think about if/how your understanding of this tension between the *khodi* and *ghayre-khodi* has developed throughout this book, I will delve deeper into this tension. In the first section I will discuss the role of the Islamic Republic and the wall it has established at the end of the participants' academic journey to keep them within the *khodi* parameters. The findings in this section are significant for three reasons. First, the Islamic Republic plays a role, in various capacities, in most of my participants' narratives throughout this book. Second, this role is a key (f)actor in how the participants' aspirations have been shaped throughout their lives. And third, the role of the Islamic Republic of Iran as an unamenable government whose control has impacted the lives of these young men presents further discussion to the wider literature on youth struggles, aspirational attainment, employability, and the broken promises of human capital theory. Thus, in the second section of this chapter I discuss the effects of the Islamic Republic's one-dimensional path in shaping the participants' aspirations and the subsequent tensions that resulted. Then, in the third section, I expound on how this book has revealed deeper limitations to the human capital argument and adds to the broken promise argument by Brown et al. (2010) vis-à-vis the Islamic Republic.

The Role of the State and the State's Ceiling

This book has offered evidence, from the perspective of a *ghayre-khodi* context, of a school system, university system, job market, and society, navigated by the participants, that appear to be subordinate to, influenced by, operated by, and/or controlled by the Islamic Republic and its tentacles of influence: the *khodi* and *khusulati*. The control exhibited by the Islamic Republic, along with the dominant role of the *khodi*, has impacted the participants' lived experiences as they attempted to explore, identify, and achieve their aspirations inside Iran. The Islamic Republic has established a status quo within Iran based on security, religious affiliation, and ideological beliefs that enables it to control and/or influence the country's school system, higher education system, and job market, as well as the banking sector, commerce, media outlets, and tech industry, to name a few. Additionally, the *khodi* has its influence in the different mafias (education, *konkur*, trade, water, energy, and monetary, to name a few), the *khusulati* companies that monopolize vast sections of Iran's job market, and governmental and government-linked entities. Moreover, the *khodi* operates as the regime's resistance to change while profiting and benefiting from the country's status quo; their machinations include continuing to push for the one-dimensional path of the *ghayre-khodi* in order to keep them from amassing enough wealth, influence, or followers to possibly challenge the status quo and threaten the existence of the Islamic Republic.

As a result, the role of the Islamic Republic within this context appears to be one of self-preservation and preemptive calculation in thwarting existential threats to its power and controlling the population through overt and covert resistance to change. The elements of the regime's overt resistance for self-preservation are well documented in public reports—especially with the 2025–2026 protests. However, an underresearched aspect is the covert resistance with preemptive calculations that include psychological elements. For example, if children within Iran were raised believing they could be and do whatever they wanted as long as they worked hard and obeyed the law, many would grow up with aspirations that the regime would see as potential threats to the status quo. Moreover, cultivating generations to think in such a way also increases the likelihood of like-minded individuals mobilizing in opposition to the regime. The lived experiences of my participants, on the other hand, highlight tensions between the *khodi* and *ghayre-khodi,* where constraints and opportunities balance on a tightrope, with ideological conformity on the one side and the ability to develop highly critical perspectives on the other. And the Islamic Republic plays a significant part as a key (f)actor in that tension. Even after the participants discovered these limitations, searched for ways to overcome or bypass them, and worked on improving their own shortcomings and weaknesses, they were unable to ascend the professional ladder beyond the ceiling that was set in place for them as *ghayre-khodi.*

Thus, the foundational contribution of this book is to challenge the assumption of the extent to which a government allows or provides space for professional growth, societal progress, and institutional change. The failure to thoroughly investigate, or take into consideration, the role of an uncompromising government—e.g., the Islamic Republic, Russia, China, Nicaragua, or North Korea—has left a void that up to this point has been filled by a global north or human capital argument of agency, soft skills, aspirational attainment, employability, and job market returns that may not fully capture the *ghayre-khodi* context. In other words, my participants' aspirations, pressures, and disappointments are no different than those of any young person trying to navigate their academic and professional journeys. And there are many examples from Italy (Genova, 2023), Greece (Vatikiotis and Nikolakaki, 2013), Spain (Tejerina, 2019), Hong Kong (Ma et al., 2018), Canada (Ang et al., 2009), and South Korea (Aibao et al., 2007) that relate similar experiences as those shared by my participants. Moreover, some of my participants who decided to leave Iran share even more similarities with their global cohort because now they have entered the global north—i.e., developed nations—where the human capital argument is more applicable, even despite the broken promise argument put forth by Brown et al. (2010). However, the focus of this book has been to catalog my participants' journey within Iran and through that lens explore how the government plays a significant role—especially considering how Iran's government shares similarities with such governments as those found in Russia, China, Nicaragua, and North Korea (or with many dictatorships, oligarchies, and monarchies). As a result, this book's investigation into the role of the Islamic Republic not only sheds light on an aspect of the regime that has been underdocumented but also contributes further to the discussion on how we think about youth struggles via-à-vis aspirations, employability, and job market returns. I will elaborate on three ways we can think about this problem in the following three sections.

The Effects of the State's One-Dimensional Path and Subsequent Tensions

The Islamic Republic's one-dimensional path shaped the participants' aspirations in three ways. First, it blurred the participants' ability to differentiate between their own aspirations and the expectations of school, university, family, and society. This blurring of aspirational awareness adversely affected the participants throughout their formative and younger years, during which they could have experimented, failed, and tried a myriad of endeavors to explore their likes, dislikes, and goals. Rather, the participants increasingly experienced the push to remain one-dimensional, short-sighted, and oblivious to the ideas of their future selves. This push manifested in the form of an educational system and a society that reinforced the one-dimensional path that superficially appeared to be championing the human capital argument of investing in education—I will discuss later in the chapter how the human capital promise was broken and empty for the participants.

Moreover, if the participants found ways to challenge this one-dimensional push, they still felt overpowered with the added pressures and expectations from certain tentacles of the State. These tentacles included governmental entities, State-run media outlets, and the influence of the *khodi* throughout the participants' lives. Thus, the hope they had in continuing to envisage and explore alternative ideas to their aspirations was worn away. And, slowly, the one-dimensional path manifested itself internally for them, metastasizing into their psyche. As a result, a tension formed between the participants and the institutions and people pushing them on this pathway, further complicating the participants' journey toward realizing their aspirations inside Iran.

The second way the one-dimensional path shaped the participants' aspirations was through the tense relationship the participants had with the *khodi*. As the participants unclouded the distinction between their own aspirations and State expectations, they no longer simply questioned the purpose of the one-dimensional push but defied it. As a result, if the *khodi*'s covert resistance in keeping the participants on the one-dimensional path was insufficient, it became directly involved in preventing the participants' attempts in trying to accomplish aspirations that conflicted with the regime's status quo or deviated from the pathway.

Thus, the continued struggles and tension the participants felt throughout their young lives increasingly became more tactile as they drew closer to and navigated Iran's job market. They found that each tentacle of the State prevented their pursuits of realizing their own aspirations inside Iran and further pushed the participants back toward the one-dimensional path. Despite the participants' continued professional maturation, enhanced employability, and deft navigational maneuvering within the *khodi* parameters, they concluded that there was a limit to the extent to which they felt they could realize their own aspirations inside Iran.

The third way the one-dimensional path shaped the participants' aspirations was through circumstantial conditions. In other words, either the participants accepted their circumstances within the parameters set by the *khodi* or the participants chose to pursue their own aspirations outside of Iran. Regardless of whether the participants chose to stay in Iran or relocate abroad, either option appears to be acceptable to the *khodi* because the alternatives—challenging, resisting, or rising up against the regime—are not viable. However, the participants preferred neither of these options. While there may be variations of the one-dimensional path depending on an individual's educational attainment—i.e., obtaining a high school diploma versus an elite university degree—the one-dimensional path is solely distinguishable by the *khodi*-versus-*ghayre-khodi* divide through ideological affiliations and status networks.

According to my findings, the one-dimensional path for a *ghayre-khodi* eventually concludes with two options of either (a) acquiescing to the status quo and getting a job within the accepted parameters or (b) leaving the country. And according to the participants, it is only a matter of time before a *ghayre-khodi* reaches this inevitable moment. In Cyrus's case, for example, he completed his bachelor's, tried and failed with two startups, completed his master's, tried and failed with two more startups, then worked on bypassing his *sarbazi* and then got a job. While the experiences and the duration may be different for each *ghayre-khodi* individual, the end result is the same. After all the attempts by the participants to deviate from the one-dimensional path, they eventually were steered back onto it. This is the defining difference between a *khodi*'s pathway versus a *ghayre-khodi*'s.

The argument can be made that a *khodi* graduate also has to follow a one-dimensional pathway because of his relational proximity to the Islamic Republic. However, the pathway for a *khodi* includes off-ramps and on-ramps that provide the individual certain concessions, advantages, leniencies, and privileges. For example, they could be allowed to attend the university they want and major in the subject they want regardless of their *konkur* score, or even whether they take the *konkur* exam at all. They could obtain their passport and travel outside Iran without having to complete their *sarbazi*; they may not even have to enlist in the *sarbazi*. They also have more options in regard to their profession because they are a part of the system and not a threat to the status quo. For example, the types of startups the participants were prevented or denied from pursuing were later established by a *khodi* or *khusulati*. The wall at the end of a *ghayre-khodi*'s one-dimensional path ensures that they remain within a certain socioeconomic demographic that does not threaten the regime's sphere of influence and control.

Thus, the second contribution of this book is to argue that aspirational attainment is perhaps dependent more on what the youth are *allowed* to aspire to, and only then is the question asked if they will be able to attain it within the parameters. To think about this differently, let us consider the following: If a government's primary concerns are (a) holding on to power because their legitimacy is under question, (b) procuring and controlling major revenue streams to help them stay in power and circumvent economic sanctions, and (c) superimposing ideological, social, political, and religious norms in order to influence its citizens' thought processes and behaviors to counteract threats to (a) and (b), then individuals considered outsiders, or *ghayre-khodi*, will not be allowed to attain aspirations the government deems threatening to (a) and (b).

When discussing this scenario within the broader literature on aspiration, we see a scarcity in debating how State control impacts a youth's exploration, identification, and pursuit of aspirations. As a result, notions of goal-setting theory (Forster & Souvignier, 2014; Locke & Latham, 2006; Schunk, 2001), or social cognitive career theory (Ingram, 2017; Lent et al., 1994; Locke & Latham, 1990; Sawitri et al., 2014), for example, are limited in explaining aspirations within the *ghayre-khodi* context due to the role of the Islamic Republic. Moreover, personal initiative (Fay & Frese, 2001), extracurricular activities—e.g., sports, music, social and academic clubs, volunteering—(Larson et al., 2006; Seow & Pan, 2014), or achievement motivation (Gregor & O'Brien, 2016; Lens et al., 2002; Ryan & Deci, 2000), for example, all come up short when considering the one-dimensional push by an unamenable regime and its tentacles of influence.

This book has shown that while my participants tried the aforementioned theories and strategies to attain their aspirations inside Iran, the role of the State was not adequately accounted for. The ceiling or wall the participants hit and the resistance they perceived from the State's tentacles of influence prevented the fruition of these theories and strategies. The limitation in these strategies is also seen in the works of Pettit (2017) in Egypt and Mains (2012) in Ethiopia. Pettit's and Mains's participants repeatedly attempted to set goals and stay motivated but constantly encountered failure. But again, the area where my book presents an alternative understanding of youth struggles is the role of the State as an unamenable actor resistant to change.

That is why Tomlinson's (2008, p. 59) argument on the limitations in the capital theories/framework was applicable to this book because my participants did "understand their future job market outcomes as being more complex than simply possessing extra credentials and technical knowledge from higher education." They also later realized that the complex nature in their future job market outcomes involved the Islamic Republic and its tentacles of influence. As a result of this added complexity, we may have to rethink how we discuss aspirations. For example, an additional fifth variation to Spenner and Featherman's (1978) four variations of aspiration (as discussed in chapter 1) may be necessary in order to incorporate the role of an adversarial government and better understand the context of one's aspirational pathway. Or we may need to rethink Appadurai's (2013) capacity to aspire (also discussed in chapter 1) beyond just nodes and pathways for those less or more fortunate and consider also those who are less or more connected to the State. Perhaps ideological nodes and pathways are a necessary addition for us to understand how a *khodi* versus a *ghayre-khodi* has the capacity to aspire for academic and professional goals. As a result, questions can be raised as to how effective one's employability and human capital investments are when the State is deciding who is allowed to aspire for what and if the individual will be allowed to attain that aspiration inside their own country.

Limitations to Employability in a *Ghayre-Khodi* Context

Thus, what we did not know about employability in Iran is the extent to which it seems contingent upon, and oftentimes at the mercy of, the Islamic Republic as it decides how much to suppress the *ghayre-khodi*'s aspirational attainment inside Iran. The global debates do not deeply examine an individual's employability within a governing system such as the Islamic Republic (or Russia, North Korea, Nicaragua, and China, as these countries do not allow such research to be conducted). While the participants increasingly strengthened and exercised their employability, they perceived a reciprocal counterbalance of restrictions enacted by the *khodi*. On the one hand, as the participants matured, they discovered the full potential of their agency. They analyzed aspects of their lives that they believed required alteration in order for them to increase the possibility of realizing their own aspirations inside Iran. For example, the participants became multidimensional, changed their environment, pursued extracurricular activities, strengthened their mental health, became self-critical and self-reliant, and enhanced their employability. All these examples are no different from their global cohort throughout the world.

On the other hand, however, the Islamic Republic's heightened counterbalance to the participants' agentic maturation and improved employability led the participants to feel that their efforts were not being reflected in the trajectory of the path they were on. Rather, the participants felt that the extent to which they were able to exert their employability was limited within *khodi* parameters, which often positioned the participants at odds with the very institutions they were told to pursue and to trust would lead them to a guaranteed and successful life. And this is different from the majority of their global cohort, at least throughout the global north. The participants were repeatedly told to fulfill the one-dimensional aspiration, and if they did, they were reassured that their future would be a guaranteed success. As a result, there was a mismatch between the lived reality for the participants and the postgraduation expectations they had as a result of their adolescent obedience to the one-dimensional path. This mismatch ties to the aforementioned blurring of aspirational awareness. The continued assurance the participants heard signified a reframing of the human capital argument in order to keep the participants on the one-dimensional path, but without the outcomes that the human capital theory discusses.

Similar to how Brown et al. (2010) discovered a broken promise in the human capital argument due to the globalized economy, there is also a broken promise in the human capital argument on a domestic scale due to uncompromising governmental control. For example, Russia's government has been criticized for its crony-backed sectors of the job market, similar to Iran's *khodi* (Balzer, 2003), as well as for its mandatory conscription, which undermines human capital gains (Kolesnikov, 2023). Nicaragua's government has been criticized in a similar way to Iran for inducing a brain drain (Divergentes, 2025), as well as favoring regime loyalists similar to the Iran's *khodi* (United Nations, 2024).

Thus, the third contribution of this book is to argue that an aspect of enhancing one's employability is dependent on one's proximal relationship to their government. This book has brought forth the argument that employability within a nondemocratic global south context may have less to do with skills and attributes or economic and job market intangibles that are attractive to employers and more to do in the Islamic Republic with where one resides on the ideological scale of being considered a *ghayre-khodi* or a *khodi*. To think about this differently, let us consider the argument by Standing (2011) that the rise of the precariat, or the precarious worker, in OECD[1] countries (of which Iran is not a member) is posing a threat to social and political stability and may lead to extremism. Standing's argument stems from the globalization of the job market that Brown et al. (2010) discusses in his criticism of human capital theory. Therefore, as youth struggle to compete for low-wage jobs in a race to the bottom of a middle-class life (as Brown argues), they simultaneously run the risk of evolving into precarious workers during that journey and becoming more susceptible to extremist beliefs and tendencies. And if that happens, they pose a threat to a country's and a government's stability (as Standing argues).

However, what if parts or all of a country's society and politics are already considered to be extreme and/or unstable? And what if the youth are already seen as a threat to social and political stability even before they become precarious workers? Standing briefly defines the "bad precariat" as those who "lash out at governments and [demonize] those who seem favored by them" (2011, p. 156). So while the bad precariat within OECD countries should be prevented from posing a threat to their society, government, and country, it is exactly these types of youth that are actively mobilizing and protesting their governments and demanding change—like Iran's Green Movement of 2009, the Bloody November protest in 2019, the Women, Life, Freedom movement of 2022, and the 2025–2026 protests. But not all youth inside Iran are active in this resistance. What Standing calls the "bad precariat" I call the active *ghayre-khodi*, and with that, there are gradations of the *ghayre-khodi* as well as the *khodi*. Table 7.1 outlines this gradation.

This ideological-employability scale highlights the range in which citizens of Iran can be categorized based on their ideological and status network in relation to the Islamic Republic and the *khodi*. Given the findings of this book, the participants would be categorized as passive *ghayre-khodi*. Other examples of passive *ghayre-khodi* include the women in Shahrokni (2019) who bypassed gender segregation in public places and, more recently, the women of Iran not wearing the hijab in public. On the other hand, most individuals who participated in the protests of 2009, 2019, 2022, and 2025 (there were smaller protests in between these as well) could be categorized as active *ghayre-khodi*. Of my forty-six participants and sixty-two stakeholders, Mr. Sadiq (a high school counselor), Ms. Arya (from the IRPHE), and Dr. Mahdi (from the Ministry of Education) are passive *khodi*, while Dr. Amir is an active *khodi*. The way these four stakeholders described life in Iran was indicative of where they stood on the ideological-employability scale. For example, Mr. Sadiq and Dr. Mahdi spoke of the benefits of being a *khodi*—more job opportunities, better pay, job security—while stressing the uneasiness of being part of a system they do not believe in. Ms. Arya was more subtle in her storytelling in order to avoid reproach while still ensuring that I understood her point. Dr. Amir, on the other hand, conveyed a strong, uncompromising disposition against expressing any empathy for my participants' criticism of society, the school system, the job market, or the regime. At times he vehemently dismissed

Table 7.1. Ideological-Employability Scale Within the Islamic Republic Context

***Active* ghayre-khodi**	***Passive* ghayre-khodi**	***Passive* khodi**	***Active* khodi**
Actively and ideologically oppose the State often through public displays of defiance.	Disagree with all or most of what the State does.	Benefit from their proximal relationship to the State, so they go along with the State's policies and agendas.	Zealots of the State for ideological and/or financial reasons.
Have no affiliation or allegiance to the State.	May know some people within the State's orbit. May find nonconfrontational ways to oppose the State.	Or, have no viable financial alternative in providing for their loved ones, so they remain employees of the State.	Actively support and defend the State and its policies and agendas by any means necessary.
Disagree with what the State does. Have direct encounters with the State, which often threatens their safety.	Often keep to themselves but are directly impacted by the *khodi*'s parameters and limitations.	(These are potential defectors.)	

the criticisms and defended the way life is in Iran as a defiant posture against the United States and sanctions imposed upon his country.

Thus, perhaps the ideological-employability scale can better help us explain other contributions that may be a factor when an individual perceivably fails in the job market. It is particularly useful when the individual (a) evaluates themselves and discovers their weaknesses; (b) finds ways to remedy their shortcomings; (c) searches for ways to overcome or bypass external barriers; and (d) improves their employability, hard/soft-skills, and the like yet still ends up struggling in the country's job market. In other words, the dominant discourse on employability may require a broader discussion, beyond the human capital argument, that investing in oneself—by means of education, training, and mastering skills—can lead to the realization of one's aspirations. The existing literature that places the onus on the individual (Baruch, 2001; Garavan, 1999) to either (a) "move self-sufficiently" within the job market (Hillage & Pollard, 1998, p. 2), (b) find ways to enhance their attractiveness within that job market (Iles et al., 1996), (c) "anticipate changes in tasks and work environment and react to these changes in a proactive way" (Sanders & de Grip, 2004, p. 76), and/or (d) exercise an "active adaptability that enables them to identify and realize job opportunities" (Fugate et al., 2004, p. 16) must be reevaluated to consider the circumstances this book has revealed regarding an adversarial government.

The global north argument that continues to focus on the individual, maintaining that one's employability derives from the different types of capital one can invest in, such as human, cultural, personal, reputational, and/or social (Tholen, 2017), should also consider the added ideological element to enhancing one's employability that this book puts forth. In other words, the current argument—that if an individual's environment and conditions are not conducive, they will find a way to realize their aspirations; and if they do not, then there is something wrong with their approach and they must restrategize—does not take us far enough within a *ghayre-khodi* context or a nondemocratic context. These debates in explaining my participants' lived experiences would be accurate if this book examined their migration to an OECD country, for example, but when focusing on their lived experiences inside Iran and their interactions with the parameters of the *khodi*, these arguments come up short, and the concept of ideological capital must also be considered.

Conclusion

In summary, the Islamic Republic of Iran reframes human capital theory to enforce a one-dimensional path: obedience to the regime, with the alternative being emigration. This path is shaped by the insider/outsider dynamic of the *khodi* (regime-affiliated insiders) versus the *ghayre-khodi* (outsiders) and enforced through monopolized institutions, ideological indoctrination, and covert resistance to change. The education system, controlled by the Supreme Council of the Cultural Revolution, mandates Islamic courses and restricts academic freedom. Even elite institutions like Sharif University are shown to be disconnected from industry, resistant to reform, and complicit in perpetuating the regime's ideological framework.

Through vivid participant narratives, the book traces the journey from pre-university pressures and misguidance, through university disillusionment, to postgraduation realities marked by unemployment, underemployment, and an ideological ceiling. Many participants reported being pushed toward emigration, while those who remained often lowered their aspirations or accepted routine jobs within regime-sanctioned industries. The concept of ideological capital emerges as a critical lens through which to understand how employability and success are contingent not on education or skill but on proximity to the regime's ideological core.

Pre-University

The participants described an education system that they perceived to be counterintuitive in their middle school and high school years. Instead of feeling that the system was working with them to explore their talents, interests, and aspirations, they perceived instead that the system was creating (and sometimes deciding) their aspirations for them. The participants also described how school curricula were disproportionately focused on teaching students the regime's ideology instead of offering variety to expand their minds and explore their options. Simultaneously, schools and society both minimized the importance of discovering one's aspirations and interests. Rather, an emphasis was placed on the *konkur*. This was exacerbated by the mafia's, or *khodi*'s, persistence in magnifying the *konkur*'s grandeur for, seemingly, their own monetary gains. Moreover, the participants felt that these institutions and actors pushed them toward a one-dimensional mentality, leaving them short-sighted in their planning and convincing them that life did not begin until after graduating with a bachelor's degree. As Darius explained it, "They frequently postponed living."

The participants went on to explain why they felt school, family, and society did not help them in discovering what their interests were in order to determine what course of action to take regarding their academic trajectory and the probability of realizing their aspirations. The participants described the neglect or misguidance they perceived from their school and particularly their guidance counselors, but they also highlighted their own immaturities and ignorance to the point they just followed what they were told. The participants believed that the assistance they received was primarily based on their *konkur* ranking, their expected major, and the university to which they were most likely to gain admission. This underdeveloped counseling infrastructure led to uncertainties about the participants' plans for the future as they continued down a one-dimensional human capital path. This situation also demonstrated how society had perpetuated this culture while the Islamic Republic seemingly enabled it to continue. And while local research and literature debated the problems and shortcomings of this path, the State enabled such barriers to exist and ignored calls for change. As a result, a covert resistance to change, led by the regime and the *khodi*, along with the overt resistance by school, family, and society, reveals itself through the participants' stories. The participants also discussed how the disconnect between their high schools and universities added to the difficulties they faced in exploring not only their aspirations but the major they liked and the university they wanted to attend.

Finally, the participants discussed how their schools pushed them to become one-dimensional. In other words, the participants' sole focus during this first stage of their lives was ranking high on the *konkur* and gaining acceptance into a top-tier university. The participants recounted growing up in a school system where they believed they could not think about anything beyond what was in front of them, and what was in front of them came with its own limitations and stipulations. First, they were forced to follow a pathway with at least, but not limited to, three milestones: (1) the gifted school exam, (2) the Science Olympiad exam, and (3) the *konkur* exam. Second, they had to reach these milestones in order to ensure a successful life. However, irrespective of their successes or failures, they felt pushed toward this one-dimensional human capital mentality. If they passed these milestones, they were labeled as gifted students and pressured to major in a STEMM program at a university like Sharif. If they failed, they were labeled as unintelligent and felt neglected, but they were still pushed toward the *konkur* because it was the only path to success. Either way, the participants did not feel encouraged to contemplate their future, thus remaining oblivious to what their true aspirations may be. As a result, they felt their individual aspirations and agency had not yet begun to take shape. Instead of discussing options and debating scenarios about their future, they were told not to think or worry about it.

Within-University

The participants relayed stories of their time at higher education institutions, and particularly at Sharif, where they encountered tension and conflict, both externally and internally. Externally, they continued to feel a sense of being pushed toward the one-dimensional human capital path. They were also continually reassured that if they followed this distorted version of human capital investment, they would attain a nonspecified, guaranteed, and successful life. This tension reached an apex for the participants as they were maturing and starting to fully grasp the one-dimensionality of their upbringing and how their aspirations were shaped to that point. The participants went on to detail the realization of, and response to, the tension of the *khodi*-versus-*ghayre-khodi* dynamic throughout higher education. As a result, the participants actively pursued their own aspirations and continued to strengthen their agency and improve their different types of capital. However, they were still beset by the inequities of a distorted human capital path that was set before them, pushing them to remain one-dimensional and short-sighted.

This external tension led to the internal tension that many of the participants felt as they realized their own uncertainty in the kind of future they wanted for themselves. To complicate matters further, the participants also discovered that they had more power and control over their lives than they thought, but there appeared to be limitations on the extent to which they could manifest that power and control in shaping and realizing their own professional aspirations inside Iran. This realization was coupled with the feeling that it was too late to change course now that they were in their mid-twenties.

Thus, they experienced a continuous tension between constraints and opportunities balanced on a tightrope with ideological conformity on one side and the ability to develop highly critical perspectives on the other. And as they drew closer to transitioning into the job market, the participants experienced additional limitations.

The participants described the lack of a significant support structure as they matured as higher education students, or as transitional graduates intent on identifying their professional aspirations. On the one hand, the university was isolated from the job market; on the other hand, *Sharifis* were isolated from one another. The participants reflected on how many professors and students were adversarial toward or exploited one another for personal gain—professors used students to write their articles, and students used professors for a recommendation in their applications to foreign universities. This fostered a feeling that no one was interested in improving the problems at Sharif. And since my participants did not exploit their relationships, they felt neglected, left to maneuver through these obstacles on their own.

Moreover, the participants experienced the following: (a) Their professors showed little to no interest in building connections with the industry; (b) these professors also focused their teaching on theoretical, outdated, and/or irrelevant material that participants found inapplicable within their country's job market; (c) other professors tried to seek positive change only to be turned away by the mafia, which aimed to maintain the status quo; (d) their university was incapable (or perhaps unwilling) of upgrading its equipment (e.g., lab equipment from 1966), add updated resources (career services center), and increase its effectiveness (professor evaluations); (e) while these issues were being identified, local debates highlighted them, along with the reasons that no meaningful change had occurred. Thus, not only did positive change seem difficult to accomplish for the participants, but the mafia and *khodi* also benefited from the status quo while resisting change. And what resulted from all this was a hopelessness born out of the broken promise that their human capital investment in the very institutions they were told to pursue and trust would lead to a guaranteed successful life.

While most of these issues are not unique to my participants or to Iran, and have been documented throughout many countries, there is one particular aspect of my participants' narrative that offers a deeper explanation and understanding of nondemocratic governments. And that is how a government can play an adverse role toward certain demographics of its citizenry while being unamenable to change for the betterment of that demographic. As the participants grew older, they realized two conflicting certainties. The first was the complexity of the tension between the *khodi* and *ghayre-khodi*.

The second was the full potential of their agency. And the conflict resided in the realization that the extent to which they were able to exert their agency inside Iran was limited within the parameters that developed from this tension between the *khodi* and the *ghayre-khodi*. While these parameters existed throughout the participants' lives, they were unaware, until they had almost finished their bachelor's degrees, of the full extent to which their lives were influenced and their aspirations shaped. Thus, while on the precipice of entering the workforce, the participants were entangled in their own tense navigation—in other words, they were excavating the recesses of their minds in search of their own aspirations while simultaneously assessing how they could exert their agency within the *khodi*'s parameters in the hopes of actualizing their desired future inside Iran.

Postgraduation

Moving forward into their postgraduation time, we see how the participants' aspirations devolved as a result of their realizations, thus leading to further struggles and obstacles despite their continued efforts in strengthening and/or changing their agency, capital, efficacy, environment, mindset, and the like. The participants' stories revealed a temporal significance in the way they described a weak and highly structured job market that seemingly favored certain types of professions for the *ghayre-khodi*—retail stores and restaurants that sell/provide goods/services—while benefiting the *khodi* and protecting the regime's existence, control, and power. Subsidiaries of the Islamic Republic like the Sazman Sanjesh (or the education mafia), *khusulati* companies, and the IRGC, for example, have monopolized vast sectors of the job market and economy. As a result, they—along with the mullahs' religious theocratic order—have too much wealth, power, influence, and control to lose if generations of the country's youth—and in particular, the *ghayre-khodi*—were to accomplish great financial and professional success, thus shifting the balance of influence and power away from the regime. My participants' perceived ability, therefore, to shape and achieve their own aspirations, with the aim of realizing a better standard of living inside Iran, was limited within the *khodi* parameters. Thus, similar to Brown et al.'s (2010) argument of broken promises of human capital theory through globalization, nondemocratic governments like the Islamic Republic appear to break their return-on-investment promises, eventually limiting those returns in accordance with the *khodi*'s expectations and job market stipulations.

With the job market working against them, my participants found their options of realizing their professional aspirations inside Iran narrowed down to three: (1) become an employee of a company that is either wholly or partly owned by the State, (2) become an employee of a private company, or (3) start your own company—while keeping in mind that the types of companies in options 2 and 3 may eventually become partly or wholly owned by the State depending on what they do, how lucrative they become, and/or how popular/influential they become. However, the obstacles and challenges that categorically fit within one or more of these three options are broadly understood and explained through the concept of *khodi* versus *ghayre-khodi.*

Most of my participants reported direct involvement by governmental offices and personnel, as well as branches of the State, in denying them the realization of their professional aspirations inside Iran. They also explained the *khodi* as being afforded certain privileges, concessions, and preferences—depending on the extent of their connection to the State—that *ghayre-khodi* individuals, like themselves, do not receive. Therefore, the *khodi* not only served as an additional factor in denying my participants the realization of their professional aspirations but also maintained the status quo within the job market. My participants' lived experiences throughout their postgraduation time demonstrated a complex dichotomy: On the one hand, they tried to break away from the one-dimensional human capital path; on the other, they tried to realize their professional aspirations inside Iran. According to the participants, these two paths intersected only if the individual was a member of the *khodi.* Thus, the time and effort my participants placed on strengthening their agency, capital, and efficacy as *ghayre-khodi* would eventually be counteracted by the ceiling that would prevent them from doing anything but acquiescing to a job with little to no professional or financial growth. But even this possibility was uncertain. This resulted in lowered aspirations and accepting their current state of affairs—which was understood as becoming a simple employee and an obedient citizen. As Cyrus put it, "If you want to raise your head just a little, they hit you back down," and the alternative is leaving the country or fighting back as an active *ghayre-khodi* and running the risk of being imprisoned or killed.

Now, the counterargument could be made that my participants are young (all in their mid-twenties at the time of the interviews), with plenty of time to work toward their professional aspirations inside Iran. Moreover, they are among the highly educated within Iran and therefore could form the basis of a movement toward cultural and possibly systemic change. My participants' rebuttal to this claim—and that of many of my stakeholders as well—is multifaceted. First, the impact of the country's brain drain is causing difficulty in mobilizing a large enough movement. Second, some *ghayre-khodi* who are still in Iran are trying to leave, and so they are unwilling to actively participate (see table 7.1) in order to avoid jeopardizing their chances of emigrating. And in the meantime, they focus on carving out a place for themselves within the job market and society while simultaneously fulfilling their exit strategy. Third, others considered passive *ghayre-khodi* that are also still in Iran (see table 7.1) just want to be left alone so they can live their lives the best they can. They may find private ways to resist the *khodi*'s status quo but are not willing to risk detention or death by publicly protesting. Fourth, a small number of the highly educated demographic have decided to become passive *khodi*—examples include three of my stakeholders: Mr. Sadiq (a high school counselor), Ms. Arya (from the IRPHE), and Dr. Mahdi (from the Ministry of Education)—and invest in their ideological capital in order to reach a higher standard of living.

More recently, with the 2025–2026 protests, we have witnessed a new aspect. For the first time in the Islamic Republic's history, Iran's current population is split between four generations that are all active within the ideological-employability scale: the baby boomer generation, who were a part of the revolution, and Generations X, Y, and Z. The baby boomers, for the most part, are passive *ghayre-khodi* or passive *khodi* and are staying out of the recent tension and uprisings between the people and the Islamic Republic. The majority of Generations X and Y are *ghayre-khodi*, but they are split between the passive and active. And members of Generation Z are mostly active *ghayre-khodi*. There is much disagreement among these generations regarding how they should deal with the regime. Those that have lived through the revolution and the eight-year war with Iraq have a dichotomous view on foreign help in changing or overthrowing the Islamic Republic. The primary reason for the hesitancy in accepting outside assistance is rooted in the past embarrassment of foreign nations helping the Pahlavi monarchy stay in power, which showed Iran as a weak nation. That is why some want regime change while others want reform. But then, members of the new Generation Z only know of these events through books and stories. They were not alive during any of these historical events, and so they carry no baggage when deciding that foreign help is needed and welcomed to overthrow this regime.

Interestingly, either as a result of or irrespective of these factors, little to no significant change has materialized from the massive movements of the 2009 Green Movement, the 2019 Bloody November protests, the 2022 Women, Life, Freedom movement, or the 2025–2026 protests. Having personally lived in and/or visited Iran from 2000 to 2020, I can attest to the participants' rebuttal. Living conditions have significantly worsened, and no real systemic change has occurred. In fact, the regime has become increasingly brutal due to the 2026 war versus the US and Israel.

A New Broken Promise in Human Capital?

The role of the Islamic Republic highlights the three limitations of the human capital theory. The first limitation is the current global arguments that have disproved the human capital argument vis-à-vis economic insufficiencies, like in Italy (Pozzoli, 2009); or a job-skills mismatch, like in Greece (Liagouras et al., 2003); or a disconnect between higher education and the job market, like in Tanzania (Al-Dosary, 2006); or the positional conflict within a globalized job market (Brown et al., 2010). Although Iran is no exception to these issues, it is in the second and third limitations where this book further problematizes the human capital argument.

The second limitation in the human capital argument is the claim that irrespective of the global criticisms just listed, individuals should rely on and invest in themselves to acquire the needed skills, attributes, and knowledge to see returns on their investment in the job market. Schultz (1961), for example, argues that investment in education leads to the socioeconomic development of one's society and the increased well-being of its citizenry. Becker (1993) adds that individuals decide on their education and training by analyzing the pros and cons of each. Thus, there is a promise or guarantee that if one were to follow this path, they will succeed. This argument is also perpetuated throughout Iran by the country's school system, higher education system, society, mass media, and the government. However, the Islamic Republic's propagation of this argument—according to my participants—appears to be a façade or an illusion that masks the fears of the *khodi* in their attempts to reduce the aspirations of the *ghayre-khodi* to one dimension. This goes beyond just education and follows the youth deep into their postgraduation life of finding a career, becoming independent, starting a family, and sustaining a standard of living conducive to such endeavors, thereby curbing their successes so they remain within certain parameters to limit financial, social, and influential growth. This results in *ghayre-khodi* remaining below a ceiling that the *khodi* does not want them to go beyond, because that would be a threat to the *khodi*'s power and influence.

In other words, squarely placing the burden on the individual is problematic when, (a) the State takes on an adversarial role; (b) a ceiling is put in place to block an individual's professional, socioeconomic, and civic growth; and (c) the *khodi* enforces limitations. According to participant narratives, no amount of restrategizing by enhancing agency, types of capital, and employability was able to lead them to remedy their situation inside Iran. If the arguments of Schultz (1961) and Becker (1993) are examined further within the *ghayre-khodi* context, then the human capital argument is applicable for the twenty-two participants who left Iran. However, while inside Iran, the guaranteed and successful life they were continuously promised was eventually revealed to them as a broken promise due to the limited parameters within which they were allowed to navigate.

The third limitation is the role of the State in an adversarial capacity. Becker's (1993, p. 17) approach to countries like Iran is one of universal application, where he concentrates on showing "how the analysis of investments in human capital helps in understanding a large and varied class of behavior even in developing countries and countries with very different cultures." This assertion may be accurate in analyzing some developing or non-Western countries like India (Jeffrey, 2010), Ethiopia (Mains, 2012), Egypt (Pettit, 2017), and Nairobi (Thieme, 2017), but not countries like Russia, China, North Korea, Nicaragua, or Iran for example. These studies, which are similar to my own, discovered that their participants were able to manifest their agency and employability in order to draw closer to realizing their aspirations inside their own country, with the help of investments in human capital.

There is an assumption, however, that individuals who navigate their country's education system, job market, and society in pursuit of realizing their own aspirations are doing so within a system where the country's government is receptive to criticism, collaboration, reciprocity, and change, to name a few. The role of such a government is critical in supporting the human capital argument. However, a different argument has emerged from this book. My participants' accounts of the Islamic Republic appearing to be unamenable toward the *ghayre-khodi* show the limits to human capital investment returns and introduce a new type of capital investment that may be beneficial to a *ghayre-khodi* Iranian navigating the country's job market and society: ideological capital.

Investing in ideological capital requires one to adopt certain elements of the *khodi* lifestyle. Now, the extent to which one is willing to embody the *khodi* lifestyle is dependent on how many compromises they are willing to make. In other words, what aspects of their defining traits are they willing to sacrifice in order to invest ideological capital? At a minimum, the individual needs to present an outward facade where their choice of clothing, grooming, and demeanor is aligned with what society believes a *khodi* to be. I discussed this in chapter 3: staying within a monochromatic color scheme (gray, brown, black, dark blue, and green for example), wearing plain, nongraphic long-sleeve shirts, never wearing a necktie, always wearing pants, maintaining a short beard and a basic short hair style, and keeping one's gaze down in public. Furthermore, projecting oneself as a pious Shia Muslim is another way to invest in ideological capital. Other ways include attending public events held by the regime and religious ceremonies, as well as regularly going to the mosque in order to build personal relationships. Additional ways to invest in ideological capital would be publicly showing support for the regime on social media and joining specific *khodi* organizations like the Basij—which is a paramilitary volunteer militia of the IRGC that staunchly supports the regime. Also, applying to jobs within the government is another way to invest in ideological capital. I have been told by many that during the job interview process, one's ideology is just as important as—if not more so than—their credentials and qualifications. If you recall in chapter 6, Nader spoke about his job interview and being asked if he prays five times a day and fasts during the month of Ramadan. He could have lied in order to get the job and would have secured an income conducive to a domestic life. But of course, he was not willing to compromise his beliefs and values for such a trade off.

I have also met many individuals who are considered *khodi* that confessed to me in private that they are just pretending in order to financially benefit from their association. I also had to pretend at times in order to gain access to certain offices, officials, and documents during my research. I was even verbally accosted on two occasions due to my outward appearance resembling that of a *khodi*. So while there may be benefits to investing in ideological capital, for a *ghayre-khodi* this investment can be seen as a betrayal against all those who have fought and died for change inside Iran. When confronted with the decision to either compromise one's principles in order to reach a higher status (financially and/or professionally) or choose the noble path of defiance only to struggle, there are many factors to consider (none more important, perhaps, than caring for a child). But whatever the reason, these are the struggles a passive *ghayre-khodi* and a passive *khodi* must wrestle with as they rationalize their choices; and such decisions are not often easy. And my participants, for example, were not willing to lie and pretend to be *khodi*, especially since they despise the government. That is why the ideological-employability scale (table 7.1) helps identify the range in which an individual is willing to or must invest in their ideological capital to then see returns on their investment.

Thus, in addition to human capital—as well as social, cultural, and religious—ideological capital also needs to be considered when investigating an individual's efforts in strengthening all forms of capital. This investigation into an individual's ideological capital fills in the details of the ideological-employability scale in table 7.1 in regards to how, where, why, and if an individual chooses to invest in ideological capital in order to increase their chances of successfully navigating their country's job market, realizing their aspirations inside their country, securing gainful employment, purchasing a home, contributing to the betterment of society, and starting and supporting a family, to name a few. If more of my participants invested in their ideological capital and at least adopted some of the attributes of a passive *khodi* on the ideological-employability scale, perhaps their job market experiences and their ability to realize their aspirations inside Iran would have had a more fruitful return.

However, the 2026 war that Israel and the United States started against Iran has changed the Islamic Republic in many respects, seemingly increasing the gulf between not only the *ghayre-khodi* and *khodi* but also between the passive and the active. On the one side, many passive *khodi* are increasingly looking for an exit strategy to unite, mobilize, and defect with the hopes of regime change. But the decision to do so is dependent on their cost-benefit analysis and if it is in their best interest to sacrifice the livelihood of their family—especially at a time when the new rulers of the regime are looking to stifle even the smallest of deviations. On the other side, the passive *ghayre-khodi* are finding it harder to justify not joining the active *ghayre-khodi* in the hopes of engendering real, positive change. What complicates this matter further is Generation Z and their uncompromising valiance to rid their country of this regime. While the Generation X *khodi* have taken over the Islamic Republic as a result of this war, the Generation Z *ghayre-khodi* have taken over the protests, and neither side is showing signs of compromise. This tension, however, is not new in modern Iranian history because during the 2009 Green Movement, it was the *khodi* Baby Boomer Generation versus the *ghayre-khodi* Generation Y. So, while on the surface it may seem that no significant change has occurred from one generation to the next, for the *ghayre-khodi*—with the standard of living on the constant decline and the regime still in power—with each major protest, there have been small victories in which the *khodi* slightly ease some restrictions and suppressions in attempts to pacify the active *ghayre-khodi* and extend their rule over the country. But time is not on the side of the Islamic Republic, and with every new generation, protests will continue to worsen until real change occurs.

APPENDIX A

List of Graduates Interviewed

Pseudonym	*Education level*	*Most notable comments*
Afshin	BS in Computer Engr. in Shiraz	All the hard work you do is in vain because there are other entities at play that have set these limitations, so regardless of what you do there's a limit to how far you can advance.
Ahmad	2010 MD from Shiraz University	Your *konkur* ranking dictates what you can major in and which universities you can attend. It's not like America, where you take the SAT and submit other documents like transcript and personal statement and the university looks at all these different factors about who you are. Here, it's just based off your *konkur* score. But if you have enough money, you can pay to go to a private university and major in almost whatever you want, but the majority of people don't have that kind of money, and there isn't student loans like in America.
Aram	2019 BS in Mechanical Engr. from Sharif	Although there is a strong entrepreneur culture in Iran, failure is a higher likelihood for us partly due to the regime's interference and restrictions.
Azariah	Former Director of Sharif Student Body	You forget sometimes that Sharif belongs to the regime, but when we tried to write an article in the university newspaper criticizing some internal policies we were quickly silenced.

(*continued*)

Pseudonym	*Education level*	*Most notable comments*
Behrouz	Tehran U. Graduate; Snapp Driver	Almost every student tries to see if they can go abroad, but even from that number there is still a large percentage who do end up leaving. And for those of us still trying to leave, we work any jobs we can get to save up and leave, but our weak economy and currency and high inflation makes it hard to save up enough money.
Bethuel	2020 BS in Civil Engr. from Sharif	It's not an exaggeration when we say success in this country depends heavily on which boxes you can check from the regime's preapproved list.
Camran	BS in Mechanical Engr. in Shiraz	High school counselors force you to pick certain majors based on your *konkur* ranking. If you're smart, you'll look elsewhere for guidance but most kids don't do that. . . . When you're seventeen, eighteen years old, how do you know what questions to ask and who to ask?
Cyrus	2017 BS in Computer Engr. & 2022 MBA from Sharif	The *khodi* don't allow you to grow in this society. They beat the hell out of you. . . . If you want to raise your head just a little, they hit you back down. Either shut up and live in this society . . . or else.
Darius	2017 BS in Mechanical Engr. from Sharif 2020 MBA from Amirkabir U.	We were kids, our breath still smelled like milk. No one told us why we have to take this path—we were like soldiers marching there and back just following orders—years later it is revealed why but we've come so far with blisters on our feet, so surely this has not been a mistake? But so what if it is? No one cares.
Davood	2011 BS in Accounting from Shiraz Azad U.	High school guidance counselors are a joke! They are not qualified because they don't have formal training in being a counselor, they don't have enough experience, they're young recent graduates who just tell you how to fill out your 150 list of majors and universities based on your *konkur* ranking. I'm envious of those American high schools where the counselor helps the student figure out what they like and what to major in. Even our elite and well-funded high schools don't have that.

Pseudonym	*Education level*	*Most notable comments*
Ebrahim	BS in Computer Engr. in Shiraz	I didn't like my major. I wanted to major in physical education, but today's society looks down at such a profession, so I felt pressured to pursue something in engineering and it was awful.
Elam	2018 BS in Mechanical Engr. & 2020 MBA from Sharif	Most of us work hard during our time at Sharif just so we can leverage that to help us leave [Iran], and I'm one of them.
Elkanah	2019 BS in Electrical Engr. & 2021 MBA from Sharif	Have you noticed how many of us are pursuing an MBA? We're like sheep; we follow this linear path without fully understanding why and we come out the other end still confused.
Farsheed	BS in Computer Engr. in Shiraz	I don't have much to say . . . my time at university was normal. Nothing sticks out. I have a regular job. I live with my parents. I go out and have fun with my friends. I don't know . . . that's it.
Farzan	2021 MS in Civil Engr. from Sharif *sarbazi* in 2023	I worked so hard to find this *sarbazi* job so I don't have to go to boot camp. You can't imagine the stress the *sarbazi* causes. It's always there waiting for you, and it provides no value to your future.
Ghaffar	BS in Architecture in Shiraz	Incoming freshmen are so excited, full of energy, hopeful for a better tomorrow, but after four years we're beaten down and more lost than we started out.
Gholam	BS in Computer Engr. in Shiraz	I enjoyed my time at university. It was fun. I'm working now, nothing to be proud of, but it's a good start, I guess, considering how most of us are unemployed.
Habib	2010 BS in Computer Science from Shiraz Azad U.	Most boys go to university for just about every reason except education. To avoid the *sarbazi* and find a way out of it. To help them get a student visa to leave Iran. To help pass the time and avoid boredom. Even with a degree there's no jobs out there.
Hafez	2019 BS & 2021 MS in Industrial Engr. from Sharif	I'm studying for the master's *konkur* in industrial engineering because I want to postpone the *sarbazi* and see if maybe I can leave Iran on a student visa.

(*continued*)

Pseudonym	*Education level*	*Most notable comments*
Hamid	2022 BA in Art from Tehran U.	I pursued my dreams and majored in the arts but society looks at us like we're panhandling vagabonds just wasting our life, so there's very little space within the job market for graduates like me, and if we try to create a space for ourselves, we encounter harsh crackdowns by the regime since they view us a part of the problem that continues to protest against them
Hezekiah	2019 BS in Computer Engr. from Sharif	I entered Sharif in 2012 and left seven years later. . . . It is unsettling when you realize the things you've been told up to this point were not for your maturation but to keep you in line. Then you have to start all over again to figure out what you want to do with your life.
Iraj	BS in Urban Planning in Shiraz	I wanted to major in the humanities, but my family had negative opinions about it, so I gave up on that desire.
Isa	2021 BS in Industrial Engr. from Sharif	We did our own research and saw that roughly seventy percent of Sharif graduates end up working a job unrelated to their field of study. I'm still going to try to make it!
Ismail	2015 BS in Chemical Engr. from Sharif	I will accept to start at a lower position with a lower salary, but what about my future? There's no job growth or salary increase. . . . You can make progress only to a certain extent, but if you want to be a manager, you will need some other factors that are not ethical. You can't buy a house and start a family with this salary.
Jafar	Unemployed Graduate in Isfahan	I would like to go abroad just to get a better education and then come back and help my country, but I don't know how realistic that is. The older I get, the more I discover how corrupt this country is.
Jahan	2023 BS in Industrial Engr. from Sharif	My friend and I started interviewing *Sharifis* who started their own company and failed. We too have a startup idea but want to learn from others' experiences.

Pseudonym	Education level	Most notable comments
Jahleel	2019 MS in Mechanical Engr. from Sharif	There's not much more I can say that you don't already know. I'm surprised and confused as to why you're even doing this research. Everyone knows this stuff. Life is difficult here for many reasons: inflation, sanctions, corruption, mismanagement, nepotism, stealing, lying, low wages, a shrinking labor market versus an expanding labor force . . . and that's just the economy. Then we have religious, political, social, cultural, ethnic, and gender issues with their own long list of difficulties.
Karim	2018 BS in Industrial Engr. from Sharif 2021 MBA from Amirkabir U.	A scary amount [of people expect you to apply and leave]. . . . The youth and even more from society, they kept saying, "Why don't you go? Why don't you go? Why don't you go?" it is very bad, maybe you like to stay here! I mean society constantly . . . if they find out you are a *Sharifi* they ask you, "Why don't you leave?"
Majid	2018 BS in Computer Engr. from Salman Farsi U. (Kazerun)	The *konkur* is a life-changing decision. You may go into it with no knowledge of what you want to do with your life and end up in a major but later realize you want to pursue something else. You can't just change majors. The are so many rules, and it feels like they change every year and there's no one to help you.
Maziyar	2020 PhD in Education from Tehran U.	I've done the research. There is almost no data on university students and graduates regarding the most pivotal issues: dropout rates, transfer rates, going abroad, job market success and failures. The government either doesn't collect such data or doesn't make it public. The best we can get is this pamphlet.
Mohamad	2023 BA in Art from Tehran U.	The economy is so bad that many companies are in debt just so they can stay open. Therefore, they're either not hiring, they're only hiring interns (because it's free), or they are hiring but with very low wages (not enough to save up considering the high inflation).

(*continued*)

Pseudonym	*Education level*	*Most notable comments*
Musa	BS in Chemistry in Shiraz	Iranian students have a lot of talent that is not nurtured; this is not what they deserve. Most should be in a better place but are not because of lack of fairness. Most are forced to study a major they don't like, and since they don't like their major, they don't succeed.
Nader	2018 BS in Mechanical Engr. & 2021 MBA from Sharif	Everybody was in agreement that you have to choose this path. There was no place to doubt, there was no place to even think about other things. Everybody told me you will go to Sharif and after that you will either leave Iran or there will be a good job for you.
Nima	2010 BS & 2013 MS in Industrial Engr. from Sharif *sarbazi* in 2015	I've been trying to leave [Iran] for four years and something always comes up to slow the process. More sanctions causing an increase in cost that I can't afford; the Muslim travel ban by Trump preventing me in getting a visa; the possibility of war and the fear of being on a plane; or just myself not being ready when the moment is right.
Osman	BS in Computer Engr. in Shiraz	My high school experience was a bit difficult, but university was great! I really enjoyed my time. I liked my major, and now I'm trying to find a job in my field . . . we'll see what happens . . . *inshallah* I'll find something.
Parsa	BS in Mechanical Engr. in Shiraz	Only with life experience, determination, and hard work can you become successful. Having a university degree is just one of the pieces.
Qasem	2011 BS in Mechanical Engr. from Sharif	Similar to American debates about systemic racism, there are many in Iran who experience systemic othering based on the *khodi*'s criteria of who is allowed to hold power, influence, and wealth.
Rasool	BS in Urban Planning in Shiraz	The country's youth are oppressed. I don't think there's any debate on that . . . unless, I guess, if you ask those from wealthy and powerful families or those within the *khodi*. They probably don't feel oppressed like the rest of us do . . . or maybe they're oppressed in a different way.
Rumi	2017 BS in Industrial Engr. & 2021 MBA from Sharif	I couldn't find a long-term job. I was hired at one place, but it only lasted two months due to a lot of reasons beyond our control, but it all stems from our shitty government—sorry for my language.

Pseudonym	*Education level*	*Most notable comments*
Shadrach	2015 BS & 2021 MS in Chemical Engr. from Sharif	I love my job! I'm a writer for a Canadian firm, and things are going great! My wife and I have a modest living, but we don't mind, and we're just enjoying what we're doing right now. Of course, we're always thinking of leaving [Iran].
Sohrab	2016 BS in Electrical Engr. in Isfahan *sarbazi* in 2018	Every time I save up enough money to leave [Iran], our economy gets worse, prices increase, the inflation gets worse, and our currency to the [US] dollar gets worse so I have to keep working with the hopes that one day I'll have enough money to leave.
Talmai	2019 BS in Mechanical Engr. from Sharif *sarbazi* in 2021	I'm just working where I can until I figure out what I can do. It seems that all of the jobs the government will let us do are not conducive to reaching your aspirations but rather making enough money to just get by. Unless your aspirations are in the retail or food industry; then you can make a lot of money, but that's because the regime isn't threatened by a successful store or restaurant.
Tooraj	2019 BS in Mechanical Engr. from Sharif	I hope my startup will be successful. The vast majority of my classmates have left [Iran]. I may, too, if my company doesn't make it.
Vahid	2021 PhD in Education from Shiraz U.	There is a lot of research to be done on Iran's education system and youth . . . and a lot of other issues, too, but people don't research it out of fear of being detained and accused of treason since the majority of our problems stem from the government.
Zechariah	2017 BS in Material Science and Engr. from Sharif	My startup is doing well so far. I'm hopeful that I can be allowed to import and export, but there are a few hurdles I have to jump over so the regime doesn't shut me down. Since the regime has monopolized the import/export business, there's only a few items I can import and export. Most items are off limits.
Ziba	2019 BS in Electrical Engr. & 2021 MBA from Sharif	After I earn my MBA, I'm going to start my own business and see what happens. I'm not naïve about the risks and complications, but I think I can make it if I choose the right industry.

APPENDIX B

List of Stakeholders Interviewed

Pseudonym	*Profession*	*Most notable comment*
Mr. Abbas	Sharif Career Counselor	Iran has weak laws and weaker enforcement on NDAs, so many students would lose their ideas to stronger entities . . . primarily the *khusulati* companies.
Mr. Abtin	Sharif Career Counselor	More than half of Sharif students and graduates apply to go abroad. Not all of them make it on their first attempt but they try for many years until they can go.
Dr. Adnan	Education Professor at Shiraz U.	Iran's higher education system is greatly influenced by the Sazman Sanjesh. Universities don't have much freedom in how they want to build their own culture and what kind of disciplines to teach.
Dr. Ali	Sharif Economics Professor	I believe the political and economic mess we're in is because of this regime, and that's why so many graduates are unemployed. It's fascinating to watch a government like Iran's work so hard to keep most of its citizens down.
Mr. Amin	Journalist (Tehran)	Most students' inability in deciding their field of study or profession is a result of obeying the adults and institutions in their life growing up and not properly learning how to think independently and question things.

(*continued*)

Pseudonym	*Profession*	*Most notable comment*
Dr. Amir	Ministry of Health (Tehran)	The youth have high expectations and are not willing to work hard to incrementally prosper. The struggles in Iran are manageable because after about forty days the people will get use to whatever the next struggle is and learn to move on and adapt. Just look at the increased gas prices . . . some protested for a while but now we're back to our regular routine.
Dr. Amjad	Economics Professor at Isfahan U.	Students care very little . . . probably not at all . . . about the field they're majoring in. They don't know what questions to ask to learn more because they are kids, and the adults around them don't teach them much of value in relation to real-world knowledge that can link their major to a career.
Ms. Arezoo	Sharif Guidance Counselor	I believe many of the problems my students face can be traced back to their upbringing and how their home, school, or society limited their potential. When students come to me confused, anxious, or scared and we talk about things, we discover that they are just starting life and everything before was just studying and schoolwork with no long-term goal in sight.
Ms. Arya	Institute for Research & Planning in Higher Education (IRPHE) (Tehran)	Students are powerless in thinking about their future, their dreams or goals, or making long-term plans. Instead, they do what they are told.
Mr. Asad	Isfahan U. Guidance Counselor	Students are unaware of what the job market is like and have unrealistic expectations as a result.
Mr. Asghar	Cofounder of an Employment Website (Tehran)	We provide resume and cover letter workshops and mock job interviews to prepare new graduates in the job market. I think you've noticed by now that most of what we do [in Iran] is copy what America does. You guys have Netflix, we have Namava. You have Uber, we have Snapp. Your universities have career service centers, ours don't but that's why I started this company because our youth need help.

Pseudonym	*Profession*	*Most notable comment*
Mr. Askari	Cofounder of a Startup Accelerator & Employment Website (Tehran)	One reason why most startups in Iran fail is because all the team members have an engineering background with no one willing or able to perform administrative, marketing, accounting, or business duties. It's difficult to find people with degrees in these fields because growing up everyone tells you these are a waste of time, but that's definitely not true.
Dr. Aziz	Computer Science Professor at Salman Farsi U. (Kazerun)	Because our economy is so weak, students feel obligated to major in a field where the profession pays well enough so they can live an independent life, buy a house, start a family, but the problem with that strategy is our economy is so weak that buying a house and living an independent life to support your own family is almost impossible unless you're a doctor or dentist . . . or if you are part of the *khodi*.
Dr. Babak	Education Professor at Tehran U.	You have to become like [the *khodi*] if you want to succeed. If you don't become like them, they will keep you down, and if you fight them, they can make your life difficult.
Ms. Bahar	Statistician (Isfahan)	I don't think the youth struggle is as difficult as many of us describe it. If you work hard enough, you can live a comfortable life . . . you just have to be realistic in what you want to accomplish in this country.
Mr. Bahman	Sharif Career Counselor	Iran is volatile because of domestic and international problems. There is no routine, and you cannot plan for the future. You were here when they raised the price of gas in the middle of the night and then people started protesting . . . or even the price of milk, eggs, or meat that doubles or triples within a week.
Dr. Bahram	Sharif Research Faculty	Obstacles exist in Iran, but they exist everywhere. I do not believe going abroad would improve conditions. The youth need to stay here and improve our country.

(*continued*)

Pseudonym	*Profession*	*Most notable comment*
Dr. Baqir	Sharif Aerospace Engr. Professor	There are obstacles that limit *Sharifis* from realizing their aspirations. There is a mafia in every vital aspect of our economy: the ports, higher education, the media, banking, automotive, and the list goes on. When they have a monopoly and there's no room for competition, they control who does what and for how much.
Dr. Bijan	Admissions Counselor at Tehran U.	I don't know of any literature that discusses what you're researching. All the debates inside Iran are through an economic lens. No one has taken the time to speak with the youth to learn what their grievances are.
Mr. Bilal	The Iranian Research Institute for Information Science and Technology (IranDoc) (Tehran)	Your research is interesting, but be careful whom you talk to. Many issues in Iran are highly sensitive, and the regime doesn't want bad things said about them . . . please be careful.
Dr. Emad	Computer Science Professor at Salman Farsi U. (Kazerun)	There is no guidance or support for our youth to help them understand and determine what discipline to major in. There is only pressure and/or limitations.
Dr. Esfandyar	Education Professor at Tehran U.	We just opened a career service center . . . can you believe that? In 2018 we just opened a career services center! That should tell you how little our institutions care about the youth and helping them find gainful employment.
Dr. Esmail	Sharif Computer Engr. Professor	My department is an exception, but Sharif does nothing to assist our students in preparing for the job market. We recently opened up a career services center, so it's not well established yet to fully help our students, but we could have done this decades ago.
Dr. Ferdowsi	Statistics Professor at Farhangian U. (Isfahan)	We really don't have reliable data on dropout rates, transfer rates, or failed students. The Sazman Sanjesh has these numbers, but they don't make them public.

Pseudonym	Profession	Most notable comment
Dr. Firooz	Economics Professor at Ferdowsi U. (Mashhad)	I'm sure we have the same problems that most countries have. Like students not knowing what kind of careers they can have from the different university majors. So I guess the difference is, while other countries have been trying to remedy this, [Iran] has just started paying attention to this issue, so we've had multiple generations almost wondering aimlessly.
Mr. Hadi	Founder of an HR company in Tehran	I don't agree with your participants' criticism of the job market or the government. If you work hard enough and are resilient to carve out a place for yourself, you can make it. Nothing worth having comes easy.
Dr. Hamed	Education Professor at Tehran U.	It doesn't matter who is in charge of the job market. You can argue it's highly centralized with the government but there are other sectors like restaurants, grocery stores, and some retail industries that are not controlled by the government. But regardless of who is in charge, the job market changes when the regime wants it to change . . . or, if a phenomenon like Snapp happens . . . but even then, the regime takes over.
Dr. Hassan	Sharif Industrial Engr. Professor	The majority of Iranians were pessimistic, negative, and hopeless about their standard of living and their future inside Iran . . . it's become like this virus that's spread to everyone.
Dr. Hossain	Sharif Industrial Engr. Professor	It is difficult to earn a wage to have a stable independent life, but I don't think it's impossible.
Dr. Jalal	Humanities Professor at Ferdowsi U. (Mashhad)	There is a disconnect between higher education and the job market. We don't have career fairs, career services centers, places to help with your résumé and cover letter, networking events, and things like that. Sure, there are some places that started to do this, but universities are like an island, very much detached from the job market and what the country needs.

(*continued*)

Pseudonym	*Profession*	*Most notable comment*
Mr. Jawad	Cofounder of an Employment Website (Tehran)	There is a disconnect between companies and graduates, so some companies bypassed universities and developed their own academies where they train their employees.
Mr. Kamran	Sharif Administrator	If graduates learned to write a proper résumé, strengthen their network, and improve their interviewing skills, they would have no trouble getting hired.
Mr. Kayvon	Sharif Research Faculty	In most areas, meritocracy has been replaced with ideology.
Mr. Kazim	Sharif Career Counselor	Those providing the funding and acquiring up to eighty percent stake in the startup are affiliated with the Islamic Republic.
Dr. Khosrow	Sharif Economics Professor	Iran is a very unstable country due to politics, economy, and ideological issues.
Mr. Kourosh	Salman Farsi U. (Kazerun) Administrator	Most universities don't have an official "rule book"—so to speak—that details how a student can change their major.
Dr. Mahdi	Ministry of Education (Tehran)	Regarding the Islamic Republic, there is much resistance to change, and in most cases, they don't allow for change to happen.
Dr. Mahmood	Education Professor at Shiraz U.	Universities are not independent entities even when they are private and separate from the government. We still have to follow guidelines from the regime, but we can change small things like the number of credits each course can have.
Mr. Mansoor	The Statistical Centre of Iran (Tehran)	There's no data on how or why high school students pick their university major, or how they come up with their 150-major list for the Sazman Sanjesh. Also, the Sazman Sanjesh is the only organization that has the data you're looking for, but they do not share it publicly. They only provide some information to some university administrators.

Pseudonym	*Profession*	*Most notable comment*
Dr. Mehran	Political Science Professor at Ferdowsi U. (Mashhad)	Look at the *konkur*... the country has been talking about removing it or changing it for over a decade. There are bills at Parliament ready to be voted on and ratified, but the Sazman Sanjesh is preventing it. Why? Because they're a mafia that makes billions of dollars from the *konkur*.
Mr. Milad	Tehran U. Undergraduate Admissions	There is no admissions application to our—or any—university. It's all done through the Sazman Sanjesh and their *konkur* system. And I'm not sure if anyone has told you this already, but they [the Sazman Sanjesh] are one of the mafias in this country that control a billion-dollar enterprise, so they are with the *khodi* and manipulating where our youth go and don't go.
Mr. Mohsen	Tehran U. Librarian	There are a lot of great master's and doctoral dissertations that speak to the problems that youth have in Iran, and they could be published as articles or books, but none of them will be because it shows the country—and most often, the government—in a bad light, so they just sit here in our library collecting dust.
Dr. Morteza	Political Science Professor at Tehran U.	I would highly advise against contacting the Sazman Sanjesh. First, they won't help you, but more importantly, once they discover what you're doing here, they can make your life very difficult. Let the higher-ups know and they'll come get you.
Dr. Mostafa	Cofounder of Policy Think Tank in Tehran	I remember during the Shah, the government helped Sharif graduates find a job. Now, almost eighty percent go abroad . . . this is just from my observation . . . there's no real data on this.
Mr. Naser	Tehran U. Librarian	There are high school guidance counselors that tell you what to major in in university just based off your *konkur* ranking. They don't help you figure out what subjects you like or what jobs you like.
Dr. Omid	Researcher at IRPHE	I agree with most of what your participants say about higher education, the job market, and the government. There's really nothing most of us in the government can do about it. These powers are held in the hands of a few.

(*continued*)

Pseudonym	*Profession*	*Most notable comment*
Dr. Parvez	Public Policy Think Tank in Tehran	We operate under the auspices of the regime so our research and recommendations can't contradict what they want to do . . . I mean, we have some space to offer diverging recommendations.
Dr. Raheel	Math Professor at Amirkabir U.	There was a baby boom because of our war against Iraq and the regime needing families to have more children because so many people were dying from the war. As a result, all those babies became university graduates, and the government wasn't prepared for them in the job market.
Dr. Reza	Sharif Industrial Engr. Professor	Look . . . I can't tell you the truth because it won't be good for me if anyone finds out. My position is too visible . . . I'll introduce you to other professors who can speak more freely.
Mr. Rida	Sharif Career Counselor	We have a mentorship program because the most pressing issue for our current students is about ninety percent do not know what their interests, abilities, and skills are, and they feel lost.
Ms. Roksanne	Sharif Administrator	It's unfortunate, but planning to go broad has more of a consistency from one day to the next when compared to planning for a future in this country. . . . If rules and laws were abided by and living conditions didn't change on a weekly basis, perhaps you could prosper with hard work.
Mr. Saadi	The Institute of Humanities and Cultural Studies (Tehran)	You have to be careful whom you talk to and whom you explain your research to because if the wrong person finds out, the government can come after you, and you could be in a lot of trouble.
Mr. Sadiq	High School Guidance Counselor (Tehran)	My students were pressured by their parents to either become doctors or engineers. I advised and challenged them to view the positive and negative to every major they thought about selecting. Counselors just glance at the student's *konkur* ranking and tell them which major to select. The younger generation of professors and counselors, however, were more active and interactive with their students to ensure the same mistakes were not repeated.

Pseudonym	*Profession*	*Most notable comment*
Dr. Saheb	Political Science Professor at Isfahan U.	There's even politics involved with many companies in Iran. The regime keeps many companies open even when they have little to no work due to sanctions, inflation, et cetera. There are a lot of companies that have a skeleton crew that sit around and do nothing, but they stay operational just to show everyone that the economy is good and companies are still thriving.
Dr. Sajjad	Sharif Computer Engr. Professor	I strongly believe that with proper faith, prayer, and being a good Muslim, you can succeed in this country. Our youth are steering in the wrong direction and then complain when they don't get the job they want. It is only through God that we attain that which we desire.
Dr. Shahram	Psychology Professor at Isfahan Azad U.	Let's imagine that students didn't have the problems of the *konkur*, the *sarbazi*, lack of support and guidance . . . even if they are able to pursue their dream job, there's still a high likelihood they won't find that job in Iran because of how polluted the job market and society is with the regime's tentacles.
Mr. Shahriar	Researcher at IRPHE	There are branches and individuals within the Islamic Republic that support and elevate specific careers and businesses over others . . . these are the mafia or members of the *khodi*.
Dr. Shayan	Biology Professor at Tehran U.	We can say that students choose their majors, but if you really examine it, they don't really have viable options with the path. It mostly comes down to picking whatever you dislike the least.
Ms. Shirin	Sharif Administrator	The Iranian government is excessively involved in the job market. We don't have a free market. We don't have an antimonopolistic system . . . the regime is in control.

(*continued*)

Pseudonym	*Profession*	*Most notable comment*
Mr. Sina	Tehran U. Administrator	Universities in Iran could be much more beneficial to the country if they each customized areas of their academics to focus on their locality and partner with the local government and companies to help their town and province flourish. Not every university in Iran needs to be pushing the boundaries of knowledge, science, and education. Look at the University of Kurdistan . . . that area is known for agriculture and farming and they have a great agriculture program.
Ms. Yazmine	Sharif Research Faculty	A one-dimensional mentality was imposed upon the youth where they followed a specific path, and for most it didn't occur to them that they could try other things.
Dr. Zaynab	Sharif Guidance Counselor	There were pressures and competition of having to be the top student while simultaneously being unaware to what they were interested in pursuing academically and professionally.

Notes

Introduction

1. (a) Twice as many women graduate from universities and twice as many are un(der)employed (Bahramitash, 2013); (b) overall, the number of un(der)employed women aged fifteen to twenty-five is double that of men (Khosravi, 2017); and (c) in 2006, the rate of un(der)employment among women in urban areas was 2.3 percent greater than men (Khosravi, 2017).

2. The specific path the participants detailed was: attending a school for the gifted → participate in the Science Olympiad → earn a top *konkur* ranking → enroll in a top-tier university like Sharif → graduate from Sharif (and perhaps enroll in a master's program and then a doctoral program) → complete their *sarbazi* → find any job, regardless of degree or interest → find a place to live → get married → have kids → live "a quiet life" that is not a threat to the Islamic Republic.

Chapter 2. Setting the Scene Within Iran's Modern History

1. When Pezeshkian took office on July 28, 2024, Israel was nine months into its military campaign as a response to the October 7, 2023, terrórist attack by Hamas. This military campaign consisted of a genocidal ethnic cleansing of the Palestinian people while also fighting Iran's Axis of Resistance (or Axis of Evil depending on the storyteller). This Axis consisted of Hamas from Gaza, Hezbollah from Lebanon, Houthis from Yemen, militias in Syria and Iraq, and certain elements of the IRGC.

2. Habibi, N. (1989). Allocation of educational and occupational opportunities in the Islamic republic of Iran: A case study in the political screening of human capital. *Iranian Studies, 22*(4), 19–46.

Chapter 7. The Role of the State and Ideological Capital

1. The Organization for Economic Cooperation and Development helps member countries develop economic policies and standards to improve quality of life for their citizens. The OECD consists of thirty-eight members, from the United States to Türkiye. Countries like Russia, China, and Iran are not members of the OECD.

Glossary of Key Persian Terms

aberu Honor or reputation.

bekar Unemployed.

dalal Literal translation is "broker." However, in Iran, it has been stigmatized with labels of thievery, chicanery, and immorality.

Daneshgah Azad Islami Islamic Azad University.

dolati A State- or government-owned-and-operated company.

gaj A corporation that provides *konkur*-related services through—but not limited to—programs, classes, training, and preparation.

galamchi A corporation that provides *konkur*-related services through—but not limited to—programs, classes, training, and preparation.

ghayre-khodi The literal translation is "not of us" or "other," but it commonly refers to "outsider." These are individuals who do not have a connection to the Islamic Republic. Therefore they, unlike the *khodi,* do not necessarily have access to or cannot gain advantages from that connection. Moreover, they may also experience a denial or limitation of certain aspects of life inside Iran because they are considered *ghayre-khodi.* Within the demographic, there are active and passive *ghayre-khodi.* An active *ghayre-khodi* is someone who outwardly opposes the Islamic Republic and actively participates in public displays of defiance and resistance—which often leads to imprisonment, abuse, and/or death. A passive *ghayre-khodi* is someone who also opposes the regime but whose acts of defiance and resistance are more subtle or covert in order to minimize the chances and degree to which their livelihood will be at risk.

khodi The literal translation is "of us" or "us," but it commonly refers to "insiders" or the "establishment." These are individuals with a connection to the Islamic Republic. This connection can be through, but is not limited to, employment, family, marriage, association, or allegiance. With this connection, certain social, economic, religious, political, financial, business, or cultural, among other, investments, concessions, privileges, advantages, and benefits are available to these individuals. As a member of the *khodi,* one theoretically upholds, advocates, and at times enforces the ideology of the *khodi* and the Islamic Republic. This ensures their existential longevity, financial security, and power and influence over how the government is run and what direction the nation is headed.

khusulati This word derives from a combination of private (***khususi***) and State (***dolati***). It is a company that is partially owned by the private sector and partially owned by the State or *khodi*. *Khusulati* companies have aided the *khodi* in monopolizing the business sector in a similar way to how it has monopolized the religious, financial, and media sectors.

khususi A private company.

konkur The country's higher education entrance exam. It is a derivative of the French *concour*, meaning "competition," an exam that is similar to Iran's *konkur*.

payām-e Nur State distance-learning university.

sarbazi The literal translation is "military." It is also the two-year mandatory service every adult male of sound mind and body must complete.

Sazman Sanjesh The National Organization for Educational Testing, a branch of the Islamic Republic that administers the *konkur* and decides what major/university each applicant is eligible for and offers admissions into four-year universities.

Sharifi Individuals with a current or prior affiliation to the University of Sharif, either as a student or graduate.

Velayat-e Faqih supreme leader—the ruler of Iran.

References

24 Online. (2014, May 7). Ijad-e faseleh ziad beyn-e hoqooq va maza'ye a'za-ye hay'at elmi ba karkanan daneshgah-ha [Creating a large gap between the salaries and benefits of faculty members and university staff]. Khabar Online. khabaronline.ir/x52mH

Abedi, M. (2018, September 14). Tanasob-e mohtava-ye amoozeshi kotob-darsi ba niyaz-haye keshvar [The alignment of educational content in textbooks with the needs of the country]. IRIB News. https://www.iribnews.ir/009KrD

Abrahamian, E. (2008). *A history of modern Iran*. Cambridge University Press.

Abrahamian, E. (2013). *The coup 1953, the CIA, and the roots of modern U.S.–Iranian relations*. New Press.

Abu-Lughod, L. (1991). Writing against culture. In T. S. Oakes & P. L. Price (Eds.), *The culture geography reader* (pp. 50–59). Routledge.

Adler, P. A., & Adler, P. (1998). *Peer power: Preadolescent culture and identity*. Rutgers University Press.

Afkar News. (2018, August 19). Pishnahad mali mafiay-e konkour be pazirofte-shodeh konkour 97 [The financial offer of the entrance exam mafia to the 97 entrance exam admittees]. Afkar News. https://www.afkarnews.com/fa/tiny/news-777443

Afrooz, G. (2002). Zarurate baznegari dar nizame motovast va reshteh-haye tasili [The need to review secondary education and fields of study]. *Peyvand*, Article 272. http://ensani.ir/fa/article/105240/

Agah, V. (2019, March 26). *Tahlil nizam sodoor mojavez ejrah sahnehaye moseghi va nezarat bar an dar Iran* [The analysis procedure in issuing a license for music performances and the monitoring of it in Iran]. Ekhtebar. https://www.ekhtebar.com

Agarwala, T. (2008). Factors influencing career choice of management students in India. *Career Development International, 13*(4), 362–376. https://doi.org/10.1108/13620430810880844

Ahearn, L. M. (2001). Language and agency. *Annual Review of Anthropology, 30*(1), 109–137. https://doi.org/10.1146/annurev.anthro.30.1.109

Aibao, Z., Xiaofeng, M., & Hajime, A. (2007). Parental expectation of early childhood education: Comparison between China, Japan, and Korea. *Frontiers of Education in China*, *2*(1), 140–147. https://doi.org/10.1007/s11516-007-0011-1

Al-Agha, F., Keshavarz, M., & Rahimi, M. (2009). Ravand roshd kami amuzesh aali khususi va dolati dar jomhuri eslaami Iran [Quantitative growth of private and public higher education in the Islamic Republic of Iran]. *Institute for Research and Planning in Higher Education, 22*(20), 73–110.

Al Ahmad, J., Campbell, R., & Algar, H. (1984). *Occidentosis: A plague from the West.* Mizan Press.

Al-Dosary, A. S. (2006). A communicative planning approach to combat graduate unemployment in Saudi Arabia. *Human Resources Development International, 9*(3), 397–414. https://www.tandfonline.com/doi/abs/10.1080/13678860600893581

Alashloo, F. R., Castka, P., & Sharp, J. M. (2005). Towards understanding the impeders of strategy implementation in higher education (HE): A case of HE institutes in Iran. *Quality Assurance in Education, 13*(2), 132–147. https://doi.org/10.1108/09684880510594382

Alibaygi, A. H., Barani, S., Karamidehkordi, E., & Pouya, M. (2013). Employability determinants of senior agricultural students in Iran. *Journal of Agricultural Science and Technology, 15*(4), 673–683. http://journals-old.modares.ac.ir/article_4989.html

Alijani, M. (2019, July 8). Oloum-e tajrobi entekhab-e aval-e danesh-amoozan [Biological sciences are the first choice of students]. ISNA. isna.ir/xd56qD

Alizadeh, P. (Ed.). (2000). *The economy of Iran: Dilemmas of an Islamic state.* I. B. Tauris.

Amini, H., Moghaddam, Y., Nejatisafa, A., Esmaeili, S., Kaviani, H., Shoar, S., Shabani, A., Samimi-Ardestani, M., Keshavarz Akhlaghi, A. A., Noroozi, A., & Mafi, M. (2013). Senior medical students' attitudes toward psychiatry as a career choice before and after an undergraduate psychiatry internship in Iran. *Academic Psychiatry, 37*(3), 196–201. https://doi.org/10.1176/appi.ap.10120171

Amuzegar, J. (2004). Iran's unemployment crisis. *Middle East Economic Survey, 47*(41). http://archives.mees.com/issues/401/articles/16809

Amuzegar, J. (2007). The Ahmadinejad era: Preparing for the apocalypse. *Journal of International Affairs, 60*(2), 35–53. http://www.jstor.org/stable/24357969

Ang, R. P., Klassen, R. M., Chong, W. H., Huan, V. S., Wong, I. Y. F., Yeo, L. S., & Krawchuk, L. L. (2009). Cross-cultural invariance of the Academic Expectations Stress Inventory: Adolescent samples from Canada and Singapore. *Journal of Adolescence, 32*(5), 1225–1237. https://doi.org/10.1016/j.adolescence.2009.01.009

Ansari, P., Kabiri, A. H., & Naderi, M. (2008, May 13). *Ahamiate darse ulume ejtemaei* [The importance of social science classes]. Tebyan. https://article.tebyan.net/68392

Appadurai, A. (2013). *The future as cultural fact: Essays on the global condition.* Verso.

Arabestani, M. (2018, November 1–3). *Ethnographic practice in Iran: Politics and precarity* [Paper presentation]. Institut für Sozialanthropologie und Empirische Kulturwissenschaft conference, Zurich, Switzerland. https://www.isek.uzh.ch/de/ethnologie/Veranstaltungen/Archiv/nocountryforanthropologists2018/abstracts.html#arabestani

Arani, A. M., Kakia, L., & Jafari Malek, M. (2018). Higher education research in Iran: Quantitative development and qualitative challenges. In J. Jung, H. Horta, & A. Yonezawa (Eds.), *Researching higher education in Asia: History, development and future* (pp. 315–326). Springer.

Arasteh, H. R. (2004, September 23). Ertebat daneshgah va san'at [University-industry relations]. Office of the Preservation and Publication of the Works of Ayatollah Ali Khamenei. https://khl.ink/f/11601

Archer, M. S. (2007). *Making our way through the world: Human reflexivity and social mobility*. Cambridge University Press.

Armstrong, T. A. (2007). *The human odyssey: Navigating the twelve stages of life*. Sterling Publishing.

Ashwin, P. (2020). *Transforming university education: A manifesto*. Bloomsbury Publishing.

Asiyai, R. I. (2012). Assessing school facilities in public secondary schools in Delta State, Nigeria. *African Research Review, 6*(2), 192–205. https://doi.org/10.4314/afrrev.v6i2.17

Aslani, E. (2009). Raqabat bad ast! [Competition is bad!]. *Mahnameh Roshd Amuzeshe Ebtedaii, 13*(4), 46. https://www.magiran.com/p838619

Asriran. (2020, August 22). Rahkar hazf-e gonkoor reshte-haye portarfadar az zaban-e vizir-e oloum [The solution to eliminating the entrance exam for popular fields from the Minister of Science]. Asriran. https://www.asriran.com/fa/news/743490

Azimi, F. (2009). *The quest for democracy in Iran: A century of struggle against authoritarian rule*. Harvard University Press.

Bahramitash, R. (2003). Islamic fundamentalism and women's employment in Iran. *International Journal of Politics, Culture, and Society, 16*(4), 551–568. https://doi.org/10.1023/A:1023043308813

Bahramitash, R. (2013). *Gender and entrepreneurship in Iran: Microenterprise and the informal sector*. Palgrave Macmillan.

Bahramitash, R., & Esfahani, H. S. (Eds.). (2011). *Veiled employment: Islamism and the political economy of women's employment in Iran*. Syracuse University Press.

Bai, L. (2006). Unemployment: Dilemmas and challenges in China's move to mass higher education. *The China Quarterly, 185,* 128–144. https://doi.org/10.1017/S0305741006000087

Balzer, H. (2003). Demography and democracy in Russia: human capital challenges to democratic consolidation. *Demokratizatsiya, 11*(1).

Barker, F. (2007). *The South African job market: Theory & practice* (5th ed.). Van Schaik Publishers.

Barsamian, D. (2020). *Retargeting Iran*. City Lights Books.

Baruch, Y. (2001). Employability: A substitute for loyalty? *Human Resource Development International, 4*(4), 543–566. https://doi.org/10.1080/13678860010024518

Bayat, A. (2009). *Life as politics: How ordinary people change the Middle East*. Stanford University Press.

Bazargan, A. (2000). Internal evaluation as an approach to revitalize university systems: The case of the Islamic Republic of Iran. *Higher Education Policy, 13*(2), 173–180. https://doi.org/10.1016/S0952-8733(99)00024-0

Beck, U. (1992). *Risk society: Towards a new modernity*. Sage Publications.

Becker, G. S. (1964). *Human capital*. Columbia University Press.

Becker, G. S. (1993). *Human capital: A theoretical and empirical analysis, with special reference to education* (3rd ed.). University of Chicago Press.

Bee, M., & Dolton, P. (1990). Patterns of change in U.K. unemployment, 1962–87. *Higher Education, 20*(1), 25–45. https://doi.org/10.1007/BF00162203

Behdad, S., & Nomani, F. (2012). Women's Labour in the Islamic Republic of Iran: Losers and Survivors. *Middle Eastern Studies, 48*(5), 707–733.

Behnia, M. (n.d.). Ta'adol-e bazar kar dar gero-ye amalkard-e sayer-e bazarha [The balance of the labor market depends on the performance of other markets]. Tejarat-e-Farda. https://www.tejaratefarda.com/fa/tiny/news-26248

Berlant, L. (2011). *Cruel Optimism.* Duke University Press.

Blustein, D. L., Duffy, R., Ferreira, J. A., Cohen-Scali, V., Cinamon, R. G., & Allan, B. A. (2020). Unemployment in the time of COVID-19: A research agenda. *Journal of Vocational Behavior, 119,* Article 103436. https://doi.org/10.1016/j.jvb.2020.103436

Bogdan, R., & Biklen, S. (2007). *Qualitative research for education: An introduction to theory and methods* (5th ed.). Pearson.

Bonyad-e Amuzesh-e Majazi-ye Iranians. (2014, February 18). Asib-shenasi entekhab reshte-haye daneshgah-i ba niyaz-haye bazar kar-e danesh-amooxtagan nabalad [Pathology of choosing university fields with the labor market needs of unqualified graduates]. Bonyad-e Amuzesh-e Majazi-ye Iranians. https://iranelearn.com/بازار-کار-دانش-آموختگان/html

Borker, H. (2018). *Madrasas and the making of Islamic womanhood.* Oxford University Press.

Boroujerdi, M. (1996). *Iranian intellectuals and the West: The tormented triumph of nativism.* Syracuse University Press.

Bourdieu, P. (1977). *Outline of a theory of practice* (R. Nice, Trans.). Cambridge University Press. (Original work published 1972)

Bourdieu, P. (1990). *In other words: Essays towards a reflexive sociology* (M. Adamson, Trans.). Stanford University Press.

Bourdieu, P. (2000). *Pascalian meditations* (R. Nice, Trans.). Stanford University Press. (Original work published 1997)

Bowen, G. A. (2009). Document analysis as a qualitative research method. *Qualitative Research Journal, 9*(2), 27–40. https://doi.org/10.3316/QRJ0902027

Bowers-Brown, T., & Harvey, L. (2004). Are there too many graduates in the UK? A literature review and an analysis of employability. *Industry and Higher Education, 18*(4), 243–254. https://doi.org/10.5367/0000000041667538

Braun, V., & Clarke, V. (2013). *Successful qualitative research: A practical guide for beginners.* SAGE.

Bromberger, C. (2009). Usual topics: Tabooed themes and new objects in Iranian anthropology. In S. R. Nadjmabadi (Ed.), *Conceptualizing Iranian anthropology: Past and present perspectives* (pp. 195–206). Berghahn Books.

Bron, A., & Thunborg, C. (2015). *Biographical interviewing: The case of non-traditional students in higher education.* SAGE. https://doi.org/10.4135/978144627305014549309

Brown, P., Green, A., & Lauder, H. (2001). *High skills: Globalization, competitiveness, and skill formation.* Oxford University Press.

Brown, P., Lauder, H., & Aston, D. (2010). *The global auction: The broken promises of education, jobs and incomes.* Oxford University Press.

Burke, C. T. (2014). *Biographical narrative interview method: Tracing graduates' futures.* SAGE. https://doi.org/10.4135/978144627305013510257

Caddell, M. (2006). Private schools as battlefields: Contested visions of learning and livelihood in Nepal. *Compare, 36*(4), 463–479. https://doi.org/10.1080/03057920601024909

Cassell, J. (1982). Harms, benefits, wrongs, and rights in fieldwork. In J. E. Sieber (Ed.), *The ethics of social research: Fieldwork, regulation, and publication* (pp. 7–31). Springer-Verlag.

Chabook, M. (2019, October 8). Jehat-giri jadid daneshgah-ha baray-e ertebat ba san'at [New direction of universities for connecting with industry]. Mehr News. mehrnews .com/xQj6F

Chera daneshamuzane nokhbeh az ulume ensani farari hastand? [Why are elite students fleeing the humanities?]. (2014, February 22). Farhang Emrooz. http://farhangemrooz.com/news/12601/

Chodorow-Reich, G., & Coglianese, J. (2021). Projecting unemployment durations: A factor-flows simulation approach with application to the COVID-19 recession. *Journal of Public Economics, 197,* Article 104398. https://doi.org/10.1016/j.jpubeco .2021.104398

Civilica. (n.d.). Hedayat shoghli tahsili va tasir-eh an dar entekhab-e shoghl [Career guidance and its impact on career choice]. Civilica. https://s-hasht.ir/13/04/1398 //هدایت-شغلی-تحصیلی-و-تاثیر-آن-در-انتخاب-ر

Clandinin, D. J., & Connelly, F. M. (2004). *Narrative inquiry: Experience and story in qualitative research.* John Wiley & Sons.

Clark, N. (2017). Education in Iran. *World Education News & Reviews.* Retrieved March 3, 2020, from https://wenr.wes.org/2017/02/education-in-iran

Clarke, M. (2008). Understanding and managing employability in changing career contexts. *Journal of European Industrial Training, 32*(4), 258–284. https://doi.org/10 .1108/03090590810871379

Connelly, F. M., & Clandinin, D. J. (1990). Stories of experience and narrative inquiry. *Educational Researcher, 19*(5), 2–14. https://doi.org/10.3102/0013189X019005002

Corwin, Z. B., Venegas, K. M., Oliverez, P. M., & Colyar, J. E. (2004). School counsel: How appropriate guidance affects educational equity. *Urban Education, 39*(4), 442–457. https://doi.org/10.1177/0042085904265107

Creswell, J. W. (2007). *Qualitative inquiry and research design: Choosing among five approaches* (2nd ed.). SAGE.

Creswell, J. W. (2009). Mapping the field of mixed methods research. *Journal of Mixed Methods Research, 3*(2), 95–108. https://doi.org/10.1177/1558689808330883

Dabalen, A., Oni, B., & Adekola, O. (2001) Job market prospects for university graduates in Nigeria. *Higher Education Policy, 14,* 141–159. https://doi.org/10.1016/S0952 -8733(01)00010-1

DANA News Agency. (2019, December 7). Tadrees reshte-haye faqed bazar-kar va mansookh shodeh dar daneshgah-ha-ye keshvar [Teaching fields without job markets and outdated fields in universities of the country]. DANA News Agency. https://dana.ir/1552831

Dari, P. (n.d.). Madarres-e farhang va ehtemam be oloum-e ensani [Culture schools and commitment to humanities] [Interview]. Markaz-e Taroje Oloum-e Ensani. https://workshopday.ir/مصاحبه-با-دکتر-پانته%E2%80%8Cآ-دری/

Darling-Hammond, L. (2000). Teacher quality and student achievement: A review of state policy evidence. *Education Policy Analysis Archives, 8*(1). https://doi.org/10 .14507/epaa.v8n1.2000

Darvishi, Y. (2017, September 4). Elat-e omdeh-ye bikari dar keshvar, nabood-e saz-o-kar-e sahih-e estekhdami ast [The main reason for unemployment in the country is the lack of a proper hiring mechanism]. IRNA. www.irna.ir/xjmz35

Davies, B., & Gannon, S. (2006). *Doing collective biography: Investigating the production of subjectivity.* McGraw-Hill Education.

De Certeau, M. (1984). *The practice of everyday life*. University of California Press.

Denny, K., & Harmon, C. (2000). *The impact of education and training on the labor market experiences of young adults* (IFS Working Papers W00/08). Institute for Fiscal Studies. https://ifs.org.uk/wps/wp0008.pdf

Denzin, N. K. (1989). *Interpretive biography*. SAGE.

Denzin, N. K., & Lincoln, Y. S. (Eds.). (2005). *The SAGE handbook of qualitative research* (3rd ed.). SAGE.

Department of Statistics & Information Technology. (2017). *Amar Amuzesh Aali Iran: Sal Tahsili 1394–95* [Statistics of Higher Education in Iran: Academic Year 2015–2016]. Iran Ministry of Science, Research & Technology.

Deresiewicz, W. (2008). The disadvantages of an elite education. *The American Scholar, 77*(3), 20–31.

Divergentes. (2025, June 18). The brain drain hitting Nicaragua. https://www.divergentes.com/the-brain-drain-hitting-nicaragua/

Dolat.ir. (n.d.). Tose'e keyfiyat madarres dolati asli-tarin siyasat amoozesh va parvaresh ast [Improving the quality of public schools is the primary policy of education]. Dolat.ir. https://dolat.ir/detail/350145

Donya-e-Eqtesad. (2018, February 15). Dalayel-e vaghe'i narezayati karkonan az shoghl-shan [The real reasons for employee dissatisfaction with their job]. Special Issue. (M. Rezaei, Trans.). https://donya-e-eqtesad.com/fa/tiny/news-3354287

Dronkers, J., & Robert, P. (2003). *The effectiveness of public and private schools from a comparative perspective*. European University Institute. https://cadmus.eui.eu/bitstream/handle/1814/1360/

Dube, V. (2004). Sidelined in the job market. *Perspectives on Labour and Income, 16*(2), 25–31. https://www150.statcan.gc.ca/n1/en/pub/75-001-x/10404/6844-eng.pdf

Eccles, J. S., & Barber, B. L. (1999). Student council, volunteering, basketball, or marching band: What kind of extracurricular involvement matters? *Journal of Adolescent Research, 14*(1), 10–43. https://doi.org/10.1177/0743558499141003

Eghtesad Online. (2019, April 23). Moshkel-e asli-ye bazar kar kambood-e taghaza ast, na arze [The main problem of the labor market is the lack of demand, not supply]. Eghtesad Online. https://www.eghtesadonline.com/001SfK

Eghtesad Online. (2019, July 22). Sargardani faregh-al-tahsilan bad az daneshgah [Confusion of graduates after university]. Eghtesad Online. https://www.eghtesadonline.com/001Xlp

Eghtesad Online. (2019, August 31). Taghyir-e algooye karyabi [Changing the job-seeking pattern]. Eghtesad Online. https://www.eghtesadonline.com/001aA1

Eghtesad Online. (2020, May 10). Tarh-e sarkari baray-e eshghal-e faregh-al-tahsilan [Government plan for employment of graduates]. Eghtesad Online. https://www.eghtesadonline.com/001pww

Eisa Zadeh, S., & Hosseini, S. A. S. (2014). Barrasi tatbiqi bikari faregh-al-tahsilan daneshgah-i dar Iran dar moghayeseh ba digar keshvar-ha [Comparative study of unemployment among university graduates in Iran compared to other countries]. Kar va Jame'a, 176. https://ensani.ir/fa/article/356432

Ejraie siasate tosiye motavazine reshteh-haye tasili be manzure ertegha kayfiate amuzeshi dar ostane markazi [Implement the policy of a balanced development of fields of study in order to improve the quality of education in Markazi Province]. (2019, May 12). http://www.pana.ir/news/914473

Emirbayer, M., & Mische, A. (1998). What is agency? *American Journal of Sociology, 103*(4), 962–1023. https://doi.org/10.1086/231294

Entekhab News Agency. (n.d.). Bazar kar danesh-amooghtagan reshte-haye ensani [Job market for graduates of humanities fields]. Entekhab News Agency. https://www.iranmodares.com/article-index.php?ID=295

Entezarian, N., & Tahmasebi, T. (2012). Barrasi mizan-e hamahangi va entebagh nezam-e amoozesh 'ali va amoozesh-haye fanni va herfahi ba niyaz-haye bazar kar [Examining the alignment and compatibility of higher education and technical and vocational training systems with labor market needs]. *Kar va Jame'a, 140*, 59–71. http://noo.rs/nnFY5

Erben, M. (Ed.). (1998). *Biography and education: A reader* (Vol. 19). Psychology Press.

Erlandson, D. A., Harris, E. L., Skipper, B. L., & Allen, S. D. (1993). *Doing naturalistic inquiry: A guide to methods*. SAGE.

Ertebate madares ba daneshghaha taghriban ghat ast [Schools and universities are nearly disconnected]. (2018, December 16). Moallem Press. https://moallempress.ir/2018/12/16/

Eskohi, F., Afzali, A. G., & Movahhed Mohammdi, H. (2012). Avamel mo'asser bar ertebat daneshgah va bazar-e kar az didgah-e daneshjuyan-e Pardis Keshavarzi va Manabe' Tabi'i Daneshgah-e Tehran [Factors influencing the university-industry relationship from the perspective of students at the College of Agriculture and Natural Resources, University of Tehran]. 4th Congress of Agricultural and Natural Resources Education and Extension Sciences, Iran. https://www.sid.ir/paper/844676/fa

Estienne, M. (1997). An organizational culture compatible with employability. *Industrial and Commercial Training, 29*(6), 194–199. https://doi.org/10.1108/00197859710177486

Evans, K. (2007). Concepts of bounded agency in education, work, and the personal lives of young adults. *International Journal of Psychology, 42*(2), 85–93. https://doi.org/10.1080/00207590600991237

Faez, A., & Shahabi, A. (2010). Arzyabi va olaviat-bandi mavane-e ertebat-e daneshgah va san'at (motale'e moredi shahrestan-e Semnan) [Evaluation and prioritization of barriers to university-industry collaboration: A case study of Semnan city]. *Quarterly Journal of Educational Leadership and Management, 4*(2), 97–124. https://journals.iau.ir/article_538788.html

Fahim, K. (2021, August 5). Shortages, sanctions, protests and pandemic: Daunting challenges await Iran's new president. *The Washington Post*. https://www.washingtonpost.com/world/middle_east/iran-raisi-protests-khuzestan-inauguration/2021/08/05/2fb4593a-f55a-11eb-a636-18cac59a98dc_story.html

Falah Tafti, M. H. (2020, August 21). Chara bishtar danesh-amoozan be reshteh-ye tajrobi alaghe darand? [Why do most students prefer the experimental sciences major?]. IRNA. https://www.irna.ir/news/83916397

Farasatkhah, M., Ghazi, M., & Bazargan, A. (2008). Quality challenge in Iran's higher education: A historical review. *Iranian Studies, 41*(2), 115–138. https://doi.org/10.1080/00210860801913321

Farhikhtegan Online. (2019, February 3). Hoqooq-e asatid oloum-e pezeshki 33 darsad bishtar az vizarat-e oloum [The salaries of medical sciences professors are 33% higher than those of the Ministry of Science]. Farhikhtegan Online. fdn.ir/25580

Fars News. (2020, August 31). Tarh-e do-foriyati Majles darbareh mafiay-e konkour [The urgent proposal by Parliament regarding the entrance exam mafia]. Fars News. https://farsnews.ir/politics/1599108300000076764

Fay, D., & Frese, M. (2001). The concept of personal initiative: An overview of validity studies. *Human Performance, 14*(1), 97–124. https://doi.org/10.1207/S15327043HUP1401_06

Feldman, D. C. (2003). The antecedents and consequences of early career indecision among young adults. *Human Resource Management Review, 13*(3), 499–531. https://doi.org/10.1016/S1053-4822(03)00048-2

Flinders, D. J. (1992). In search of ethical guidance: Constructing a basis for dialogue. *Qualitative Studies in Education, 5*(2), 101–115. https://doi.org/10.1080/0951839920050202

Forster, N., & Souvignier, E. (2014). Learning progress assessment and goal setting: Effects on reading achievement, reading motivation and reading self-concept. *Learning and Instruction, 32,* 91–100. https://doi.org/10.1016/j.learninstruc.2014.02.002

Fugate, M., Kinicki, A. J., & Ashforth, B. E. (2004). Employability: A psycho-social construct, its dimensions, and applications. *Journal of Vocational Behavior, 65*(1), 14–38. https://doi.org/10.1016/j.jvb.2003.10.005

Garavan, T. N. (1999). Employability, the emerging new deal? *Journal of European Industrial Training, 23*(1). https://doi.org/10.1108/jeit.1999.00323aaa.001

Genova, C. (2023). Wearing protest: Youth clothing and appearance in the evolution of radical social movements in Italy. *Partecipazione e Conflitto, 16*(2), 319–338. https://doi.org/10.1285/i20356609v16i2p319

Ghanuni, R., & Ghaltash, A. (2019). Moghayese democracye amuzish, forsudegi tahsili va maharat-haye shahrundi madarese dolati va gheyre dolati [A comparison of democratic education, academic burnout and citizen skills in public and nonpublic schools]. *Faslename Elmi, 39*(3), 209–224. http://ensani.ir/fa/article/417922/

Ghanyatpishe, A. A. (2005). Moghayese asar reghabate fardi, talash fardi va reghabate gorohi dar pishrafte tahsili [A comparison on the effect of individual competition, individual effort and group competition on academic achievement]. *Talim va tarbiat, 81*(1). http://ensani.ir/fa/article/417922/

Ghasempour Dehaghani, A., Liaghatdar, M. J., & Jafari, S. E. (2011). Tahlili bar boomi sazi va beyn-ol-melali shodan barname-darsi daneshgah-ha dar asr-e jahan-goyayi [An analysis of localization and internationalization of university curricula in the age of globalization]. *Journal of Iranian Cultural Research, 4*(4), 1–24. https://www.jicr.ir/article_182.html

Ghezelloo, M. (2019, October 20). Aya tahsilat daneshgah-i hanooz ham daneshjuyan ra baray-e bazar kar amadeh mikonad? [Does higher education still prepare students for the labor market?]. Tejarat News. https://tejaratnews.com/n/24WL

Giddens, A. (1984). *The constitution of society: Outline of the theory of structuration.* University of California Press.

Giddens, A. (1991). *Modernity and self-identity: Self and society in the late modern age.* Polity Press.

Glesne, C., & Peshkin, A. (1992). *Becoming a qualitative researcher: An introduction.* Longman.

Gonick, M., Walsh, S., & Brown, M. (2011). Collective biography and the question of difference. *Qualitative Inquiry, 17*(8), 741–749. https://doi.org/10.1177/1077800411421118

Goodson, I. F., & Sikes, P. (2001). *Life history research in educational settings: Learning from lives.* Open University Press.

Granovetter, M. (1995). Coase revisited: Business groups in the modern economy. *Industrial and Corporate Change, 4*(1), 93–130. https://doi.org/10.1093/icc/4.1.93

Gregor, M. A., & O'Brien, K. M. (2016). Understanding career aspirations among young women: Improving instrumentation. *Journal of Career Assessment, 24*(3), 559–572. https://doi.org/10.1177/1069072715599537

Grint, K. (1991). *The sociology of work: An introduction.* Polity Press.

Guba, E. G. (1981). Criteria for assessing the trustworthiness of naturalistic inquiries. *Educational Communication and Technology, 29*(2), 75–91. https://www.jstor.org/stable/30219811

Haas, T. (1992). *What can I become: Educational aspirations of students in rural America* (ED345931). ERIC. https://files.eric.ed.gov/fulltext/ED345931.pdf

Habibi, N. (1989). Allocation of educational and occupational opportunities in the Islamic republic of Iran: A case study in the political screening of human capital. *Iranian Studies, 22*(4), 19–46. https://doi.org/10.1080/00210868908701739

Habibi, N. (2015). Iran's overeducation crisis: Causes and ramifications. *Middle East Brief, 89,* 1–7. https://www.brandeis.edu/crown/publications/middle-east-briefs/pdfs/1-100/meb89.pdf

Hajforoush, A. (2019, February 25). Shenasayi va anhalal-e sazman-e makhof mafiay-e konkour va payamad-haye aan [Identifying and dissolving the notorious entrance exam mafia and its consequences]. Khabar Online. https://www.khabaronline.ir/news/1234737

Hakim Sabzevari University. (n.d.). Arzeshiabi-ye asatid [Faculty evaluation]. Hakim Sabzevari University. https://www.hsu.ac.ir/amozesh/2-سوالات-متداول-آموزشي/نظارت-وارزيابي/

Haller, A. O., & Miller, I. W. (1971). *The Occupational Aspiration Scale: Theory, structure and correlates* (ED016712). ERIC. https://files.eric.ed.gov/fulltext/ED016712.pdf

Hamdhaidari, S., Agahi, H., & Papzan, A. (2008). Higher education during the Islamic government of Iran (1979–2004). *International Journal of Educational Development, 28*(3), 231–245. https://doi.org/10.1016/j.ijedudev.2006.11.001

Hammersley, M., & Atkinson, P. (2007). *Ethnography: Principles in practice* (3rd ed.). Routledge.

Hansen, D. M., & Larson, R. W. (2007). Amplifiers of developmental and negative experiences in organized activities: Dosage, motivation, lead roles, and adult youth ratios. *Journal of Applied Developmental Psychology, 28*(4), 360–374. https://doi.org/10.1016/j.appdev.2007.04.006

Harvey, L. (2001). Defining and measuring employability. *Quality in Higher Education, 7*(2), 97–109. https://doi.org/10.1080/13538320120059990

Hasan Nia, F. (n.d.). Ayeen nameh hedayat-e tahsili danesh-amoozan va zovabet-e aan [Regulations for student educational guidance and its criteria]. Shoraye Aalai Amuzeshe va Parvaresh. https://bayanbox.ir/view/8485555315111388957

Hashemi, H. (2020). Konkur, kiseaye baraye daramade amuzesh [Konkur, a bag for educational income]. *Iran,* Article 7477. https://www.magiran.com/article/4107533

Hashemi, S. M. K., Hosseini, S. M., & Rezvanfar, A. (2012). Explaining entrepreneurial intention among agricultural students: Effects of entrepreneurial self-efficacy and college entrepreneurial orientation. *Research Journal of Business Management, 6*(3), 94–102. https://doi.org/10.3923/rjbm.2012.94.102

Hassani, M., & Mir Ghasemi, S. J. (2016). Investigating stratification within higher education through examining the status of students in different academic majors in terms of cultural, social and economic capital. *Educational Research and Reviews, 11*(8), 676–685. https://doi.org/10.5897/ERR2016.2629

Hastings, S. L. (2010). Triangulation. In N. J. Salkind (Ed.), *Encyclopedia of research design* (pp. 1538–1541). SAGE.

Haydari, S. Z. (2016, December 15). Vazayef-e moshavaran dar madarres; az hedayat-e tahsili ta erteqa-ye 'elmi/Lezom-e taghyir-e nengarish nasbat be naqsh-e moshavaran [The duties of counselors in schools; from academic guidance to scientific advancement/The necessity of changing the perception of the role of counselors]. DANA News Agency. https://dana.ir/976285

Heiatelmi. (2019, November 5). Daramad-e payin; mohim-tarin moshkel-e asatid daneshgah [Low income; the biggest problem of university professors]. Heiatelmi. https://heiatelmi.ir/1398/08/میزان-درامد-هیات-علمی-سراسری/

Hemmati, Sh. (2019, September 22). Aya shakh mafiay-e gonkoor shekaste mishavad? [Will the power of the entrance exam mafia be broken?]. Eghtesad Online. https://www.eghtesadonline.com/fa/news/382429/

Hesarkhi, E. (2022, February 23). Madrak bi-maharet ya maharet bi-madrak; daneshgah ya amoozesh online [Unskilled degree or degree without skills; university or online education]. Faradars. https://b.fdrs.ir/5ja

Hillage, J., & Pollard, E. (1998). *Employability: Developing a framework for policy analysis.* Department for Education and Employment.

Hochschild, A. R. (2016). *Strangers in their own land: Anger and mourning on the American right.* The New Press.

Hodis, F. A., Johnston, M., Meyer, L. H., Mcclure, J., Hodis, G. M., & Starkey, L. (2015). Maximal levels of aspiration, minimal boundary goals, and their relationships with academic achievement: The case of secondary-school students. *British Educational Research Journal, 41*(6), 1125–1141. https://doi.org/10.1002/berj.3189

Hoffman, A. (1974). *Unwanted Mexican Americans in the Great Depression: Repatriation pressures, 1929–1939.* University of Arizona Press.

Holloway, I., & Freshwater, D. (2009). *Narrative research in nursing.* Wiley.

Holmes, L. (2001). Reconsidering employability: The "graduate identity" approach. *Quality in Higher Education, 7*(2), 111–119. https://doi.org/10.1080/13538320120060006

House, R. M., & Hayes, R. L. (2002). School counselors: Becoming key players in school reform. *Professional School Counseling, 5*(4), 249–256.

Hunter, S. T. (1992). *Iran after Khomeini.* Praeger Publishers.

Iles, P., Forster, A., & Tinline, G. (1996). The changing relationships between work commitment, personal flexibility and employability: An evaluation of a field experiment in executive development. *Journal of Managerial Psychology, 11*(8), 18–34. https://doi.org/10.1108/02683949610150033

ILNA. (2018, September 9). Bandbazi dar jazb-e heyat elmi daneshgah-ha: Az esrar ta enkar/"Eraye asnad" faqat dar monazereh-ye televiziyoni [Cliques in hiring university faculty: From insistence to denial/"Presenting documents" only in the televised debate]. ILNA. https://www.ilna.ir/fa/tiny/news-677788

ILNA. (2020, November 14). Mafiay-e gonkoor baray-e jolo-giri az hazf-e gonkoor besyar fa'al va ghadaratmand ast/Savaq-e tahsili feli mowed-e etemad-e jame'e nist [The entrance exam mafia is very active and powerful in preventing its elimination/ Current academic records are not trusted by society]. ILNA. https://www.ilna.ir/fa/tiny/news-995340

Ingram, C. L. (2017). *An examination of collegiate extracurricular activities and career aspiration levels* [Master's thesis, Rowan University]. Rowan Digital Works. https://rdw.rowan.edu/etd/2444/

International Labor Organization (ILO). (n.d.). *Forms of work: An overview of the new statistical standards.* https://ilostat.ilo.org/methods/concepts-and-definitions/forms-of-work/

International Labor Organization (ILO). (2013). *Global Employment Trends for Youth 2013: A generation at risk.* https://www.ilo.org/wcmsp5/groups/public/@dgreports/@dcomm/documents/publication/wcms_212423.pdf

International Labor Organization (ILO). (2019). *Quick guide on interpreting the unemployment rate.* https://ilo.org/wcmsp5/groups/public/---dgreports/---stat/documents/publication/wcms_675155.pdf

Ireh, M. (1999). Career development theories and their implications for high school career guidance and counseling. *The High School Journal, 83*(2), 28–40. https://www.jstor.org/stable/i40015760

IRIB News Agency. (2019, October 13). Movaafeqat Majles ba hazf tanavoe madarres [Parliament's approval to eliminate school diversity]. IRIB News Agency. https://www.iribnews.ir/fa/news/2547568

IRNA. (2020, March 1). Ehya-ye e'temad-e mardom [Restoring public trust]. IRNA. www.irna.ir/xjxrdT

IRNA. (2018, October 17). Maharat-amoozi; peyvand-e daneshgah va bazar kar [Skill development; the link between university and the labor market]. IRNA. www.irna.ir/xjr5BF

IRNA. (2019, June 30). Oloum-e ensani dar Iran jaddi gerefte nashodeh ast [Humanities are not taken seriously in Iran]. IRNA. https://www.irna.ir/xjtBXL

Islamic Parliament Research Center of the Islamic Republic of Iran. (2006, October). *Barrsi vaziat doreh peesh daneshghahi dar nezam amuzeshi* [Investigating the status of pre-university in the education system].

Islamic Parliament Research Center of the Islamic Republic of Iran. (2018, September 1). *Moshavere: neyaz faramush shode dar amuzesh va parvarsh* [Counseling: The need has been forgotten by the Ministry of Education]. Iran Parliament. https://rc.majlis.ir/fa/news/show/1074849

Islamic Parliament Research Center of the Islamic Republic of Iran. (2019a, June 11). *Barname-reizi amuzesh va parvarsh baraye hedayat danesh amuzan* [Ministry of Education's plan for guiding students]. Iran Parliament. https://rc.majlis.ir/fa/news/show/1148017

Islamic Parliament Research Center of the Islamic Republic of Iran. (2019b, July 28). *Moshavere va hedayat tahsili bayad be doreh haye paien tar beyayad* [Academic counseling and guidance must begin earlier]. Iran Parliament. https://rc.majlis.ir/fa/news/show/1205194

Islamic Parliament Research Center of the Islamic Republic of Iran. (2019c, July 27). *Zarurat ahamiat dadan be mozu hedayat tahsili* [The need to pay attention to the issue of academic guidance]. Iran Parliament. https://rc.majlis.ir/fa/news/show/1202770

ISNA. (2010, January 13). Aghlab daneshjuyan IT bad az faregh al-tahsili dochar-e sardargomi mishavand [Most IT students get confused after graduation]. ISNA. isna.ir/xdtKR8

ISNA. (2014, September 20). Elal-e bikari az negah-e yek jame'e shenas [Causes of unemployment from the perspective of a sociologist]. ISNA. isna.ir/x8d3Fz

ISNA. (2013, November 8). Estefadeh az ravabet, parti-bazi, rant va zir-mizi az mosadiq-e fesad-e edari ast [Using connections, favoritism, privilege, and under-the-table dealings (bribes) are examples of administrative corruption]. ISNA. isna.ir/x6fLtT

ISNA. (2020, March 25). Parvandeh natamam "hazf-e gonkoor" va edameh nakami dar ta'yin-eh ravesh-e jaygozin [The unfinished case of "eliminating the entrance exam" and continued failure in determining a replacement method]. ISNA. https://www.isna.ir/news/98122620088/

ISNA. (2017, December 5). Ra'is-e daneshgah-e azad: Konkour ra hazf nemikonand chon 8 hezar milyard gorgesh mali darad [The president of Azad University: The entrance exam will not be eliminated because it has an 8 trillion financial turnover]. Jamaran. https://www.jamaran.news/fa/tiny/news-805818

ISNA. (2017, May 13). Sharayet sabt-nam faregh-al-tahsilan e'lam shod [The registration conditions for graduates have been announced]. ISNA. isna.ir/xcZ4Yd

IUS News. (2018, October 29). Jang-e qodrat dar goruh-e falsafeh-ye 'ilm daneshgah-e Sharif dar ghiyab-e ostaad [Power struggle in the philosophy of science group at Sharif University in the absence of a professor]. IUS News. https://iusnews.ir/fa/news-details/289249/جنگ-قدرت-در-گروه-فلسفه-علم-دانشگاه-شریف-در-غیاب-استاد/

Izadi, A. A. (2017). Tarahi masir-e shoghli danesh-amoozan [Career path design for students]. *Roshd-e Amuzeshe - Moshaver Madreseh, 12*(3), 46–52. https://www.roshdmag.ir/Roshdmag_content/media/article/26.32%20from%20MATN%20Moshvere%20madreseh%2046-2_0.pdf

Jackson, E. L., Crawford, D. W., & Godbey, G. (1993). Negotiation of leisure constraints. *Leisure Sciences, 15*(1), 1–11. https://doi.org/10.1080/01490409309513182

Jafari, M. S. (2020, July 5). Chara danesh-amoozan fard-gera mishavand?! [Why do students become individualistic?!]. *Roshd Magazine.* https://www.roshdmag.ir/Roshdmag_content/media/article/43.44%20from%20(98-99)%20MATN%20OLOM%20AJTAMAEE%2082-10_-1.pdf

Jafarshoar, M. (2018, January 11). Dar daneshgah ba hich movajeh hastim! [We face nothing at the university!]. ISNA. isna.ir/xd4dpd

Jandaghi, M. (2019, June 15). Sharayet ma'afiat bime-i karfarmaiyan dar soorat-e jazb faregh-al-tahsilan bikar [Conditions for insurance exemption for employers hiring unemployed graduates]. Mehr News. https://www.mehrnews.com/news/4640642

Janesick, V. J. (1999). A journal about journal writing as a qualitative research technique: History, issues, and reflections. *Qualitative Inquiry, 5*(4), 505–524. https://doi.org/10.1177/107780049900500404

Janesick, V. J. (2011). *"Stretching" exercises for qualitative researchers* (3rd ed.). SAGE.

Jeffrey, C. (2010). *Timepass: Youth, class, and the politics of waiting in India.* Stanford University Press.

Johnson, J., & Rochkind, J. (2010). *Can I get a little advice here? How an overstretched high school guidance system is undermining students' college aspirations.* Public Agenda. https://files.eric.ed.gov/fulltext/ED508672.pdf

Johnson, M. (1976). That was your life: A biographical approach to later life. In J. M. A. Munnichs & W. J. A. Van Den Heuvel (Eds.), *Dependency or interdependency in old age* (pp. 147–161). Springer.

Kahl, J. A. (1953). Educational and occupational aspirations of "common man" boys. *Harvard Educational Review, 23*(3), 186–203.

Kalb, Z. (2017). Neither *Dowlati* nor *Khosusi*: Islam, education and civil society in contemporary Iran. *Iranian Studies, 50*(4), 575–600. https://doi.org/10.1080/00210862.2017.1295345

Kamyab, S. (2008). The university entrance exam crisis in Iran. *International Higher Education, 51,* 22–23. https://doi.org/10.6017/ihe.2008.51.8010

Kanoon-e Faregh-al-Tahsilan-e Daneshgah Azad Eslami. (2019, November 8). Vaziyat-e bikari-e danesh-amooxtegan-e daneshgah-ha [The unemployment status of university graduates]. Kanoon-e Faregh-al-Tahsilan-e Daneshgah Azad Eslami. http://www.aiau.ir/News/8680/وضعیت_بیکاری_دانش_موختگان_دانشگاه_ها

Karimi, E. (2011, November 28). Elal va rahkarhaye padideh-e mohajerat-e nokhbegan [Causes and solutions of the brain drain phenomenon]. Tabnak. https://www.tabnak.ir/fa/news/206524

Karimi, S., & Sharif, M. (2014). Chalesh-haye amoozesh 'ali dar tadvin-e mohtava-ye barname-ye darsi ba roykard-e jame'e yadgiri [Challenges in higher education in designing curriculum content with a learning community approach]. *Rookardhaye Novin Amuzeshi, 9*(1), 107–142. https://nea.ui.ac.ir/article_19114.html

Karimi, Z. (2020, October 3). Bazar kar che moshkelati darad? [What problems does the labor market have?]. Otagh Iran Online. https://otaghiranonline.ir/news2/34830

Kashan University. (n.d.). Zaroorat-e ta'amol daneshgah ba san'at [The necessity of university-industry interaction]. Kashan University Website. https://karafarini.kashanu.ac.ir/fa/page/2541

Katzman, K. (2014). Iran sanctions. *Current Politics and Economics of the Middle East, 5*(1), 41–156.

Kawohl, W., & Nordt, C. (2020). COVID-19, unemployment, and suicide. *The Lancet Psychiatry, 7*(5), 389–390. https://doi.org/10.1016/S2215-0366(20)30141-3

Keramati, M. R. (2001). Raqabat ya refaqat dar kelas-dars [Competition or friendship in the classroom]. *Psychology and Educational Sciences, 31*(2), 139–156. https://www.sid.ir/paper/55603/fa

Khabar Online. (2019, July 31). Avamel-e mohem-e manfi-negari dar jame'e-ye Iran chist? [What are the main factors of negativity in Iranian society?]. Khabar Online. khabaronline.ir/xdW39

Khabar Online. (2019, November 10). Kahesh-e farar-e maghzha-ye Irani; varooneh-namayi hamchenan edameh darad [Reduction of Iranian brain drain; misrepresentation continues]. Khabar Online. khabaronline.ir/xfdwC

Khabar Online. (2014, March 10). Mazaya'i baray-e chap maqalat ISI, keh monjar be atash-e daneshgahiyan shodeh ast [Advantages of publishing ISI articles, which have led to the thirst among academics]. Khabar Online. khabaronline.ir/x4W3f

Khan, H. I., & Wenk, K. L. (1974). *The educational system of Iran* (ED104741). ERIC. https://files.eric.ed.gov/fulltext/ED104741.pdf

Khandan, E. (2013, July 20). Farar-e maghzha az Iran; hekayat hamchenan baqi [Brain drain from Iran; the story continues]. BBC Persian. https://www.bbc.com/persian/iran/2013/07/130720_l01_brain_drain_iran

Khomeini, I. (2005). *Islamic government: Governance of the jurist* (H. Algar, Trans.). Institute for the Compilation and Publication of Imam Khomeini's works. (Original work published 1970)

Khosravi, S. (2008). *Young and defiant in Tehran*. University of Pennsylvania Press.

Khosravi, S. (2017). *Precarious lives: Waiting and hope in Iran*. University of Pennsylvania Press.

Khosrowshahi, N. (2019, August 15). Chand darsad mardan az peyda kardan-e kar na'omidand? [What percentage of men are hopeless about finding a job?]. ISNA. isna.ir/xd5hg9

Kinzer, S. (2003). *All the Shah's men: An American coup and the roots of Middle East terror*. John Wiley & Sons.

Knowles, C. (2017). *Winning the peace: The British in occupied Germany, 1945–1948*. Bloomsbury Publishing.

Kohlbacher, F. (2006). The use of qualitative content analysis in case study research. *Forum Qualitative Social Research, 7*(1), 1–30. https://doi.org/10.17169/fqs-7.1.75

Kolesnikov, A. (2023, February 8). Russia's second, silent war against its human capital. Carnegie Endowment for International Peace. https://carnegieendowment.org/russia-eurasia/politika/2023/01/russias-second-silent-war-against-its-human-capital?lang=en

Kousha, K., & Abdoli, M. (2004, August 22–27). *Iran's national ICT education plan: An overview of the possibilities, problems and programs* [Paper presentation]. World Library and Information Congress: 70th International Federation of Library Associations and Institutions General Conference and Council. Buenos Aires, Argentina. http://origin-archive.ifla.org/IV/ifla70/papers/084e-Kousha_Abdoli.pdf

Kukla, A. (2000). *Social constructivism and the philosophy of science*. Routledge.

Kwiatkowski, E., & Kucharski, L. (2010). Long-term unemployment in Poland in the years 1995–2007. *Comparative Economic Research, 12*(3), 5–27. https://doi.org/10.2478/v10103-009-0009-4

Labaft Zadeh, M. (2011, November 30). Sarfasl-haye doros daneshgah-i oloum-e ensani dar Iran ghadimi ast [The course outlines of humanities subjects in Iranian universities are outdated]. Magiran. https://www.magiran.com/article/2407483

Lareau, A. (2003). *Unequal childhoods*. University of California Press.

Larson, R. W., Hansen, D. M., & Moneta, G. (2006). Differing profiles of developmental experiences across types of organized youth activities. *Developmental Psychology, 42*(5), 849–863. https://doi.org/10.1037/0012-1649.42.5.849

Leachman, M., Masterson, K., & Figueroa, E. (2017, November 29). *A punishing decade for school funding*. Center on Budget and Policy Priorities. https://www.cbpp.org/sites/default/files/atoms/files/11-29-17sfp.pdf

Lee, V. E., & Ekstrom, R. B. (1987). Student access to guidance counseling in high school. *American Educational Research Journal, 24*(2), 287–310. https://doi.org/10.3102/00028312024002287

Lens, W., Simons, J., & Dewitt, S. (2002). From duty to desire: The role of students' future time perspective and instrumentality perceptions for study motivation and self-regulation. In F. Pajares & T. Urdan (Eds.), *Academic motivation of adolescents* (pp. 221–245). Information Age Publishing.

Lent, R. W., & Brown, S. D. (1996). Social cognitive approach to career development: An overview. *The Career Development Quarterly, 44*(4), 310–321. https://doi.org/10.1002/j.2161-0045.1996.tb00448.x

Lent, R. W., Brown, S. D., & Hackett, G. (1994). Toward a unifying social cognitive theory of career and academic interest, choice, and performance. *Journal of Vocational Behavior, 45*(1), 79–122. https://doi.org/10.1006/jvbe.1994.1027

Lewin, K., Dembo, T., Festinger, L., & Sears, P. S. (1944). Level of aspiration. In J. M. Hunt (Ed.), *Personality and behavior disorders: A handbook based on experimental and clinical research* (pp. 333–378). The Ronald Press.

Liagouras, G., Protogerou, A., & Caloghirou, Y. (2003). Exploring mismatches between higher education and the job market in Greece. *European Journal of Education, 38*(4), 413–426. https://doi.org/10.1111/j.0141-8211.2003.00158.x

Lincoln, Y. S., & Guba, E. G. (1985). *Naturalistic inquiry.* SAGE.

Livanos, I. (2010). The relationship between higher education and job market in Greece: The weakest link? *Higher Education, 60*(5), 473–489. https://doi.org/10.1007/s10734-010-9310-1

Locke, E. A., & Latham, G. P. (1990). *A theory of goal setting and task performance.* Prentice-Hall.

Locke, E. A., & Latham, G. P (2006). New directions in goal-setting theory. *Current Directions in Psychological Science, 15*(5), 265–268. https://doi.org/10.1111/j.1467-8721.2006.00449.x

Ma, Y., Siu, A., & Tse, W. S. (2018). The role of high parental expectations in adolescents' academic performance and depression in Hong Kong. *Journal of Family Issues, 39*(9), 2505–2522. https://doi-org.mutex.gmu.edu/10.1177/0192513X18755194

Madares farhang va ehtemam be ulume ensani [Schools of culture and concern for the humanities]. (n.d.). Center for the Promotion of the Humanities. https://bit.ly/2ZtKB3r

Mafi, M. S., & Mafi, Y. (1999). Tashvigh va tanbie: ra-haye pishrafte aari az reghabat [Encouragement and punishment: Ways to progress without competition]. *Masael Amuzish, 3,* 63–65. http://ensani.ir/fa/article/276137/

Mahdavi, P. (2009). *Passionate uprisings: Iran's sexual revolution.* Stanford University Press.

Mahdi, A. A. (1999). The student movement in the Islamic Republic of Iran. *Journal of Iranian Research and Analysis, 15*(2), 5–32. http://go.owu.edu/~aamahdi/students.htm

Mahdi, R. (2016). Barrasi avamel-e mo'aser bar bikari va bahrehvari bazar kar dar Iran [Examining factors influencing unemployment and labor market productivity in Iran]. International Conference on Management and Economics in the 21st Century, 2nd Edition. https://sid.ir/paper/833301/fa

Mahoney, J. L., Cairns, B. D., & Farmer, T. W. (2003). Promoting interpersonal competence and educational success through extracurricular activity participation. *Journal of Educational Psychology, 95*(2), 409–418. https://doi.org/10.1037/0022-0663.95.2.409

Mains, D. (2012). *Hope is cut: Youth, unemployment, and the future in urban Ethiopia.* Temple University Press.

Majdi, M. (2019, February 10). Mafiay-e konkour che kassan-i hastand va chegooneh tamame keshvar ra gereftar-e konkour karde-and? [Who are the entrance exam mafia and how have they trapped the entire country in the entrance exam?]. Dinu. https://dinu.ir/مافیای-کنکور-چه-کسانی-هستند؟/

Majdifar, S. (2020, September 2). Darkhast eslah-e hoqooq a'za-ye hay'at elmi vizarat-e ATF [Request for correcting the salaries of faculty members of the Ministry of Science, Research, and Technology]. Karzar. https://www.karzar.net/2943

Maleki, H. (2019, September 16). Dah mas'aleh-ye asasi barname-rizi darsi dar Iran [Ten fundamental issues in curriculum planning in Iran]. Research and Educational Planning Organization. http://old.oerp.ir/node/10025

Malekpour, A., & Mohammadi, F. (2013). Barrasi zamine-ha va mavan-e eshghal-e fargh-al-tahsilat daneshgah-i maqta' karshenas-i reshte-haye oloum-e ensani shahrestan-e Bijar [Examining the factors and obstacles to employment for graduates of humanities fields in Bijar county]. *Kar va Jame'a, 157*, 24–37. https://ensani.ir/fa/article/356320

Malekzadeh, S. (2016). Paranoia and perspective, or how I learned to stop worrying and start loving research in the Islamic Republic of Iran. *Social Science Quarterly, 97*(4), 862–875. https://doi.org/10.1111/ssqu.12342

Mann, S. (2016). *The research interview: Reflective practice and reflexivity in research processes*. Palgrave Macmillan.

Maqsoudgerdavan, A., & Abdollahi, D. (2017). Che reshteh-i entekhab mikonid va chera? Barrasi avamel-e mo'aser bar entekhab-e reshteh-ye tahsili-ye danesh-amoozan [What major do you choose and why? Examining factors influencing students' selection of academic majors]. *Roshd Amuzesh Oloum Ejtemaei, 74*, 54–57. https://www.noormags.ir/view/fa/articlepage/1268159

Marginson, S. (2019). Limitations of human capital theory. *Studies in Higher Education, 44*(2), 287–301. https://doi.org/10.1080/03075079.2017.1359823

Markaz-e Pazhouhesh-haye Majles-e Shoraye Islami [Research Center of the Islamic Consultative Assembly]. (2018, November 17). Behtor kardan-e sathe keyfiat amoozesh dar madarres dolati az ahdaf-e kahesh tanavoe madarres dar keshvar [Improving the quality of education in public schools as a goal to reduce school diversity in the country]. Research Center of the Islamic Consultative Assembly. https://rc.majlis.ir/fa/news/show/1083729

Markus, H., & Nurius, P. (1986). Possible selves. *American Psychologist, 41*(9), 954–969. https://doi.org/10.1037/0003-066X.41.9.954

Marshall, C., & Rossman G. (1999). *Designing qualitative research* (3rd ed.). SAGE.

Mashregh News. (2018, January 14). Barname-ye dolat baray-e kahesh-eh amar-e tahsil-kordegan bikar chist? [What is the government's plan to reduce the number of unemployed graduates?]. Sobh No. mshrgh.ir/820410

Mashregh News. (2019, January 31). Bisheshtin sha'ghal-ha az kodam reshte-ha va daneshgah-ha hastand [Which fields and universities have the most employees]. Mahr News Agency. https://www.mashreghnews.ir/news/933278

Mashregh News. (2016, July 17). Mo'azali be nameh "hedayat tahsili" va sargardani danesh-amoozan [An issue called "educational guidance" and the confusion of students]. Fars News Agency. https://www.mashreghnews.ir/news/604616/

Mashregh News. (2020, May 10). Tarh-e sarkari baray-e eshghal-e faregh-al-tahsilan + amār [Government plan for employment of graduates + statistics]. Farhikhtegan Newspaper. mshrgh.ir/1071032

Matthews, M., & Lord, M. (2017). Brain gain. *ASEE Prism, 26*(7), 24–29. http://www.jstor.org/stable/44160963

Maxwell, A. (2005). *Qualitative research design: An interactive approach* (2nd ed.). SAGE.

McGaha, V., & Fitzpatrick, J. (2010). Employment, academic and extracurricular contributors to college aspirations. *Journal of College Admission, 207*, 22–29. https://files.eric.ed.gov/fulltext/EJ886927.pdf

McQuaid, R. W., & Lindsay, C. (2005). The concept of employability. *Urban Studies, 42*(2), 197–219. https://doi.org/10.1080/0042098042000316100

Mehr News. (2019, November 24). Chara danesh-amoozan be "dars-e tareekh" alaghe neshan nemidahand? [Why do students show no interest in "history lessons"?]. Mehr News Agency. http://old.oerp.ir/news/10370/

Mehr News. (2015, August 23). Sarfasl-haye ghadimi doros 'amel rukoode pajoohesh dar oloum-e ensani [Outdated course outlines as a factor in the stagnation of research in the humanities]. Mehr News. mehrnews.com/xwCnf

Menashri, D. (1992). *Education and the making of modern Iran.* Cornell University Press.

Menninger, K. A. (1930). *The human mind.* New York: Alfred A. Knopf.

Merriam, S. B. (1998). *Qualitative research and case study applications in education* (2nd ed.). Jossey-Bass Publishers.

Merriam, S. B. (2009). *Qualitative research: A guide to design and implementation.* Jossey-Bass.

Merrill, B., & West, L. (2009). *Using biographical methods in social research.* SAGE.

Milani, A. (2011). *The shah.* Palgrave Macmillan.

Milani, M. (2018). *The making of Iran's Islamic revolution: From monarchy to Islamic republic* (2nd ed.). Routledge.

Miles, M. B., & Huberman, A. M. (1994). *Qualitative data: An expanded sourcebook analysis* (2nd ed.). SAGE.

Mills, D., & Borker, H. (2018). *Educational portraits and their anthropological readers: Ethnography and analytical "double vision."* University of Oxford Department of Education.

Ministry of Culture and Islamic Guidance. (n.d.). *Guidance on licenses.* https://www.farhang.gov.ir/fa/memberhelp/mojavez

Mirzaei, N. (2020, July 2). Hedayat tahsili danesh-amoozan va mas'ooliyat-e modiran-e madarres [Educational guidance for students and the responsibility of school administrators]. IRNA. www.irna.ir/xjyFDJ

Mirzaei, N. (2019, October 21). *Maharate Amuzi dar madares va daneshgaha zarurat nizame amuzeshe ast* [Skills training in schools and universities is a necessity of the education system]. Islamic Republic News Agency. https://www.irna.ir/news/83523473/

Moallem Press. (n.d.). Ertebat-e madarres ba daneshgah-ha taqriban ghat' ast [The connection between schools and universities is almost cut off]. Moallem Press. https://moallempress.ir/?p=10001

Moazami, A. (2019, April 30). A'za-ye hay'at elmi daneshgah-ha dar sal-e 1398 cheghadr hoqooq migirand? [How much do university faculty members earn in 2019?]. Meidaan. https://meidaan.com/archive/61524

Moghadam, F. E. (2009). Undercounting women's work in Iran. *Iranian Studies, 42*(1), 81–95.

Mohammadi, J. (2020, July 27). Oloum-e ensani: Mazloom hatta dar vizarat-e fakhimeh amoozesh va parvaresh [Humanities: Oppressed even in the esteemed Ministry of Education]. Asriran. https://www.asriran.com/fa/news/748504

Mojgan, F. N., Kadir, R. A., & Soheil, S. (2011). The relationship between state and trait anxiety with career indecision of undergraduate students. *International Education Studies, 4*(3), 31–35. https://doi.org/10.5539/ies.v4n3p31

Molanouri, M. (2020). Hanoozam dostesh dari? [Do you still love it?]. *Sharif Newspaper*. https://vrgl.ir/P1res

Mortezaei Mahini, M. Y. (2019, July 29). Shaakhes-e jam'garayi dar Iran payin-tar az motevaset-e jahani ast [The index of collectivism in Iran is lower than the global average]. IRNA. www.irna.ir/xjv36w

Moshaver Group. (n.d.). Rahnamay-e taghyir reshteh dar Daneshgah San'ati Sharif 1402–1403 [Guide to changing majors at Sharif University of Technology, 2023–2024]. Moshaver Group. https://moshavergroup.com /تغییر-رشته-دانشگاه-صنعتی-شریف/

Moss, G. (2004). Provisions of trustworthiness in critical narrative research: Bridging intersubjectivity and fidelity. *The Qualitative Report, 9*(2), 359–374. https://doi.org/10.46743/2160-3715/2004.1933

Murphy, J. P. (2017). *Yearning to labor: Youth, unemployment, and social destiny in urban France*. University of Nebraska Press.

Naderi, A. (2006). Paradox-e kambod-e nirooye ensani motakhasses va bikari faregh-al-tahsilan daneshgah-i [The paradox of the shortage of specialized human resources and unemployment among university graduates]. *Kar va Jame'a, 75–76*, 4–39. http://noo.rs/wmH4r

Nadjmabadi, S. R. (2009). *Conceptualizing Iranian anthropology: Past and present perspectives*. Berghahn Books.

Naficy, N. (2018). From Rice University to the University of Tehran: Reflections on working as an American-trained anthropologist in Iran. *American Anthropologist, 120*(1), 137–142. https://anthrosource.onlinelibrary.wiley.com/doi/full/10.1111/aman.12995.

Naghdi, M., Torabi, N., Erfan, A., & Banisi, V. (2014). Taghyir va eslah barname-haye darsi [Changes and reforms in curriculum programs]. First International Symposium on Management Sciences with a Focus on Sustainable Development. https://civilica.com/doc/374897/

Naghshineh, A. (2011, November 29). Daneshgah va daneshjuyan-e Sharif: Az shayehh ta vaghei'at [Sharif University and its students: From rumors to reality]. Ardalan's Blog. https://ardalan.me/fa/1390/09/08/sharif-university-of-technology/

Naji, S., Nikbakht, A., Abedi, H., & Esmaeili, A. (2016). Determination of employment status and unemployment factors of nursing graduates of Islamic Azad University of Isfahan Branch (Khorasgan) in 2013. *Research Journal of Medical Sciences, 10*(4), 348–350. https://doi.org/10.36478/rjmsci.2016.348.350

Nilsson, S. (2010). Enhancing individual employability: The perspective of engineering graduates. *Education + Training, 52*(6/7), 540–551. https://doi.org/10.1108/00400911011068487

Nurmi, J. E. (2004). Socialization and self-development: Channeling, selection, adjustment, and reflection. In R. M. Lerner & L. Steinber (Eds.), *Handbook of adolescent psychology* (2nd ed., pp. 85–124). Wiley & Sons.

Olgoo. (n.d.). Tarh-e jadid-e amoozesh va parvaresh dar hedayat tahsili chegooneh ejra shod? [How was the new educational guidance plan implemented?]. Olgoo Books. https://www.olgoobooks.ir/108-طرح-جدید-آموزش-و-پرورش-در-هدایت-تحصیلی-چگونه-اجرا-شد/

Olszewska, Z. (2013). Classy kids and down-at-heel intellectuals: Status aspiration and blind spots in the contemporary ethnography of Iran. *Iranian Studies, 46*(6), 841–862. https://doi.org/10.1080/00210862.2013.810078

O'Neill, B. (2014). Cast aside: boredom, downward mobility, and homelessness in post-communist Bucharest. *Cultural Anthropology, 29*(1), 8–31. https://journal.culanth.org/index.php/ca/article/view/ca29.1.03

O'Reilly, K. (2005). *Ethnographic methods.* Routledge.

Oreopoulos, P., Von Wachter, T., & Heisz, A. (2012). The short- and long-term career effects of graduating in a recession. *American Economic Journal: Applied Economics, 4*(1), 1–29. https://doi.org/10.1257/app.4.1.1

Orndorff, R. M., & Herr, E. L. (1996). A comparative study of declared and undeclared college students on career uncertainty and involvement in career development activities. *Journal of Counseling and Development, 74*(6), 632–639. https://doi.org/10.1002/j.1556-6676.1996.tb02303.x

Osipow, S. H. (1999). Assessing career indecision. *Journal of Vocational Behavior, 55*(1), 147–154. https://doi.org/10.1006/jvbe.1999.1704

PANA News. (2019, May 12). Ejra-ye siyasat-e tose'e-ye motevazen reshte-haye tahsili be manzoreh erteqa-ye keyfiat-e amoozesh-i dar ostan-e markazi [Implementation of the balanced development policy of fields of study to enhance educational quality in Markazi province]. https://www.pana.ir/fa/tiny/news-914473

Parsine. (2010, March 24). Dalayel va ravand-e mohajerat-e daneshjuyan-e "Daneshgah-e San'ati Sharif" [Reasons and trends of student migration at "Sharif University of Technology"]. Parsine. https://www.parsine.com/fa/tiny/news-18637

Patton, M. Q. (2002). *Qualitative research & evaluation methods* (3rd ed.). SAGE.

Payne, K. J., & Biddle, B. J. (1999). Poor school funding, child poverty, and mathematics achievement. *Educational Researcher, 28*(6), 4–13. https://doi.org/10.3102/0013189X028006004

Pettigrew, A. M. (1992). The character and significance of strategy process research. *Strategic Management Journal, 13*(52), 5–16. https://doi.org/10.1002/smj.4250130903

Pettit, H. (2017). *Without hope there is no life: Class, affect, and meritocracy in middle-class Cairo* (Doctoral dissertation, London School of Economics and Political Science). LSE Theses Online. http://etheses.lse.ac.uk/3673/

Piketty, T. (2014). *Capital in the twenty-first century.* Harvard University Press.

Plummer, K. (1983). *Documents of life: An introduction to the problems and literature of a humanistic method.* Allen and Unwin.

Pouyan, A. (2016, November 11). Chera zore vazir be mafia konkur nemersad? [Why isn't the ministry stronger than the *konkur* mafia?]. *Rozname Shargh.* https://www.magiran.com/article/3831440

Pouyan, A. (2018, November 11). Ehtemal mafiay-e kharid-o-forush nmarah: Chara zor-e vizir be mafiay-e gonkoor nemi-resad? [The likelihood of a grade-buying and selling mafia: Why the minister can't defeat the entrance exam mafia?]. *Shargh Newspaper*, 3288. https://www.magiran.com/article/3831440

Pozzoli, D. (2009). The transition to work for Italian university graduates. *Labour, 23*(1), 131–169. https://onlinelibrary.wiley.com/doi/abs/10.1111/j.1467-9914.2008.00442.x

Qana'at Pish-e, A. A. (2005). Moghayese asar raqabat fardi, talash fardi va raqabat goroohee dar pishraft-e tahsili [Comparison of the effects of individual competition, individual effort, and group competition on academic achievement]. *Taleem va Tarbiyat, 81*, 120–156. https://www.noormags.ir/view/fa/articlepage/1105847

Qanuni, R., & Gholtas, A. (2019). Moghayese demokrasi amoozeshi, farsuodegi tahsili va mahaarat-haye shahrvandi madarres dolati va gheyr-e dolati [Comparison of educational democracy, academic burnout, and citizenship skills in public and private schools]. *Rahyafte No dar Modiriyat Amoozeshi, 10*(3), 39. https://ensani.ir/fa/article/417922/

Rabiei, M., & Salehi, R. (2007). Moghayese narkh-haye amuzeshi va kyfiate amuzesh va parvaresh nemunehaye bartar madarese dolati va ghayre entefayi ostan chahar mahal va bakhtiyari [Comparison of educational rates and quality of education of the best examples of public and private schools in the provinces of Chaharmahal and Bakhtiari]. *Faslname noavarihaye amuzesh, 19*. http://ensani.ir/fa/article/112877/

Radio Goftogo. (2019, November 30). Sarfasl-e basyari az doros-e memari dar daneshgah ghadimi ast [The course outlines of many architecture subjects in universities are outdated]. Seda. https://seda.ir/sh/?5541208

Rahdari, M., Nasr, A. R., Nili, M. R., & Tork Ladani, B. (2015). Arzyabi maharat-haye herfeyi va vaziyat-e eshteghal-e danesh-amookhtegan karshenasi-e mohandesi fanavari etelaat [Evaluation of professional skills and employment status of IT engineering graduates]. *Pajouhesh va Barname Rizi dar Amoozesh 'Ali, 21*(2), 1–24. https://journal.irphe.ac.ir/article_702868.html

Rahkare hazf konkure reshte-haye portarafdar az zabane vazir ulum [A solution to eliminate the *konkur* for popular majors from the mouth of minister of science]. (2020, August 22). *Asriran*. https://www.asriran.com/fa/news/743490/

Rajan, R., Servaes, H., & Zingales, L. (2000). The cost of diversity: The diversification discount and inefficient investment. *The Journal of Finance, 55*(1), 35–80. https://doi.org/10.1111/0022-1082.00200

Ralph, M. (2008). Killing time. *Social text, 26*(4), 1–29. https://read.dukeupress.edu/social-text/article-abstract/26/4%20(97)/1/33574/Killing-Time

Razavi, J. (2017, May 24). Chalash-haye ertebat san'at va daneshgah [Challenges of industry-university collaboration]. Donya-e-Eqtesad. https://donya-e-eqtesad.com/fa/tiny/news-1102113

Reissman, L. (1953). Levels of aspiration and social class. *American Sociological Review, 18*(3), 233–242. https://doi.org/10.2307/2087876

Research Center of the Islamic Consultative Assembly. (2020, June 8). Barrasi avamel mo'asser bar nakar-amadi sanjesh va pazirosh daneshjoo dar Iran [Examining the factors influencing the inefficiency of student assessment and admission in Iran]. Research Center of the Islamic Consultative Assembly. https://rc.majlis.ir/fa/report/show/1546760

Rezaei Madani, M., Kalantari Harmozi, A., & Naeimi, E. (2019). Barrasi farayand hedayat-e tahsili novin az manzar-e moshavaran-e madarres [An analysis of the modern educational guidance process from the perspective of school counselors]. *Farhang-e Moshavere va Ravand-darmani, 10*(39), 27–48. https://doi.org/10.22054/qccpc.2019.40632.2098

Rezapour, S., & Shafiei, R. (2013). Avamel-e mo'asser bar entekhab-e reshteh tahsili-ye danesh-amoozan [Factors influencing students' selection of academic majors]. First International Conference of Political Epic (Focusing on Middle East Developments) and Economic Epic (Focusing on Management and Accounting). https://civilica.com/doc/495168

Ricoeur, P. (1980). Narrative time. *Critical Inquiry, 7*(1), 169–190. https://www.jstor.org/stable/1343181

Roberts, B. (2002). *Biographical research.* Open University Press.

Rubin, H. J., & Rubin, I. S. (2004). *Qualitative interviewing: The art of hearing data* (2nd ed.). SAGE.

Ryan, R. M., & Deci, E. L. (2000). Self-determination theory and the facilitation of intrinsic motivation, social development, and well-being. *American Psychologist, 55,* 68–78. https://doi.org/10.1037/0003-066X.55.1.68

Sabouhi, F. (2015). Barrasi vaziyat-e bikari dar mian-e danesh-amoozegan-e amoozesh 'ali va tabyin-e jame'e shenakhti an (motale'e moredi: Shahrestan-e Bahmai) [Examining unemployment among higher education graduates and its sociological explanation (Case study: Bahmei county)]. International Conference on Humanities, Psychology, and Social Sciences. https://civilica.com/doc/436297/

Safi, A. (2012, October 15). Amouzeshe va parvaresh Iran dar sad sal gozashteh [Education in Iran over the past century]. Roshd Magazine. https://www.roshdmag.ir/fa/article/6487

Sajedi Sabegh, K. (2010, October 23). Araye behtarin rahkar-shokofayi estedad-haye danesh-amoozan [Presenting the best solutions for the flourishing of students' talents]. Dabestan-e Shahed-e Shohaday-e Parvin Zad. https://parvinzad.blogfa.com/post/23

Sakurai, K. (2004). University entrance examination and the making of an Islamic society in Iran: A study of the post-revolutionary Iranian approach to "*konkur.*" *Iranian Studies, 37*(3), 385–406. https://doi.org/10.1080/0021086042000287505

Salamatbakhsh, F. (2019, September 14). Eshteghal-zayi az tariq-e hamahangi beyn arze va taghaza-ye niroye kar [Job creation through balancing labor supply and demand]. IRNA. www.irna.ir/xjvxwX

Salehi-Isfahani, D., & Taghvatalab, S. (2019). Education and the allocation of time of married women in Iran. *Review of Economics of the Household, 17,* 889–921.

Sanatkhah, A. (2009). Barrasi avamel mo'asser bar bikari faregh-al-tahsilan daneshgah-ha [Examining the factors influencing unemployment among university graduates]. Kar va Jame'a, 109. https://ensani.ir/fa/article/215811

Sanders, J., & de Grip, A. (2004). Training, task flexibility and the employability of low-skilled workers. *International Journal of Manpower, 25*(1), 73–89. https://doi.org/10.1108/01437720410525009

Sawitri, D. R., Creed, P. A., & Zimmer-Gembeck, M. J. (2014). Longitudinal relations of parental influences and adolescent career aspirations and actions in a collectivist society. *Journal of Research on Adolescence, 25*(3), 551–563. https://doi.org/10.1111/jora.12145

Schielke, S. (2015). *Egypt in the future tense: Hope, frustration and ambivalence, before and after 2011.* Indiana University Press.

Schneider, M. (2003). *Linking school facility conditions to teacher satisfaction and success* (ED480552). ERIC. https://files.eric.ed.gov/fulltext/ED480552.pdf

Schultz, T. W. (1961). Investment in human capital. *The American Economic Review, 51*(1), 1–17. http://www.jstor.org/stable/1818907

Schunk, D. H. (2001). *Self-regulation through goal-setting* (ED462671). ERIC. https://files.eric.ed.gov/fulltext/ED462671.pdf

Seif, D. (2020, August 25). *Aghaze payesh tarhe tahvol dar hamkarihaye daneshgaha va moasesate pejhohesh va fanavari ba jamee va sanat* [Begin monitoring the transformation plan on the cooperation between universities and research and technology institutes with society and industry]. Ministry of Science Research and Technology.

Seifollah, S., & Sanatkhan, A. (2008). Barrasi enteqadi tahqiq-ha va manabe' esnadi mojood dar khosoos bikari fargh-al-tahsilat daneshgah-ha dar Iran [A critical review of research and available documentary sources regarding unemployment among university graduates in Iran]. *Oloum-e Ejtemai (Social Sciences), 3*(4), 15. https://ensani.ir/fa/article/407179

Seow, P., & Pan, G. (2014). A literature review of the impact of extracurricular activities participation on students' academic performance. *Journal of Education for Business, 89*(7), 361–366. https://doi.org/10.1080/08832323.2014.912195

Sewell, W. H., Haller, A., & Straus, M. (1957). Social status and educational and occupational aspiration. *American Sociological Review, 22*(1), 67–73. https://doi.org/10.2307/2088767

Sewell, W. H. (1992). A theory of structure: Duality, agency, and transformation. *American Journal of Sociology, 98*(1), 1–29. https://doi.org/10.1086/229967

Shahbazi, M. (2009). Past experiences and future perspectives of an indigenous anthropologist on anthropological work in Iran. In S. R. Nadjmabadi (Ed.), *Conceptualizing Iranian anthropology: Past and present perspectives* (pp. 143–156). Berghahn Books.

Shahnoushi, M., & Dadkhah, M. (2017). Mavaane tahaghogh-e shayesteh-salari dar sazeman-haye dolati shahr-e Shiraz az didgah-e karshenasan-e standard-e Fars [Barriers to achieving meritocracy in government organizations in Shiraz from the perspective of experts in the Fars Governorate]. *Jame'e Shenasi Karbordi, 28*(3), 195–218. https://jas.ui.ac.ir/article_21718.html

Shahraranews. (2020, July 14). Pishnahad ozv-e Shoraye Aali Enghelab Farhangi baraye hazf-e gonkoor karshenas-i-arshed va doktari [Proposal by a member of the Supreme Council of the Cultural Revolution to eliminate the master's and doctoral entrance exams]. Shahraranews. https://shahraranews.ir/fa/news/34354/

Shahrokni, N. (2019). *Women in Place: The Politics of Gender Segregation in Iran*. University of California Press.

Shank, G. F. (2006). *Qualitative research: A personal skills approach* (2nd ed.). Pearson Education.

Shariaty College of National Skills for Girls, Dr. Shiriati Tehran. (2020, September 21). Asatid-e karafarin rahkari jaddi baray-e mahart-afzayi daneshjuyan/ Karafarin-i daneshgah-ha ba'es-e roshd-e eqtesadi mishavad [The president of the Technical and Vocational University in an interview with Fars: Entrepreneurial professors are a serious solution for enhancing student skills/ University entrepreneurship leads to economic growth]. Shariaty College Website. https://www.shariaty.ac.ir/fa/news/2065

Sharif Tech Park. (2019, August 13). Karafarinan poolsaz dar majavarat daneshgah-e Sharif [Wealthy entrepreneurs near Sharif University]. Iran Newspaper. https://techpark.sharif.ir/کارآفرینان-پولساز-در-مجاورت-دانشگاه-ش/

Sharif Career School. (2019, January 1). Madreseh eshteghal-e Sharif [Sharif Employment School]. Sharif Career School. http://tsc.sharif.ir/1397/10/11/مدرسه-اشتغال-شریف/

Sharif University. (n.d.). Ayin-nameh amoozeshi dore-ye kardani va karshenasi daneshgah-e San'ati Sharif va shiveh ejraee mofad-e an [Educational regulations for associate and bachelor's degree programs at Sharif University of Technology and their implementation method]. Sharif University. http://old.sharif.ir/c/document_library/get_file?uuid=a38671e8-d58f-423a-8799-7f4fbcf3f4dc&groupId=377256

Sharif University. (2019, January 9). Sharif University Job Fair. http://jobfair.sharif.ir/

Sharif University of Technology Technology Complex. (2018, January 1). Madreseh eshteghal-e Sharif [Sharif Employment School]. Sharif University of Technology Technology Complex. tsc.sharif.ir/1397/10/11/مدرسه-اشتغال-شریف/

Shilling, C. (1992). Reconceptualising structure and agency in the sociology of education: Structuration theory and schooling. *British Journal of Sociology of Education, 13*(1), 69–87. https://www.tandfonline.com/doi/abs/10.1080/0142569920130105

Shiraz Novin Newspaper. (n.d.). Vorood-e corona ba moj-e hashtom [The arrival of COVID-19 with the eighth wave]. Shiraz Novin Newspaper. https://www.shiraznovinnews.ir/news-details/3491-مقاله-نکات-اساسی-درباره-تربیت-اجتماعی-دانش-آموزان

Singh, R., & Sarkar, S. (2012). *Teaching quality counts: How student outcomes relate to quality of teaching in private and public schools in India*. Young Lives. https://bit.ly/3jQV0xl

Sobhani, A., & Shahidi, M. (2007). Asib shenasie konkur va barrsie emkane hazf an dar nizam pazireshe daneshju [The pathology of the *konkur* and the possibility of eliminating it in the student admission system]. *Danesh va Pejhohish dar Ulume Tarbiati, 13*, 161–181. http://ensani.ir/fa/article/219229/

Sohrab Mafi, M., & Mafi, Y. (1998). Tashvigh va tanbih: Rah-haye pishraft ari az raqabat [Encouragement and punishment: Paths to progress without competition]. Loh-e Bahman, 3. https://ensani.ir/fa/article/276137

Sohrabi, A. (2017, June 18). Sarfasl-haye darsi reshte-haye honar mansookh shodeh ast/ Baznegari dar paziresh-e daneshjoo [The course outlines of art fields are outdated/ Revising student admissions]. Mehr News. mehrnews.com/xJ4Xw

Sohrabi, A. (2019, October 6). Naqsh-e 12 sal tahsil dar ta'ayin masir-e tose'e shoghli yek jame'e [The role of 12 years of education in determining the career development path of a society]. MIGNA News Agency. https://www.migna.ir/news/48471

Spenner, K., & Featherman, D. (1978). Achievement ambitions. *Annual Review of Sociology, 4*, 373–420. https://doi.org/10.1146/annurev.so.04.080178.002105

Spermann, A. (2015). How to fight long-term unemployment: Lessons from Germany. *IZA Journal of Labor Policy, 4*(15), Article 15. https://doi.org/10.1186/s40173-015-0039-4

Spradley, J. P. (1979). *The ethnographic interview*. Harcourt Brace Jovanovich College Publishers.

Staff, J., Harris, A., Sabates, R., & Briddell, L. (2010). Uncertainty in early occupational aspirations: Role exploration or aimlessness? *Social Forces, 89*(2), 659–683. https://doi.org/10.1353/sof.2010.0088

Stake, R. E. (1995). *The art of case study research*. SAGE.

Standing, G. (2011). *The precariat: the new dangerous class.* Bloomsbury Academic.

Student News Network (SSN). (2017, January 9). Arzeshiabi-ye asatid; az afsaneh ta vaghe'iat/Chara daneshjuyan nazarsanji darbari-ye asatid ra bi-ta'sir midanand? [Faculty evaluation; from myth to reality/Why do students consider faculty surveys ineffective?]. Student News Network (SSN). https://snn.ir/fa/news/574881

Student News Network (SSN). (2017, September 5). Chara 80 darsad-e Sharifi-ha az Iran miravand?/Dastan-e yek 'amel nashenaakhteh! [Why do 80% of Sharifi people leave Iran? The story of an unknown factor!]. Students News Network. https://snn.ir/002eET

Student News Network (SSN). (2020, September 30). Yeksan-engari a'za-ye hay'at-haye elmi dar ayin-nameh-ye erteqa-ye asatid/Daneshjoo, abzar-i baray-e tolid-e maqaleh-ye asatid! [Uniform treatment of faculty members in the professors' promotion regulations/Student, a tool for generating professors' articles!]. Student News Network (SSN). https://snn.ir/003giy

Suarez-Ortega, M. (2013). Performance, reflexivity, and learning through biographical-narrative research. *Qualitative Inquiry, 19*(3), 189–200. https://doi.org/10.1177/1077800412466223

Subhani, A., & Shahidi, M. (2007). Asib-shenasi-ye gonkoor va barrasi emkan-e hazf-e aan dar nizame paziresh daneshjoo [Pathology of the entrance exam and examining the possibility of its removal in the student admission system]. *Danesh va Pajoohesh dar Oloum-e Tarbiyyati, 4*(13). https://ensani.ir/fa/article/219229/

Tabnak. (2013, May 27). Moghayese hoqooq daryafti asatid daneshgah ba namayandegan majles [Comparison of the salaries of university professors with members of parliament]. Tabnak. https://www.tabnak.ir/001Lo8

Tabnak. (2020, October 23). Tarh-e hazf-e gonkoor kelid khord [The proposal to eliminate the entrance exam is underway]. Tabnak. https://www.tabnak.ir/fa/news/1010564

Tahre ertebate madares ba daneshgaha dar ostane markaze morede hamayate dastegah-haye ejraie gharar girad [A plan to connect schools with universities in Markazi province should be supported by the executive bodies]. (2018, December 22). Tasnim News. https://www.tasnimnews.com/fa/news/1397/10/01/1905080/

Tahre do foriti majlis dar bare mafia konkur [Two urgent parliamentary plans for the konkur mafia]. (2020, September 3). Fars News. https://www.farsnews.ir/news/13990608000344/

Talebi, M. (2012). *Luzume estedadiabi daneshamuzane irani dar taamin va tosiye manabeh ensani kar amad az negah jame shenasi amuzesh va parvaresh* [The need to find talented Iranian students at providing and developing human resources from the sociological view of education]. Tebyan. https://article.tebyan.net/193125/

Tamman, M. (2021, April 27). The hot list: Meet Kaveh Madani, the climate expert who fled Iran. Reuters. https://www.reuters.com/investigates/special-report/climate-change-scientists-madani/

Tasnim News. (2016, July 26). Negarani az ejbar dar entekhab reshteh-tahsili/Bi-tavajjohi be alayeg va nomarat danesh-amoozan [Concerns about being forced to choose a field of study/Disregard for students' interests and grades]. Tasnim News. https://www.tasnimnews.com/fa/news/1395/05/04/1139313

Tasnim News. (2017, July 23). Rant va parti-bazi dar edarat ghoqa mikonad/Mardom az in mozu narahat va shaki hastand [Favoritism and privilege in offices are rampant/People are upset and complaining about this issue]. Tasnim News. https://www.tasnimnews.com/fa/news/1396/05/01/1472439/

Tasnim News. (2018, September 27). Vakevi dalayel bi-tavajjohi be madarres dolati/madarres gereftaar ebtedayi-tarin moshkelat [Analysis of reasons for neglecting public schools: Schools trapped in the most basic problems]. https://www.tasnimnews.com/fa/news/1397/07/05/1837858

Tasnim News. (2018, November 9). Mubarazeh namayesh-i ba mafiay-e konkour [A show of fighting the entrance exam mafia]. Tasnim News. https://www.tasnimnews.com/fa/news/1397/08/18/1870143/

Tasnim News. (2018, December 22). Tarh-e ertebat-e madarres ba daneshgah-ha dar ostan-e markazi mowed-e hemayat-e dashtahaye ejra'i gharar gireh [The proposal for connecting schools with universities in Markazi province should be supported by executive agencies]. Tasnim News. https://www.tasnimnews.com/fa/news/1397/10/01/1905080

Tasnim News. (2019, September 15). 62 darsad danesh-amoozan dabeestani dar kelas-haye bish az 26 nafar dars mikhanand [62% of elementary school students study in classes with more than 26 students]. Tasnim. https://www.tasnimnews.com/fa/news/1398/06/24/2096585

Tasnim News. (2019, October 4). Kelas-haye dars madarres dolati dar marz-e enfejar! [Classrooms in public schools on the brink of explosion!]. Tasnim News. https://www.tasnimnews.com/fa/news/1398/07/12/2108196

Tasnim News. (2019, December 8). Hami-ye boomi sazi oloum hastam [I support the localization of sciences]. Mahr News Agency. https://www.tasnimnews.com/fa/news/1398/09/17/2155469/

Tasnim News. (2020, July 16). Pasokh be 10 soal-e danesh-amoozan darbareh entekhab-e reshteh tahsili [Answers to 10 questions students have about choosing an academic major]. Tasnim News. https://www.tasnimnews.com/fa/news/1399/04/26/2306388/

Tasnim News. (2020, July 25). Tarh-e do-foriyati Majles baray-e lagh-e gonkoor arshad dar sal-e 99 [The urgent proposal by Parliament to cancel the master's entrance exam in 2020]. Tasnim News. https://www.tasnimnews.com/fa/news/1399/05/04/2314113

Tavangar, G. (2017, October 21). Gerd-e bikari bar chohreh-ye oloum-e ensani! [The dust of unemployment on the face of humanities!]. Kayhan. https://kayhan.ir/fa/news/117006/

Tavinqoli, R. (2015). Barrasi rabeteh beyn-e san'at va daneshgah dar Iran [Examining the relationship between industry and university in Iran]. Third National Conference of Student Scientific Associations of Agricultural and Natural Resources Disciplines. https://civilica.com/doc/457729/

Taylor, S. J., Bogdan, R., & DeVault, M. L. (2016). *Introduction to qualitative research methods: A guidebook and resource*. John Wiley & Sons.

Tejerina, B. (2019). Youth and precariousness in Spain: Beyond a waiting time. In E. Colombo & P. Rebughini (Eds.), *Youth and the Politics of the Present* (pp. 88–100). Routledge.

Thieme, T. A. (2017). The hustle economy: Informality, uncertainty and the geographies of getting by. *Progress in Human Geography, 42*(4), 529–548. https://doi.org/10.1177/0309132517690039

Tholen, G. (2015). What can research into employability tell us about agency and structure? *British Journal of Sociology of Education, 36*(5), 766–784. https://doi.org/10.1080/01425692.2013.847782

Tholen, G. (2017). *Graduate work: Skills, credentials, careers, and job markets.* Oxford University Press.

Thomas, W. I., & Znaniecki, F. (1996). *The Polish peasant in Europe and America: A classic work in immigration history.* University of Illinois Press. (Original work published 1918–1920)

Tien, H. S., Lin, C., & Chen, S. (2005). A grounded analysis of career uncertainty perceived by college students in Taiwan. *The Career Development Quarterly, 54*(2), 162–174. https://doi.org/10.1002/j.2161-0045.2005.tb00148.x

Tizland. (n.d.). Shahab chist va che ahdaf-i ra donbāl mikonad? [What is Shahab and what objectives does it pursue?]. Fars News Agency. https://tizland.ir/show/?id=5152

Tomic, I. (2014). Structural unemployment in Croatia—How important is the occupational mismatch? *Economic Research–Ekonomska Istraživanja, 27*(1), 346–365. https://doi.org/10.1080/1331677X.2014.966969

Tomlinson, M. (2008). "The degree is not enough": Students' perceptions of the role of higher education credentials for graduate work and employability. *British Journal of Sociology of Education, 29*(1), 49–61. https://doi.org/10.1080/01425690701737457

Tomlinson, M. (2012). Employability: A review of conceptual and empirical themes. *Higher Education Policy, 25*(4), 407–431. https://doi.org/10.1057/hep.2011.26

Tomlinson, M. (2007). Employability and student attitudes and orientations to the job market. *Journal of Education and Work, 20*(4), 285–304. https://doi.org/10.1080/13639080701650164

Trice, A. D., & McClellan, N. (1993). Do children's career aspirations predict adult occupations? An answer from a secondary analysis of a longitudinal study. *Psychological Reports, 72*(2), 368–370. https://doi.org/10.2466/pr0.1993.72.2.368

Ulume ensani; mazlum hata dar vezarat fakhime amuzesh va parvaresh [Humanities; oppressed even in the great Ministry of Education]. (2020, September 27). Asriran. https://www.asriran.com/fa/news/748504/

Ulume ensani dar Iran jedi gerefteh nashodeh ast [Humanities have not been taken seriously in Iran]. (2019, July 1). Islamic Republic News Agency. https://www.irna.ir/news/83365010/

United Nations. (2024, November 8). Nicaragua: Alarming erosion of freedom and academic autonomy. UN News. https://news.un.org/en/story/2024/11/1156741

U.S. News & World Report. (2021, August 3). Best Global University: Sharif University of Technology. https://www.usnews.com/education/best-global-universities/sharif-university-of-technology-502898

Vaez Zadeh, H. (2011, August 2). Chara be oloum-e ensani niyaz darim? [Why do we need humanities?]. Khabar Online. https://www.khabaronline.ir/news/165779

Valero, D., Hirschi, A., & Strauss, K. (2015). Hope in adolescent careers: Mediating effects of work motivation on career outcomes in Swiss apprentices. *Journal of Career Development, 42*(5), 381–395. https://doi.org/10.1177/0894845314566866

Van Lange, P. A. M., & De Dreu, C. K. W. (2001). Social interaction: Cooperation and competition. In M. Hewstone & W. Stroebe (Eds.), *Introduction to psychology* (pp. 234–258). Blackwell Publishers Inc. https://research.vu.nl/en/publications/social-interaction-cooperation-and-competition

Van Zeyl, C. J. (1974). *Ambition and social structure: Educational structure and mobility orientation in the Netherlands and the United States*. Lexington Books.

Varzi, R. (2006). *Warring souls: Youth, media, and martyrdom in post-Revolution Iran*. Duke University Press.

Vatikiotis, L., & Nikolakaki, M. (2013). Resistance in Greece. In D. Hill (Ed.), *Immiseration capitalism and education: Austerity, resistance and revolt* (pp. 144–154). Brighton: Institute for Education Policy Studies.

Vygotsky, L. S. (2012). *Thought and language* (E. Hanfmann, G. Vakar, & A. Kozulin, Trans.). MIT Press. (Original work published 1934)

Wambu, G. W., & Fisher, T. A. (2015). School guidance and counseling in Kenya: Historical development, current status, and future prospects. *Journal of Education and Practice, 6*(11), 93–102. https://www.iiste.org/Journals/index.php/JEP/article/view/21864

WebPouya. (2024, December 24). Elal-e shekast-e bozorgtarin raqib-e Digikala [Reasons for the failure of Digikala's biggest competitor]. WebPouya. https://www.webpouya.com/blog/why-is-bamilo-closed

Wengraf, T. (2001). *Qualitative research interviewing: Biographic narrative and semi-structured methods*. SAGE.

Willig, C. (2014). Interpretation and analysis. In U. Flick (Ed.), *The SAGE handbook of qualitative data analysis interpretation and analysis* (pp. 136–150). SAGE.

Yadegarzadeh, G., Parand, K., & Kanani, E. (2012). Barrasi nazarat-e moshaveran madareseh pish-daneshgahi dar khosus niyazha va moshkelat-e davtalaban dar farayand-e entekhab-e reshteh azmoon-e sarasari (konkoor) [Examining the opinions of pre-university school counselors on the needs and problems of applicants in the process of selecting a major for the national exam (*Konkur*)]. *Amuzesh-e Ali-e Iran, 4*(4), 16. https://ensani.ir/fa/article/519312

Yaghmaian, B. (2002). *Social change in Iran: An eyewitness account of dissent, defiance and new movements*. State University of New York Press.

Yin, R. K. (2012). *Applications of case study research* (3rd ed.). SAGE.

Yin, R. K. (2014). *Case study research: Design and methods* (5th ed.). SAGE.

Yousefpour, Y. (2019, December 16). Fardiyat, mo'azali keh danesh-amoozan Irani mi-amoozand! [Individualism, a problem that Iranian students learn!]. ISNA. isna.ir/xdDSNk

Zali, F., Keramati, M. R., & Poor Karimi, J. (2017). Moghayese fazay-e amoozesh-i madarres dolati va gheyr-e dolati, mored: madarres motavasete shahr-e Karaj [Comparison of the educational environment in public and private schools: A case study of secondary schools in Karaj]. *Journal of School Administration, 5*(1), 51–72. https://www.noormags.ir/view/fa/articlepage/1780645

Zareh Saryazdi, M. (2019, February 23). Dastan-e shekast-e Bamilo; khorooj-e avalin market-place Irani che ta'siri bar bazar khahad dasht? [The story of Bamilo's failure; what impact will the exit of Iran's first marketplace have on the market?]. Zoomit. https://www.zoomit.ir/business/313130-bamilo-exit-story-consequences/

Index

Page numbers in bold and italics denote tables and figures, respectively. Page numbers followed by n denote note.

www.ingramcontent.com/pod-product-compliance
Lightning Source LLC
LaVergne TN
LVHW050620041026
849372LV00002B/37
* 9 7 8 1 4 7 7 3 3 5 7 4 1 *